e-Economy: Rhetoric or Business Reality?

As dotcom became dotbomb, the hype that surrounded the meteoric growth of the network economy gave way to a new scepticism.

But short-term downturns have obscured the real and lasting contributions that electronic communication has made to the marketplace. For academics, policy-makers and entrepreneurs, key questions remain. How should new technology be incorporated into standard models of business practice? And how much has the Internet changed those very models? What is different about the new economy?

Using a business and socio-economic framework, the authors take a rigorous approach to the new economy, its performance and prospects. With chapters on e-Leadership, e-Management, e-Retail, e-Government and e-Business processes, this book takes one of the most broad-ranging and critical approaches to the topic, including human resource management, e-Marketing, enterprise culture, digitized knowledge and technology.

Rigorous, yet retaining the accessible format and style that characterizes every volume in this series, *e-Economy: Rhetoric or Business Reality?* provides a thorough critique of the prospects facing businesses in the new economy and will be of interest to anyone studying e-Business and commerce.

Leslie Budd is Reader in Social Enterprise at the Open University Business School, where he is a member of the Centre for Public Leadership and Social Enterprise (PULSE) and the Public and Non-profit Research Unit (PiN). An academician of the Academy of Social Sciences, he is also Chair of the Regional Studies Association.

Lisa Harris is a Chartered Marketer and Lecturer in Marketing at Brunel University. She is founder of the University's e-Commerce research group and is Course Director for the BSc in e-Commerce. She is author of *Marketing the e-Business* (Routledge, 2002) and co-editor of the Routledge e-Business series.

Routledge e-Business series

Routledge e-Business is a bold new series examining key aspects of the e-Business world, designed to provide students and academics with a more structured learning resource. Introducing issues of marketing, Human Resource Management, ethics, operations management, law, design, computing and the e-Business environment, it offers a broad overview of key e-Business issues from both managerial and technical perspectives.

Marketing the e-Business
Lisa Harris and Charles Dennis

e-Business Fundamentals
Edited by Paul Jackson, Lisa Harris and Peter Eckersley

e-Retailing
Charles Dennis, Tino Fenech and Bill Merrilees

e-Economy: Rhetoric or Business Reality?
Edited by Leslie Budd and Lisa Harris

e-Economy: Rhetoric or Business Reality?

Edited by Leslie Budd
and Lisa Harris

Routledge
Taylor & Francis Group

LONDON AND NEW YORK

First published 2004
by Routledge
2 Park Square, Milton Park, Abingdon,
Oxon OX14 4RN

Simultaneously published in the USA and Canada
by Routledge
270 Madison Ave, New York NY10016

Routledge is an imprint of the Taylor & Francis Group

Typeset in Perpetua and Bell Gothic by
Keystroke, Jacaranda Lodge, Wolverhampton
Printed and bound in Great Britain by
The Cromwell Press, Trowbridge, Wiltshire

British Library Cataloguing in Publication Data
A catalogue record for this book is available from the British Library

Library of Congress Cataloging in Publication Data
E-economy: rhetoric or business reality? / edited by Leslie Budd and Lisa Harris.
    p. cm. (Routledge e-business series; 4)
  Includes bibliographical references.
  1. Electronic commerce. 2. International finance—Social aspects.
  I. Budd, Leslie, 1949– II. Harris, Lisa, 1968– III. Series.
  HF5548.32.E1866 2004
  381'.142–dc22   2004003417

ISBN 0–415–33954–5 (hbk)
ISBN 0–415–33955–3 (pbk)

Contents

CONTENTS

Illustrations

FIGURES

TABLES

Contributors

LESLIE BUDD is Reader in Social Enterprise at the Open University and formerly Lecturer in Management Studies at Brunel University where he was part of the e-Commerce Research Network. He is an economist who has published widely the relationship between international financial markets and regional economic development, and in particular the impact of electronic trading on the stability of financial centres. Leslie is an Academician of the Academy of Social Sciences and currently Chair of the Regional Studies Association.

PATRICIA LEWIS is a Lecturer in the School of Business and Management at Brunel University and a member of the research centre BRESE (Brunel Research in Enterprise, Sustainability and Ethics) also located at Brunel. Her research interests centre on the development and evolution of enterprise culture, entrepreneurial identity and gender and enterprise. She has written (as Patricia Carr) a number of papers and a book entitled *The Age of Enterprise* on these issues.

JANE VINCENT has over 20 years' experience in the UK mobile communications industry working with BT and mmO$_2$ specializing in business transformation, product marketing and strategy development. She joined the Digital World Research Centre at Surrey University in 2002. Jane studied Social Sciences at the University of Leicester and her academic interests now are in the user behaviours associated with mobile communications, particularly emotion and mobile phones, on which she has published several papers. She has presented at academic and industry conferences and is currently delivering a second project for the UMTS Forum on the Social Shaping of 3G/UMTS Products and Services.

LEFKI PAPACHARALAMBOUS is a Research Associate and Lecturer in the School of Business and Management, Brunel University. She is also a research fellow at the Technological Education Institute of Halkida, Greece. Her doctoral thesis examines issues of knowledge embeddedness within virtual teams performing in socio-technological systems. She is a board member of the International Telework Academy, a virtual organization dedicated to promote research in the field of telework and other new forms of work. Lefki is the author of conference and journal papers on management issues in the e-Business world, in particular, knowledge and learning in organizations, virtual teamwork, e-Leadership and change management.

NELARINE CORNELIUS is a Senior Lecturer in Human Resource Management and Organizational Behaviour in the School of Business and Management, Brunel University. She is also Senior Honorary Research Fellow, King's College Hospital Medical School, University of London. Her research areas include learning and change in organizations, workplace diversity and quality of life and emotional labour.

MARTIN HARRIS is a Senior Lecturer in Management at the University of Essex and formerly Lecturer in Management Studies at Brunel University. He has published widely on virtual organizations and virtual learning and the network society. His current work is looking at how scholarly communications and their underlying knowledge services are being digitally restructured in the public domain.

SIMRAN K. GREWAL is a Doctoral Researcher at the School of Business and Management, Brunel University. Her research interests are exploring the social and organizational dynamics of introducing e-Learning technology in traditional UK universities. Her publications include 'The Social Dynamics of Integrating E-Mediated Learning into Traditional UK Universities', paper presented at e-Learn 2003 World Conference on e-Learning in Corporate, Government, Healthcare and Higher Education, Phoenix, Arizona, USA, November 7–11. She has been teaching at the Brunel School of Business and Management since 2001.

NOAH CURTHOYS is a Policy Analyst with HM Treasury in the UK. He has worked on e-Government issues since 1999, within both the academic and private sectors. This included doctoral research at Brunel University, a report for the Work Foundation and commercial research for Kable and Socitm. Prior to that he studied Political Science at the LSE and UCL. His current interests include public sector reform, international e-Government and workforce re-engineering.

CHARLES DENNIS is a Chartered Marketer and a Lecturer in Marketing and Retail Management at Brunel University, where he heads up the 'Marketing' pathway of the University's BSc Business and Management degree. Originally a Chartered Chemical Engineer, he spent some years in engineering and technical posts, latterly with a 'marketing' emphasis. This was followed by seven years with 'Marketing Methods' as an Institute of Marketing approved consultant. Charles has published internationally on consumer shopping behaviour, e-Shopping and e-Retailing. The textbook *Marketing the e-Business* (Harris and Dennis) was published by Routledge in 2002.

OLIVER RICHARDSON is a Lecturer in Computing in the Brunel School of Business and Management. His research interests are in the usage of the World Wide Web by small businesses, and in the growth and development of the UK wine industry. He has built and maintained a Web site on the UK wine industry for the last 6 years, and has written widely on the utilization of the World Wide Web by small producers.

SUZANNE MIECZKOWSKA holds a Master's Degree in Information Studies from the University of Brighton, and a BA (Hons) in French from the University of Western Ontario, Canada. She has been a research assistant at the Open University Business School since 2001, where she has been investigating the impact of e-Commerce on the management of internal business processes. Her other interests include the impact of self-service technology, library operations and information retrieval, qualitative research methods and the philosophy of research.

DAVID BARNES is Senior Lecturer in Operations and Strategic Management at Royal Holloway, University of London. His research interests centre on the strategic management of operations and the impact of e-Commerce on operations. Prior to his academic career he worked in the process plant contracting and building products manufacturing industries, in engineering and line management positions for a number of organizations ranging from blue chip to small family-owned businesses. He holds a BSc (Eng.) degree from Imperial College London, an MBA from the Open University and a PhD from Staffordshire University.

MATTHEW HINTON is a Lecturer in Information and Knowledge Management at the Open University Business School. His research interests include the impact of electronic commerce on operations and information technology evaluation, especially the performance management of e-Commerce applications. In addition he is interested in the system implementation dynamics of customer relationship management (CRM) systems. He holds a PhD in Innovation and Technology Assessment from Cranfield University and a BSc (Hons) in Business Information Technology from Kingston University. Prior to his academic role he worked in the petro-chemicals industry providing computer support and IT training.

ANGELA AYIOS conducted her PhD research on cross-cultural interpersonal trust in east–west joint ventures in Russia. After a decade working as the editor of a variety of business magazines, she decided to move to academia to follow up her interest in business ethics across different cultures. She has sat on the national executive of the European Business Ethics Network-UK, acting as joint editor of the newsletter. She is the author of *Trust and Western–Russian Business Relationships* (Ashgate: 2004). She lectures on business ethics at Brunel University and has research interests in trust, the professions and parental experiences of raising autistic children.

LISA HARRIS is Course Director of Brunel's e-Commerce BSc and Deputy Director of the Brunel MBA. She worked in banking for 10 years and her PhD research examined the management of change in the banking industry in the early days of the Internet. Lisa is currently running research projects reviewing emerging trends in online marketing ethics, e-Government and public sector marketing. She is a Chartered Marketer, Education Officer for the Royal Counties branch of the Chartered Institute of Marketing and also teaches Marketing courses for the Student Support Group and Oxford College of Marketing.

Foreword

Businessmen (and politicians) famously pride themselves on inhabiting the 'real world'. In the supposedly rigorous arena that they inhabit, 'hard-nosed' and 'tough' are terms of approval, in implicit or explicit contrast with 'academic', which has become code for 'airy-fairy' or just plain 'irrelevant'. In this perspective it was a stroke of marketing genius to invent the term 'hardware' for computers. Computers have everything that the decisive real-world operator needs: they operate in 'real time', are 'platforms' or 'solutions' which 'support clients' and applications of various kinds. They are 'what works'.

Perhaps the most impressive thing that computers support, however, is blind faith. Not at all put off by the implosion of the dotcoms, the UK government has committed itself to putting all government services online by the end of 2005, and has spent around £8bn on obliging departments and the wider public sector to comply with its demanding targets. Yet there is very little evidence that customers want or need online transactions, let alone hard payback from the investment. As Sir Peter Gershon's 2004 efficiency review inelegantly put it, 'Relatively little emphasis has been given to the efficiencies that could be delivered by realising the full benefits of these investments in seeking to migrate particular customer segments to new channels.'

Even the e-governmental total will be dwarfed in the next few years, as the public sector piles into the computerisation of back offices and outsourcing (not counting the purchasing, integration and implementation consultancy that goes with them). A significant amount of the spending will be concentrated on a few mega-projects, such as the NHS National Programme for IT and the amalgamation of Customs and Excise and Inland Revenue information systems. Historically, the success rate for large-scale computer projects is reported to be around 17 per cent.

Although the private sector affects much scorn for public-sector naivety in such matters, most companies also qualify as ICT fundamentalists. Undaunted by previous unhappy experience, they have enthusiastically invested in a succession of acronyms — ERM, CRM, EDRM — each of which turns out on closer inspection to have as little real meaning as the last. Investigations by McKinsey show that in the 1990s US banks invested billions in CRM which were largely wasted because they had neglected to check whether customers wished to be cross-sold to. They didn't. In such cases ICT isn't the 'enabler' (or even 'e-enabler') of consultancy literature so much as a *dis*abler, hard-wiring (that word again) routines and processes into place that actually prevent flexibility. Outsourcing is often the same. Hardly surprising, then, that the productivity effects of computers are notoriously elusive and hard to pin down.

Perhaps a little theory might have helped companies to get *really* real.

Because ICT does matter. Its effects are real enough, even if they aren't quite what companies expected. Take the music business, which in summer 2004 was enthusiastically talking up the 50th anniversary of the birth of rock 'n' roll in 1954 as a way of bolstering sagging album sales. Actually, 2004 is more likely to be remembered as the music majors' funeral, the Old Titans shot down and then buried by iTunes and GarageBand, two innovative programmes dreamed up by a New Titan, computer company Apple, which is now not only eating the oldies' lunch but cooking up a different meal to which they are not even invited.

The new economy in action? Well, yes. But, as this book illustrates in welcome and timely fashion, the new is surprisingly often just a line-extension of the old. There was no external barrier preventing the music business from embracing file-sharing over the internet rather than fighting it, or enabling its consumers to make their own music. Push rewind, and it transpires that what has really put the music industry in such dire straits (sorry) is a repetitive pattern of behaviour that was damaging enough in the old economy. Thus, despite today's fond evocations of 1954, at the time the music industry was actually appalled and baffled by rock 'n' roll. By 1959 it had all but killed the golden goose, which was only revived by an injection of energy and drollerie from four funny-looking Liverpool lads called the Beatles. On the technology front, the industry was half-hearted about tape-recorders until it became clear that the demand for music on the move allowed it to sell people quite a lot of what they already had, a satisfying trick it pulled off again with the upgrade to CDs. But by the time the internet arrived, the music companies had long ago used up any credit they had with consumers. When the latter had at last acquired the possibility of getting what they actually wanted, how could anyone imagine they would go back to being fobbed off with what companies chose to give them? As the Who, admittedly a bit ahead of time, had once warned, 'Won't Get Fooled Again'.

In an early poem, Ted Hughes wrote, 'The future's no calamitous change/But a malingering of now.' In demystifying and making sense, as the chapters in this book do, of what we mean by the so-called 'new' and 'e-economy', it is the underlying continuities that emerge as more enlightening than the breathless assertions of change. As Leslie Budd notes, every age believes it is new and different – 'the claims made by the disciples of the Information Age, Knowledge Economy and the new and e-economies, at the end of the second millennium, are no different from those of Adam Smith and Karl Marx in the eighteenth and nineteenth centuries or the proponents of modernity at the turn of the [twentieth] century.' Technology is a constant in today's economy, and it changes many aspects of business – but not, in a capitalist system, the need for a company to sell enough things to customers at a price that allows it to cover its costs, make a return to shareholders and invest in the future.

Simon Caulkin, Management Correspondent of The Observer

The economy of virtuality and reality

LESLIE BUDD AND LISA HARRIS

Anthony Powell is an English writer whose 12-volume opus is called *Dance to the Music of Time*. The title is based on a painting by the artist Poussin that hangs in the Wallace Collection in London. The painting shows the mythical figures of Bacchus and Pan orchestrating a dance. The dancers form a circle and dance around an open fire. As they complete each circle they change positions, but each dancer only sees their new immediate partner at each turn, because their backs are to the fire. Powell's work starts from the end of the First World War and ends after the Second. It is essentially a narrative on what it is to be English. He uses the Poussin painting as a metaphor to illustrate the way in which people move in and out of each other's lives, but at each turn of existence we do not have a full picture of whom we will meet and meet again. This metaphor of *Dance to the Music of Time* is equally applicable in trying to write an analytical narrative of the transformation of economy and society in the last and this millennium.

For those born in the last 50 years, the world represents a whirling dance of new revolutionary technology, organizational and personal change. In the last two centuries, we have moved from the Industrial Revolution to the Productivity Revolution to the Managerial Revolution to the Knowledge Revolution, according to Peter Drucker, the guru of management theory. These revolutions have seen the power and the triumph of the steam engine give way to the rapid stealth of the high-speed train; the coughing of the piston engine submit to the roar of the jet engine; the large reel of computer tape bow out to the microprocessor. In everyday life the ubiquity of the television in the last half century has now almost been matched by that of the mobile phone. We appear to be more globally connected, yet locally isolated, than ever before. How do we tell the story of new times and old times? Where does the old end and the new begin? At what point will the economy of reality finally give way to the economy of virtuality?

This book attempts to tell a story about this change from different and sometimes complementary perspectives. In doing so it attempts to take the reader on a journey through the minefield of claims and counter-claims of the Information Age and the Knowledge Society. We begin with a brief overview of the history of the e-Economy in order to remind ourselves that a significant amount of change has already taken place within a relatively short timespan.

Box 1.1
POLITICS VERSUS TECHNOLOGY

The cold war fuelled the development of the Internet because the possibility of hostile nuclear powers meant the US Dept of Defense needed a 'cellular' communication system that could re-route itself wherever communication lines were blocked.

1969   ARPANET (Advanced Research Project Agency Network) was formed by a group of universities and private research groups and funded by the US Dept of Defense.

1978   Randy Seuss and Ward Christensen invented the modem which allowed two computers to exchange files without going through a host system.

1979   Tom Truscott and Steve Bellovin modified the Unix operating system to allow people to exchange files over regular telephone wires which led to USENET (ARPANET's precursor).

1982   The National Science Foundation (NSF) launched the CSFNET which was open to any research institution willing to pay the fees and ban commercial use.

1983   Tom Jennings demonstrated how to post bulletin boards on PCs and set up FIDONET – the first big PC network (by 1991 tens of thousands of users around the world were using it). ARPANET was split in two: MILNET – for military use; ARPANET – for scientific research.

1984   Berners-Lee, a British software engineer was a full-time researcher at CERN, near Geneva when he was introduced to the Internet by a colleague. He found the software 'user-nasty' and so went about simplifying it and ultimately developed what is now know as WWW.

1987   NSF awarded a 5-year contract to Michigan Educational Research Information Triad (MERIT). By the time this contract was up for renewal, a number of commercial network providers were asking to be allowed to enter the Internet market.

        By the end of the 1980s US federal government was no longer willing to finance two separate networks and approved NSFNET – a new high speed network to replace ARPANET, which was becoming technically obsolete.

1990   Pentagon closed down ARPANET and left the Internet in the hands of the NSF.

        Berners-Lee's software was ready. It 'sat on top' of the Internet using its communications protocols and packet-switching technology, existing computers and phone lines. It consisted of three elements:

- HTML (hypertext mark-up language): computer language for formatting hypertext files.
- HTTP (hypertext transfer protocol): method for jumping between files.
- URL (universal resource locator): a unique address code for each file.

To show how it worked, he created the world's first Web site (www.info. cern.ch – sadly this site is no longer available to view). He also created a primitive Web browser that allowed users to read and edit files and within 4 months the first American Web site was launched. A posting on a bulletin board attracted a few hundred people a day to Berners-Lee's site.

1991   NSF proposed creating a high speed backbone network service for scientific researchers that was supported by taxpayers' money, and all other Internet users would have to sign up with a commercial Internet Service Provider (ISP).

1992   Hits on Berners-Lee's site were plotted on a graph and the exponential curve, a characteristic of the Web, began.

1993   Gopher, an Internet browser charged an annual license fee to non-academic users. An act of treason to the Internet community! Usage dropped and Gopher never recovered. The Internet had more than 1 million computers attached to it and e-Commerce was still an oxymoron. When anyone tried to make money from the online community they were automatically 'flamed'.

        30 April 1993, CERN, the European particle physics laboratory near Geneva, who owned the intellectual property rights to Berners-Lee's programmes released their rights so that anybody, anywhere in the world could use the World Wide Web protocols without paying a royalty or observing any legal restraints.

        Berners-Lee described the Web as a market economy and the exponential curve became the talisman of Wall Street investors.

1995   NSFNET closed down and the Internet was a private sector enterprise.

From 1996 onwards private enterprise dominated the Internet and its applications where many new technologies were brought to market and new technologies were talked about in the public domain before they had even been beta-tested to keep pace with the demand for new products and services.

1996   Search engines, JAVA, Internet phone.
        Emerging technologies included: virtual environments (VRML), collaborative tools, Internet appliance (network computer).

1997   Push, multicasting.
        Emerging technologies included: push.

1998   e-Commerce, e-Auctions, portals.
       Emerging technologies included: e-Trade, XML, intrusion detection.
1999   e-Trade, online banking, MP3.
       Emerging technologies included: net-cell phones, thin computing, embedded computing.
2000   ASP, Napster.
       Emerging technologies included: wireless devices, IPv6.
       Lawsuits of the year: Napster, DeCSS.
2001   First uncompressed real-time gigabit HDTV transmission across a wide-area IP network takes place on Internet2 (12 November).
       GÉANT, the pan-European Gigabit Research and Education Network, becomes operational (23 October), replacing the TEN-155 network which was closed down (30 November).
       The first live distributed musical – *The Technophobe and The Madman* – over Internet2 networks debuts on 20 February.
       Napster forced to suspend service but comes back later in the year as a subscription service.
       European Council finalizes an international cybercrime treaty on 22 June and adopts it on 9 November. This is the first treaty addressing criminal offences committed over the Internet.
       Emerging technologies: Grid computing, P2P.
2002   Abilene (Internet2) backbone deploys native IPv6 (5 August) and has 200 university, 60 corporate and 40 affiliate members (2 September).
       Global Terabit Research Network (GTRN) is formed composed of two OC-48 2.4GB circuits connecting Internet2 Abiline, CANARIE CA*net3, and GÉANT (18 February).
       Hundreds of Internet radio stations observe a *Day of Silence* in protest of proposed song royalty rate increases (1 May).
       A new US law creates a kids-safe 'dot-kids' domain (kids.us) to be implemented in 2003 (3 December).
       The FBI teams up with Terras Lycos to disseminate virtual wanted posts across the Web portal's properties (11 December).
2003   Last Abilene segment upgraded to 10Gbps (5 November).
       Little GLORIAD (Global Ring Network for Advanced Application Development) starts operations (22 December), consisting of a networked ring across the northern hemisphere with connections in Chicago, Amsterdam, Moscow, Novosibirsk, Zabajkal'sk, Manzhouli, Beijing and Hong Kong. This is the first-ever fibre network connections across the Russia–China border.
       The first official Swiss online election takes place in Anières (7 January).

Taxes make headlines as: larger US Internet retailers begin collecting taxes on all purchases; some US states tax Internet bandwidth; and the EU requires all Internet companies to collect value added tax (VAT) on digital downloads starting 1 July.

The French Ministry of Culture bans the use of the word 'email' by government ministries, and adopts the use of the more French sounding 'courriel' (July).

The Recording Industry Association of America (RIAA) sues 261 individuals on 8 September for allegedly distributing copyright music files over peer-to-peer networks.

Data extracted from Cassidy, J. (2002) *dotcon*. London: Penguin, and updated from various online sources by Janet Wood-Farrer.

The revolutionary leader of the People's Republic of China, Mao Tse-Tung,[1] stated that every journey of a thousand miles starts with the first step. In undertaking this journey, we attempt to navigate from first principles. The Oxford English Dictionary (OED) defines the following:

- *Economy*: The administration of the concerns and resources of a community or organised system, from the Greek *oikonomia*.
- *Reality*: Property of being real, resemblance to the original, real existence, what is real, what underlies appearances, real nature of.
- *Virtuality*: That is such for practical purposes though not in name or strict definition; not physically existing as such but made by software to appear to do so from the point of view of the program or the user; applied to memory that appears to be internal although most of it is external, transfer between the two being made automatically as required.
- *Rhetoric*: Art of persuasive or impressive speaking or writing; language designed to persuade or impress (often with the implication of insincerity, exaggeration etc.); persuasiveness of looks or acts.

These definitions provide us with the building blocks of our analytical narrative.

THE DEFINITIONAL CHALLENGES OF THE E-ECONOMY

Having reviewed the background and defined what we mean by reality, virtuality and rhetoric, what do we actually mean by the 'e-Economy'? Is it just another name for the new economy or the general resource underpinnings of e-Commerce and/or e-Business? Part of the definition is taken from our opening chapter:

> A definition suggests that the new economy was created by the age of networked intelligence: an age where every economic and social exchange can take place through ICT. The flow of information was physical through paper-based transactions in the old economy. In the new economy, all flows of information are digital, flowing at faster and faster speeds across computer networks (Tapscott 1996). The e-Economy therefore relies primarily on ICT infrastructure for the production, exchange and distribution of goods and services and as such is part of the larger new economy which encompasses the wider impact of the e-Economy and its infrastructure.
>
> (Budd 2004)

This is a useful first stab at a definition of the e-Economy, but we need to be more explicit about what we mean by the new economy, before we pin down one of its major components. But does the new economy merely represent the current phase in the long run process of what the Austrian economist Joseph Schumpeter called 'creative destruction'? The new economy is closely associated with developments in Information and Communications Technologies (ICT), delivering a faster, broader and deeper system of production and consumption of goods and services on a global scale. This speeding up of what is often called 'turnover time' creates forms of organizational, consumption and cultural change. Rapid growth in the development, use and dissemination of ICT offers the opportunity to overcome the constraints of time and space in geographical terms.

Knowledge and information and networked intelligence are central to the workings of any economy. A market economy is one in which price signals provide the intelligence of how resources should be distributed across the network of individual and connected activities. The structures of a market are understood by a system of codified and tacit knowledge. The language of marketing of distribution and marketing channels articulates flows between and across networks. Central to the transactions between producers and consumers is a flow of information on which informed choices can be made over the making, selling and buying of goods. This is what constitutes 'the administration of the concerns and resources of a community or organised system': the definition of an economy.

If all economies share a relationship between knowledge and information and networked intelligence, then what is new about the new economy and what is different about the e-Economy? One could say the former has newer technology and that the latter uses this new technology in an intensively different way to produce a new business model and a new way of organizing the flow of goods and services. The *Encyclopaedia of the New Economy* defines the new economy as:

> When we talk about the new economy, we're talking about a world in which people work with their brains instead of their hands. A world in which communications

technology creates global competition – not just for running shoes and laptop computers, but also for bank loans and other services that can't be packed into a crate and shipped. A world in which innovation is more important than mass production. A world in which investment buys new concepts or the means to create them, rather than new machines. A world in which rapid change is a constant. A world at least as different from what came before it as the industrial age was from its agricultural predecessor. A world so different its emergence can only be described as a revolution.

(http://hotwired.wired.com/special/ene/)

But is this particularly new? People have worked with their brains and hands since the first mechanization of agriculture in pre-modern times. Mass production is central to gaining economies of scale and the ability to gain and maintain market share and power. Microsoft may be a leading new economy company, but it mass produces its software products.

According to Anderson Consulting, 'e-enterprises will conduct e-commerce in the e-Economy in the 21st century' (http://ac.mit.edu/classes/presentations/presentations/eCom/sld008.htm). An e-Enterprise is a 'business or government enterprise with the capability to exchange value (money, goods, services or information) electronically'. An e-Economy is 'the broad business environment in which global commerce is conducted' (op. cit.). According to this view, the take up of the e-Economy is driven by four interconnected factors:

- expanding technological infrastructure;
- compelling consumer value;
- compelling business value;
- co-operative regulatory environment.

But does this perspective compel us? Does the definition convince? Are we still in the realm of the 'Art of persuasive or impressive speaking or writing; language designed to persuade or impress (often with the implication of insincerity, exaggeration etc.) Persuasiveness of looks or acts' (our definition of 'rhetoric')? How are we going to move forward to a working definition of the new economy and the e-Economy that allows us to make the analytical journey into the domain of business reality?

Often definitions of the new economy are conflated with that of the e-Economy. The following definition goes some way to a distinct field of enquiry into the e-Economy that is complementary to the new economy:

The e-economy depends on many innovative technical and institutional arrangements. One of the more fundamental arrangements is 'integration' – the interconnection of the data, documents, systems, and business processes of the different organizations participating in the e-Economy. Integration is necessary for the e-Economy, but it is difficult and expensive to achieve and it brings with it the risks of propagating errors, crashes, and disasters.

(http://ecom.fov.uni-.si/ECBledHome.nsf/0/
83bf29aa7e48b0cfc1256b980039aa2b?OpenDocument&Click)

What is our perspective and one that tells the story of this book? Tapscott's definition provides us with a good starting point. The new economy is one in which transactions take place through digital means using ICT infrastructure. As a result of the way in which transactions are undertaken, there are large and wide-ranging impacts on investment and output decisions, consumer choices, organizational characteristics, operational decisions, business models, labour markets and access to public services. Although rooted in the economy of virtuality through digital media and ICT infrastructure, the new economy encompasses a range of activities where ICT is applied to the economy of reality (in the words of others: 'the old economy').

The e-Economy is a subset of the new economy. It is an economy in which the organization of the production, distribution and consumption of goods and services is entirely through digital means and relies entirely on the delivery capacities of ICT. These means include the Internet and mobile telephony. Therefore, the impact of the new economy is much deeper and wide-ranging than that of the e-Economy. Inevitably there will be an elision between the two as there are spillovers from the boundaries of the e-Economy into the new economy and vice versa. What connects the old economy to the new economy to the e-Economy is innovation and the constant revolutionizing of the conditions of production: Schumpeter's process of 'creative destruction'.

CREATIVE DESTRUCTION'S JOURNEY THROUGH THE E-ECONOMY

Joseph Schumpeter (1883–1950) wanted to be the world's greatest economist, the world's greatest horseman and the world's greatest lover, according to popular rumour. Whether he actually succeeded in the last two claims – or if instead this was an early example of 'sexing up' – is a matter for his biographers. He remains, however, one of the world's most influential economists. Schumpeter developed his concept of 'creative destruction' from the observation that, although capitalism was evolutionary in character, its underlining condition was revolutionary. That is, innovation and technical progress generated 'industrial mutation' and sent gales of 'creative destruction' through the economic system. New technologies, process and management innovation and the opening up of competition in global markets cause this mutation. The constant threat to the old from the new reaches every corner and touches every sinew of human experience, as well as the organization of economy and society. This process is a very useful guide for us to narrate the story of this book, how the old turns into the new and the new turns into the old. This is also the reality that businesses in market economies live with every day. The rhetoric of new ways of organizing business and the economy may influence decision-making, but the promise of the new is often just that: promise not performance delivery.

STRUCTURE OF THE BOOK

Our first two chapters are connected by their exploration of the old and the new and the impact of the creative destruction in the evolution of the e-Economy. In Chapter 1, 'Death of the "new"? Re-materializing the economy', Leslie Budd explores the claims that we now live in a new age of the 'information society' and the 'knowledge economy' and gives a sceptical account of these claims. He argues that every generation claims it is living in a new era by drawing on the analysis of the impact of art and technology on the world at the end of the nineteenth century and start of the twentieth century, using the metaphor of the 'shock of the new'. The test for any new proposition like the e-Economy is: where is the theory; where is the evidence; and where are the data? Investigating the assertion that the new economy and e-Economy has engendered a 'weightless society' and the 'death of distance', Budd finds little theory, not much evidence and almost no data. In examining the productivity miracle wrought by the new economy, he finds a variable picture in which mirages appear just as much as miracles. In reviewing the organizational implications of the e-Economy he reaches the conclusion that creative destruction and human ingenuity, rather than the digital basis of the e-Economy, is a more important determinant of the new and the overthrowing of the old: moving from technological rhetoric to the delivery of business reality.

Patricia Lewis takes up the theme of creative destruction in Chapter 2, 'Entrepreneurial chaos, entrepreneurial order and the dotcom bubble'. She undertakes a discourse analysis to argue that cultural factors are important for the emergence of the new economy and the dotcom bubble. Furthermore, she notes that the discourses of enterprise and enterprise culture are central to the relationship of the dotcom bubble to the new economy, and the explanation of the dotcom phenomenon is much more complex than the suggestion that its demise resulted from the suspension of the fundamentals of business reality. The norms of enterprise culture were rooted in the socio-economic shifts in the Anglo-Saxon economies from the late 1970s on, and its acceptance became generalized for individuals and organizations. The dotcom phenomenon is rooted in the liberation that enterprise enables, but brings with it the threat of chaos as the process of creative destruction informs every entrepreneurial activity. The opportunities created by the e-Economy have allowed many individuals to recreate themselves as entrepreneurs. Lewis draws on some evidence of women entrepreneurs to elucidate the arguments for the culturally liberating aspects of entrepreneurial activity. It is the constant shift from entrepreneurial order to entrepreneurial chaos that explains the rise and fall of the dotcom phenomenon. Lewis's perspective is similar to that of Schumpeter so that the rhetoric of the e-Economy merges with reality because of the embedding of enterprise culture in economy and society. In this view, the economy of virtuality and the economy of reality are bridged by the new cultural norms of enterprise.

Our attention moves from the role of culture to that of social shaping in Chapter 3, 'Social shaping of government: what can be learned from the adoption of mobile mediated communications?' In this chapter, Jane Vincent looks at the ubiquitous nature of the mobile phone and its role in transforming modes of communication and the delivery of e-Government services. She argues that the social shaping of technologies is an important determinant in the take-up and use of mobile telephony. Social shaping refers to the social practices that feed back into the development of technology. These include the syntax that consumers have developed for texting on mobile phones and the unwillingness to adopt WAP technologies. This has implications for the development of e-Government and the prospects of being an e-Citizen. E-Citizens, in Vincent's view, do not have to be technologically literate but have a need for electronically mediated communications. She points to the interaction of technology and society being a continuing and powerful process. Technologies may be constantly changing but our reasons for doing things changes less frequently. There is a high degree of technological entropy – a tendency for technology to race ahead of relatively stationary social practices.

Social shaping is important in how we manage new technologies and the pace of their take-up. New technologies are often introduced for marketing reasons – most of us do not need the power of a Pentium IV processor but we are persuaded that we are somehow antediluvian if we do not constantly upgrade our kit. The same applies to the latest mobile phones and associated gadgets. We may want them for what they bestow in terms of social practices – status, gadgets, toys, etc. The reality of social practices therefore determines our engagement with the economy of reality and the way in which social shaping bounds the rhetoric of business in advancing the absolute necessity of new ICT. In advancing this argument, Vincent is reminding us of the essential historical truth of Schumpeter's destructively creative insight.

The issue of governance is at the heart of contemporary debates about organizations, whether public or private. Another challenge for the contemporary organization is leadership. In Chapter 4, 'e-Leadership: challenges of new governance models', Lefki Papacharalambous takes an enthusiastic view of the organizational changes engendered by the e-Economy. Following Drucker, she claims that we live in the era of inter-dependence, in which paternalistic authority gives way to delegated and coaching styles of management. In this view, knowledge is not hierarchical, and flatter organizational structures develop within which new leaders and leadership styles are needed. Knowledge-intensive industries need creativity and innovation, but also a change in the mindset of the population of organizations, as well as society at large. Papacharalambous does make the heroic claim that we live in a era of 'e-Everything', but conditions this rhetoric with a presumption that even e-Everything will become an everyday thing in the future. She quotes work by Choudhury which claims that organizational performance

xxiii

metrics such as the return on capital invested or return on net assets will be replaced by return on talent (ROT). If this claim is verified, it has large implications for organizations in decisions over leadership and accompanying styles. Whether the rhetoric of e-Leaders and e-Leadership becomes the universal reality of business organizations is for the verdict of history, as it dances through our journey. At present, few organizations fit this profile. We wait to see whether creative destruction will overthrow the economy of reality and replace it with the economy of virtuality.

We are reminded of the realities of working in organizations that have exploited ICT and instigated forms of virtual working in Chapter 5, 'e-Management and workforce diversity'. Nelarine Cornelius points out that despite the rhetoric and hype about new ways of thinking in the organization of the workforce in e-Business, there is little reflective or empirical knowledge about the breadth of experience of employees in e-Business settings. Cornelius looks at the human side of e-Business – the 'people' issues. She takes us through the literature on e-Working, in particular the role and impact of call centres in enabling 24/7 working. In particular, she looks at how conventional human resource management practice copes with the different demands imposed on it by e-Businesses. Despite the rhetoric of the virtual organization, Cornelius shows that new practices are not evolving quickly or even being established. The shift of call centres from the developed to the underdeveloped economies complicates this issue. Cross-border operations are driven by cost considerations, but in organizations where soft assets (customer service relationships) are frequently as important as hard assets, other approaches may be needed. Cornelius points to the possibilities of applying capabilities theory to this issue. This theory suggests that freedom of opportunity, quality of life and life chances are important considerations for e-Business organizations to flourish and create the conditions for new organizational and HR practices. In this context, virtual working becomes genuinely flexible in the way in which individuals and organizations interact. There is considerable evidence to show that genuinely flexible organizations are more productive ones. In concluding, she points to the fact that e-Business is a logical extension of the mechanization of the nineteenth century. The historical realities of business remind us to treat the rhetoric of the virtual organization with caution. We are also reminded that the process of 'creative destruction' is a constant.

The impact of digital technologies in organizations, both private and public, is still relatively underresearched, particular the prospects of e-Learning. In Chapter 6, 'ICT and institutional change at the British Library', Martin Harris argues that the spread of global information networks will not necessarily undermine the role of large public sector knowledge providers. He uses a comprehensive case study of the British Library, a global library brand, to advance his argument. It has been claimed that the speed and take-up of networked technologies and associated organization forms spell the end of large public bureaucracies who are knowledge providers. The globalized private providers are the new wave in the dissemination of knowledge in education in this view. It's the 'whiz-bang' global media companies that will digitize the education universe, across the globe. As Harris argues, local reality is a little more prosaic than the global rhetoric.

He begins with a review of the academic debates on digital learning and their implications for higher education in the United Kingdom. Much of the debate has centred on the belief that global markets and ICT are transforming higher education. Therefore the new should be embraced as quickly as possible. As Harris's study of the digitization of library services at the British Library demonstrates, the old is still with us in the type of knowledge services demanded, but it is their form of dissemination that may be different. He reviews different forms of scholarly communication, electronic delivery and the digital preservation of archives. There is a detailed examination of the 'Collect Britain' project – the digitization of the entire collection – in the context of the institutional location of the library. In the apparent age of the 'hybrid library', how innovation is managed is a key issue. In conclusion, Harris notes the threat to historically embedded knowledge institutions like the British Library from 'borderless education' underwritten by powerful global corporations. Despite the rhetoric of a global information society, the relationship between knowledge and information and their digital dissemination is a complex one. Large public bureaucracies that are global knowledge providers may not appear to be part of the new reality, but they will not necessarily all be discarded as old.

The question of whether e-Learning is the educational model of the future is still an open one. Virtual learning forms co-exist alongside traditional forms in large numbers of universities throughout the world. Universities are communities of individuals in the pursuit of universal education and its dissemination to a global 'visible' college beyond campus boundaries, whether real or virtual. What is the balance between e-Mediated learning and traditional forms of learning in universities? In Chapter 7, 'Coerced evolution: a study of the integration of e-Mediated learning into a traditional university', Simran Grewal explores part of this question by taking a sociological perspective. She argues a number of social challenges are generating the gradual and incremental adoption of e-Mediated learning and its efficiency. She uses a case study of the Virtual Learning Environment (VLE) of a traditional campus university populated by a total of 15,000 full-time and part-time students and 800 academic staff. E-Mediated learning is the use of ICT-based teaching and learning infrastructure that takes manifold forms. There are many claims that the demise of universities is upon us because of VLEs and the prospect of the virtual university. Universities throughout the world have become more driven by corporate imperatives, particularly in the United Kingdom. Yet, it is not clear that the drivers for this corporate shift are ICT and associated technological infrastructures. Universities are major employers and have a large local impact. They have become more complex organizations that – in the UK at least – have been publicly underfunded for the last 25 years. Many universities have fallen for the rhetoric of the new world that the VLE engenders, as though there will be seamless transition to the new learning order. In reality, this is a fragmented and problematic process in which the old confronts the new and the new confronts the old.

In reviewing the social dynamic of the virtual university, Grewal points to the downside of modernity and the claims for the new enlightenment. Trust and governance are central to any organization and this is a key issue in any move towards virtualization of university education. Moreover, e-Learning institutions will have higher transactions costs and they seek to implement comprehensive operational procedures. In the case study, Grewal shows the assumption that all students are 'technologically literate' to be false. Moreover, there is a 'free-rider' problem of academic staff waiting for colleagues to set up local VLEs so that they can use them, but not contribute to the hard graft of their development. In this case, VLE is a support mechanism and not a substitute for conventional practice. Creative destruction may be appealing, but the set-up costs of VLEs are large and may not be suitable for traditional universities. The economy of virtuality has some way to go in matching the economy of reality that pervades most of higher education.

The prospective social transformation of ICT has implications for the way in which we are governed and the public services that enable us to maintain our social practices. The journey in the development of e-Government is narrated in Chapter 8, 'e-Government: from utopian rhetoric to practical realism'. Noah Curthoys sets out how the array of portals, targets and re-engineering that constitute e-Government has shifted from the rhetoric of technological change to the reality of management and performance. He reviews the development of e-Government, contrasting and comparing its development in the US and UK: from re-inventing e-Government in the former to the rebuilding of e-Government in the latter, beyond its developmental hype. The theory and practice of e-Government still seem distant cousins in the UK, as there appears to be little innovation since the first branding of digital government. The greatest impact has been in e-Business practices imparting commercialization in government services. The least impact has been on the general culture of the civil service. Curthoys concludes there has been a perceptual shift from 'wide-eyed hype' to a focus on 'core operability', and also a move in the control of e-Government from lead agencies to powerful departments. Finally, budgetary constraint has reined in dotcom dreams. The realities of the everyday economy have constrained the digital visions of the economy of virtuality in the e-Government universe.

In contrast to the digital dreams of revolutionizing government, the impact of the new e-Economy on retailing has been a variable. In bridging rhetoric and reality, e-Retail is on the cusp between the economy of virtuality and the economy of reality. This issue is one of a number explored in Chapter 9, 'e-Retail: paradoxes for suppliers and consumers'. Charles Dennis and Oliver Richardson point out the apparent contradiction between the 320 per cent increase in the number of Web sites and the dramatic increase in business failures of Web-based companies. They examine the use and impact of the Web on a number of small-scale rural industries – vineyards, smokeries, herb and other gardens and woodworkers. Discussions of the threats to the rural economy are current in most countries of the European Union (EU). There is a significant decay of distance in the provision of wired and wireless technology from the main urban centres. The rural economy is one then that suffers from the digital divide. Dennis and Richardson review the use of the Web and its take-up, including the different focus for small rural industries. The main purpose of these sites is marketing, affording greater access to potential market opportunities. The other purpose is educative to generate knowledge and interest in the products of these industries. The authors go on to put the development of e-Retail in context of the social and cultural importance of shopping. Will e-Retail reduce the benefits of retail therapy? Consumption is an economically rational act because it provides the means in terms of income of another individual's consumption. E-Retail will not change this economic fact. But, is the psychological benefit of shopping tied to the act of consumption, irrespective of location: real or virtual? Is it in this light that the rhetoric of having a Web site as a business 'must' needs to be viewed? There is also the cultural issue of community: as out-of-town malls destroy local shops will e-Retail help rebuild them as virtual intermediaries? Shopping is a familiar, intimate and universal experience. Is the process of destroying real shopping undermining the creativity of virtual retail? This is one of the key questions as the e-Economy develops and matures.

One of the most overlooked areas in the hype about the e-Economy is operations management. The same could equally apply to the operational considerations of retail. In Chapter 10, 'e-Business processes: information and operations for competitive advantage', Suzanne Mieczkowska, David Barnes and Mathew Hinton set out the impact of e-Business operations on organizational strategy in advancing competitive advantage. They focus on the impact of disintermediation, business process management and relationships to customers and suppliers from the use of the Internet. Drawing on case studies from different sectors, they examine the rhetoric and business reality of e-Business operations. Despite the hype surrounding e-Enterprises, Mieczkowska, Barnes and Hinton argue that many companies are not able or are unwilling to impose e-Business processes overnight. Furthermore, they suggest there is compelling evidence that companies are taking a more holistic and incremental and not 'big bang' approach to the adoption of e-Business. They conclude by arguing that sustainable competitive advantage will ensure when e-Commerce is used to support a business strategy based on differentiation or superior customer service. The economy of virtuality neither guarantees differentiation nor superior customer service. As many companies also operate within the economy of reality, the promise of e-Business processes will not necessarily deliver strategic operations. In this context, e-Business operations provide a rich seam in which the rhetoric and business reality of the e-Economy can be mined.

Throughout this book the issue of trust and governance is touched upon. These two interconnected concepts are central to the development and management of any organization in both public and private domains. In all the hype about the Internet, the stress has been on the virtual organization or the Internet entrepreneur. Little attention has been paid to one of the least mentioned stakeholders in the e-Economy: the service workers who constitute the majority of labour demand. In building trust in stakeholder relationships: are call centres sweat shops or massage parlours? Angela Ayios and Lisa Harris examine the continuum of low to high trust relationships in the evolution of e-Business operations. They set out a continuum from low (calculative) trust to intermediate (knowledge-based) trust to strong (affect-based) trust. They follow this

xxvii

with a comprehensive discussion of businesses, brands and trust. Virtual media actually increases the value of trust to a business as the role of call centre develops multi-functional characteristics. Ayios and Harris use the metaphor of sweat shops and massage parlours – in a digital and dislocated service environment, organizations that engender trust and appear to have good working practices for educated, informed and knowledgeable staff will sustain competitive advantage. Moreover, in this new environment, stakeholder relationships based on stronger trust relations is a must. They argue that a high quality integrated service provision is required for a business environment that operates through many simultaneous channels if the evolving business reality is to live up to the rhetoric of the e-Economy. The economy of virtuality does not allow organizations to escape the organizational imperatives of the economy of reality: legitimate governance and beneficial trust relations. In the hype of e-Enterprise, e-Business, e-Commerce and the e-Economy, digitized and virtual media do not substitute for these basic lessons.

In Powell's *Dance to the Music of Time*, there is a constant figure that spans the 25 years that the book covers, apart from the narrator. This figure is Widmerpool, an Everyman[2] character whose flawed personality does not prevent him from progressing up the social and economic ladder, despite humble beginnings. In the e-Economy, ICT takes on the role of Widmerpool: it appears constantly and everywhere. The dance of the economy of virtuality and the economy of reality has to negotiate more complex moves. The business reality of the e-Economy rests just as much on human ingenuity, being selectively creative in destroying the old and navigating the new. The rhetoric of the e-Economy would have us believe that all you need is ICT, and the rest follows. The long march of the history of knowledge has not stopped because of the invention of the telephone, the television, the Internet and the mobile phone. In 1930, Mao Tse-Tung wrote:

> Knowledge begins with practice, and theoretical knowledge which is acquired through practice must return to practice. The active foundations of knowledge manifest itself not only in the active leap from perceptual to rational knowledge, but – and this is more important – it must manifest itself in the leap from rational knowledge to revolutionary knowledge.[3]

The great leap from the rational knowledge underpinning the economy of reality to the revolutionary knowledge underpinning the economy of virtuality has not yet occurred despite the rhetoric of the new economy. We are still taking faltering steps in the process of creative destruction, in fits and starts as Schumpeter perceptively noted. You probably will not agree with all the opinions expressed in the chapters which follow, but more importantly, you will find yourself questioning the rhetoric and thinking about the Internet and its applications more critically and creatively.

NOTES

1   Mao Tse-Tung was the first Communist leader of China after the revolution of 1949. Mao drew his analogy from the Long March of the Communist Party to safety at a time when its army was losing the civil war in China.
2   Everyman is usually a typical character: 'the man in the street'.
3   Taken from his Collected Works published in 1930.

FURTHER READING

Cassidy, J. (2001) *Dotcon*, Harmondsworth: Penguin.
Castells, M. (1996) *The Rise of the Network Society*, Oxford: Blackwell.
Harris, L. and Dennis, C. (2002) *Marketing the e-Business*, London: Routledge.
Jackson, P., Harris, L. and Eckersley, P. M. (2003) *e-Business Fundamentals*, London: Routledge.
Woolgar, S. (ed.) (2003) *Virtual Society?*, Oxford: Oxford University Press.

Chapter 1

Death of the 'new'? Re-materializing the economy

LESLIE BUDD

KEY LEARNING POINTS

After completing this chapter you should have an understanding of:

- Historical perspectives of the so-called 'new economy'
- The impact of the 'new economy' upon growth and productivity
- Micro- and macroeconomic perspectives of the Internet age
- The organizational implications of the 'new economy'

INTRODUCTION

The title of this chapter is a combination of the title of a television series of the 1980s, *The Shock of the New*, concerning the quest for the 'new' age from the late nineteenth century onwards, and the work of the economist Danny Quah who claims that the new or 'weightless' economy has created de-materialized products, for example, software (Quah 2001). This chapter argues that these claims for the existence of a new 'e-Economy' and its weightlessness are excessive. Many economic activities are still rooted in producing manufactured goods that are to be sold in shopping malls and high streets, and also in services that do not require the intermediary of a computer for their production and delivery. One of the most enduring, and possibly global, industries is motor manufacturing. Most leading businesses in the world are still large, bureaucratic entities, displaying hierarchical organizational characteristics (du Gay 2000). What has changed, or what is possibly new, is the deeper and wider use of information and communication technologies (ICT) in the production, exchange and distribution of products and services. These technologies speed up time to market and initiate new organizational possibilities, for example **supply and value chain management**.

1

THINK POINT

Before we start our journey through this chapter by constructing a narrative, we have to ask what is e-Business and/or e-Commerce or the new economy? The British government has defined e-Commerce as: 'The exchange of information across electronic networks, at any stage in the supply chain, whether within an organization, between businesses, between businesses and consumers, or between the public and private sectors, whether paid or unpaid' (HMSO 1998). It has also been used interchangeably with the digital economy or the new economy. The term e-Economy, however, covers a much wider and deeper spectrum of activities than implied by the definition of e-Commerce, given above. We use the term e-Economy in this book (see Introduction) in order to date the development of what has been termed the new economy, so that we do not get into intricate discussion of when the old economy became the new and the new economy then becomes old.

A definition suggests that the new economy was created by the age of networked intelligence: an age where every economic and social exchange can take place through ICT. The flow of information was physical through paper-based transactions in the old economy. In the new economy, all flows of information are digital, flowing at faster and faster speeds across computer networks (Tapscott 1996). The e-Economy therefore relies primarily on ICT infrastructure for the production exchange and distribution of goods and services and as such is part of the larger new economy which encompasses the wider impact of the e-Economy and its infrastructure.

The structure of this chapter and its arguments are organized along the following lines:

- An account of the claims for a new age, which in reality corresponds to every generation believing that it lives in a new era. This introduction draws on accounts of the development of **modernity**, the process of creative destruction, long waves of innovation in economic life, the ideology of the Machine Age and the progress from the *Industrial Revolution* to the *Productivity Revolution* to the *Management Revolution* (Drucker 1998), culminating in the 'knowledge society'.
- A stringent review of the literature on the 'weightless economy', the 'thin economy' and the 'de-materialized economy'. This review establishes the context in which the claims for the superior productivity performance of the e-Economy is analysed.
- An examination of the productivity miracle that was claimed for the new economy in general and the e-Economy in particular from the late 1990s onwards. This examination includes an analysis of data and information from the United

States and Europe in order to assess the contention that there has been a permanent and universal enhancement of productivity in these countries which can be sustained.

- An exploration of the microeconomic impact of the new economy and e-Economy, in particular their implications for management of organizations.

SCENE SETTING

The 'Gottdiener Test'[1] can be used to investigate every new idea that claims to transform the world we inhabit, whether it is globalization, the age of networked intelligence or the information or knowledge society. It consists of three parts:

1 Where is the theory?
2 Where is the evidence?
3 Where are the data?

Theory

The theoretical framework used to explore whether the evolution of the e-Economy actually represents a de-materialization of the economy is transactions cost economics (TCE). This branch of economics is closely associated with institutional economics and the study of organization, both in theory and practice. That is, the comparative study of economic institutions, in particular the firm, the market and the contractual relationships between organizations. In this framework, the market and the firm are seen as organizations. TCE looks at the contractual arrangements of co-operative relationships between firms, for example investigations range from market exchange to centralized organizational hierarchies, **vertically integrated** supply chains and networks. From the perspective of TCE, economics is a science of contract, rather than of choice between competing demands and limited resources (Buchanan 1975). Transaction costs have been defined as 'the costs of running the economic system' (Arrow 1969: 4). One of the foremost exponents of TCE is the economist Oliver Williamson, who sets out four propositions that underpin TCE as a field of enquiry:

1 central to the study of transactions costs is the concept of opportunism;
2 economic activity, that includes investments in physical and human capital that is related to particular transactions, is especially important for the study of opportunism;
3 central to an understanding of opportunism is the efficient processing of information;
4 a comparative institutional framework is essential to the examination of transaction costs (Williamson 1985).

Opportunism in markets is defined as a strong form of self-seeking behaviour, of which there are two aspects. The first is *adverse selection* and the second is *moral hazard*. Adverse selection operates at the level of the organization which seeks to minimize the risk of poor decisions. Without proper safeguards in place, for example contractual arrangements, making the wrong decisions will greatly increase risk. Moral hazard relates to other agencies and economic actors, for example public authorities, bailing out the consequences of poor decision-making by organizations. The comparative institutional assessment is the study of separate alternatives, in particular what Williamson calls 'governance structures', designed to manage the impact of opportunism in economic transactions. Another element central to TCE is bounded rationality. This is the psychological assumption that economic factors intend their actions to be rational, but are actually limited in their ability to achieve rational outcomes in their decision-making. Rationality is bounded (limited) in organizations and networks because they do not operate in perfectly competitive markets.

Evidence

Evidence and data concerning the superior performance of the new economy and e-Economy are actually hard to come by. Partly it is a matter of size, and partly it is because of the methodological problems of disentangling the elements of the old economy from the new. The claims rest on the evidence of the productivity performance of the US economy between 1995 and 2000. This evidence suggested that there had been a **paradigm shift** in the performance of the US economy that had racheted up productivity and economic growth to a new higher plateau in the late 1990s. Moreover, the realities of the stock market cycle had been overcome as cyber-analysts boasted of the Dow-Jones stock market index reaching 30,000 by 2000. At the time of writing in early 2004 the Dow-Jones index measured 9,300.

The American economist Robert Gordon has questioned whether the infrastructure of the new economy and e-Economy measure up to the inventions of the past (Gordon 2000). He is sceptical because the main driver of the increased production and use of computers is associated with a ten-fold decline in their real prices between 1960 and 2000. The other main driver was the long **bull market** in stocks and shares that drove down the cost of capital, raised the role of equity to that of a messianic asset and drove institutions to seek and create higher return and risk asset classes. It also coincided with a long decline in consumer, producer and commodity prices (IMF 2003). The historical reality is that the annual average long run return on equities is 1 per cent. In other words, the dotcom into dotbomb into dotcon phenomenon was another speculative bubble that ranks alongside that of the Tulip Crisis of the seventeenth century and the South Sea Bubble of the eighteenth century.[2] Gordon's own words express his doubts about the new economy:

> The sceptic's case begins with a new interpretation of the recent productivity revival. While impressive on the surface, the revival reveals a marked imbalance in its location

within the economy, appearing to be centred in the production of computer hardware, including peripherals, and telecommunications equipment, with substantial spill-over to the rest of durable manufacturing. However, outside the 12 per cent of the economy engaged in manufacturing durable goods, the new economy's effects on productivity growth are surprisingly absent, and capital deepening has been remarkably unproductive.

(Gordon 2000: 4)

Data

A few siren voices have been heard to question the 'new'. The scepticism was founded on the Solow paradox, named after the economist, Robert Solow: 'You can see the computer age everywhere but in the productivity statistics' (Solow 1987). Critics of what can be called the 'Solow/Gordon position' have suggested that the permanent ratcheting up effect only began in 1995, a period that was not covered by their analysis. However, Gordon's later analysis of the US non-farm private growth generated the following results:

- 2.66 per cent per annum between 1950 and 1973;
- 1.42 per cent per annum between 1973 and 1995;
- 2.86 per cent per annum between 1995 and 2000.

In fact, the driver of US productivity in the late twentieth century was manufacturing, in particular the production of computers and the spillover effects from their use. The role of manufacturing in the US 'growth miracle' has been understated in the popular press. Manufacturing productivity grew by:

- 2.61 per cent per annum between 1950 and 1973;
- 2.57 per cent per annum between 1973 and 1995;
- 5.93 per cent per annum between 1995 and 2000.

Most of the latter period's performance was accounted for in the final year. The main drivers were:

- the growth in the use of computers in computer-based manufacturing;
- the expansion of electronic data processing (EDP) systems in wholesale and retail outlets, for example Wal-Mart.

The claims made for services, particularly financial services, are not well supported by the data. Productivity in services is notoriously difficult to measure, but the apparently impressive performance of financial services was merely a size effect; that is, a short-term surge in the volume of trading through the same infrastructure, but not a sustainable change in the efficiency of operations.

5

A NEW AGE OR ARE ALL AGES NEW?

In 1980, the art historian and critic Robert Hughes wrote and narrated a television series entitled *The Shock of the New: Art and the Century of Change*. In the accompanying book, Hughes examined the development of art and culture from the late nineteenth to the late twentieth century: the period known as modernism. Essentially, modernism is a view of the world that posits the progress of science and technology, and its underlying culture as the organizing principle of rational modern society. Early proponents of modernism proclaimed it had dramatically changed the world in a very short period. In the opening chapter of his book, 'The Mechanical Paradise', Hughes summarizes the prevalent view of the time:

> In 1913, the French writer Charles Péguy remarked that 'the world has changed less since the time of Jesus Christ than it has in the last thirty years'. He was speaking of all the conditions of Western capitalist society; its idea of itself, its sense of history, its beliefs, its pieties, and modes of production – and its art. In Péguy's time, the time of our grandfathers, and great-grandfathers, the visual arts had a kind of social importance they can no longer claim today, and they seemed to be in a state of utter convulsion. Did cultural turmoil predict social turmoil? Many people thought so then; today we are not so sure, but that is because we live at the end of modernism, whereas they were alive at the beginning.
>
> (Hughes 1980: 9).

Each age tends to induce the contemporary inhabitants to claim that their epoch represents 'the new'. At the very end of the twentieth century and the start of the twenty-first century, the Information Age and its supporting Internet infrastructure ushered in the new global knowledge society. Or did it? The following quote also captures the faith in the progress of new technology and its industries:

> The more a country starts its development on the foundations of modern industry, like the United States, for example, the more rapid the process of destruction. Capitalist production therefore, develops technology, and the combining together of various processes into a social whole, only by sapping the original sources of all wealth – the soil and the labourer.[3]

On asking first year undergraduates on an e-Commerce degree who was the author of this quote, many replied Bill Gates, others Tim Burners-Lee, one of the founders of the World Wide Web. The answer is in note 3, but the author was writing of the chemical and electrical industries of the new 'modern industry' of the late nineteenth century.

The reference to the destruction of industry is redolent of one of the most famous economists of the twentieth century: Joseph Schumpeter. One of Schumpeter's most repeated concepts is that of **creative destruction**. This process develops what

6

Schumpeter called 'industrial mutation', that is, the revolutionizing of the economic structure from within. The opening up of foreign competition, new technology, process and management innovation threaten to destroy the old economic structure and create a new one. Although Schumpeter viewed capitalism as having an evolutionary character, the internal structure of industries was faced by the revolutionizing of production.

The seeds of germination of the new industrial and business processes are sown from the remnants of the old ones (Schumpeter 1942). For example, the pharmaceutical industry can claim to be one of the few global industries. The constituent companies rely on patenting new drug discoveries to maintain their competitive advantage and global reach. Once the use of the new drugs becomes widespread, there is an attrition in the control of the market, as the drug can be copied easily from the moment the time limit on the patent is up. The research experience of developing, marketing and selling the drug provides the basis for developing the next generation of treatments. New treatments may require different research facilities, industrial processes and organizational change. As the old pharmaceutical order is being destroyed a new one is being created to take its place: the essence of creative destruction. The process of creative destruction is not, in Schumpeter's view, a constant one. It comes in fits and starts, and sometimes torrents. This perspective also lends itself to the proponents of **Kondratieff waves**, including Schumpeter himself in his book *Business Cycles* (Schumpeter 1939).

Nikolai Kondratieff was an economist from the Soviet Union, who argued from the Marxist perspective that capitalism tended to experience a falling rate of profit. This tendency would be experienced most strongly every 50 years, leading to major periodic crises. The only way to resolve these crises was to invest in a new set of technologies offering new profitable opportunities from the new industries these technologies offered (Kondratieff 1935). Schumpeter adapted the 50 year cycle to suggest that:

> Historically the first Kondratieff wave covered by our material means the industrial revolution, including the protracted process of its absorption. We date it from the eighties of the eighteenth century to 1842. The second stretches over what has been called the age of steam and steel. It runs its course between 1842 and 1897. And the third, the Kondratieff of electricity, chemistry and motors, we date from 1889 on.
>
> (Schumpeter 1939)

The planner Sir Peter Hall suggests the fourth wave began in the mid-1950s. Central to the third and fourth waves is innovation in communications in command and control (Hall 1998). Hall speculates on the possibility of a fifth Kondratieff wave, based on the technological infrastructure of the Information Age:

> In the mid-1990s, however, almost every observer is agreed that something really new is happening: the question is whether it represents the basis of a fifth Kondratieff long

wave or a fundamental evolution of capitalism itself from an industrial to an informational era, or – as now seems certain – both at once.

(ibid.: 945)

Hall's comment is the touchstone of this chapter. However, the stage theory of history is not confined to economists and planners.[4]

The late architectural writer Reyner Banham is most well known as the narrator of Los Angles, but more importantly for our purposes, the author of the book, *Theory and Design in the First Machine Age*. For Banham, the First Machine Age was ushered in by the invention of electricity, that created the conditions for innovations like the telephone, the gramophone, the washing machine, etc. The Second Machine Age, starting around the 1960s, is characterized by mass production techniques producing electronic devices, which are consumed universally and symbolized by a single source of mass communication – the television (Banham 1960).

Are we living through a new Kondratieff wave based on the Information Age and the Knowledge Economy? One would have thought so, given the number of times these two concepts appear in the news and the number of search counts on the Web. Quantity of repetition is no substitute for the quality of analysis, however. It is apparent that the rhetoric of the new age of the new economy and e-Economy is more powerful than the mundane nature of business reality.

THE NEW ECONOMY IN PROSPECT AND RETROSPECT

In the previous section we took a sceptical look at the claims that we are living in a new age: the Information Age, conditioned and managed by the global application of ICT. What have we learned at this juncture?

LEARNING JUNCTURE

The wonders of new technology persuade each age that it represents the 'new'. This newness is celebrated by major public events. For example, the World Fair in St Louis, Missouri in 1904, the Great Exhibition in London in 1851. The First and Second Machine Ages coincide with some of the most rapid technological developments. Two developments that have accelerated the most dramatic development are electricity and the internal combustion engine. At present, the instruments of the 'Information Age': the Web and Internet, do not stack up as great inventions, compared with the former two (Gordon 2000). However, the strongest supporters of the Information Age point to the disjuncture with the past. Their claims rest on the 'stage view' of history:

- The global and universal adoption of ICT has vindicated Auguste Comte's final positive stage of history.
- This final stage coincides with the fifth Kondratieff wave, where we have moved from an industrial to an informational era.
- Faith in technological progress, as the founding principle of modern rational society, has found full expression with the development of the new economy

The key to developments in science and knowledge, however, is human ingenuity: the way in which great inventions are created, progressed and sustained. In other words, the process of 'creative destruction' developed by Schumpeter, as described above. It can be claimed that the full development of the e-Economy will not take place until the innovations that develop out of the Internet and the Web are fully developed and absorbed. This is a reasonable position to hold, but why do so many of the new economy disciples continue to press their case for the rapid and enormous break with the past? In the rest of this section, we look at whether the rhetoric that the new economy (and the e-Economy in particular) is business reality, actually stands up to scrutiny.

The quote by Robert Hughes in the section 'A new age or are all ages new?', on the rise of the 'Mechanical Age', is echoed in Edward Luttwak's book *Turbo Capitalism: Winners and Losers in the Global Economy*. Turbo-charged capitalism or turbo-capitalism is significantly different from the period between 1945 and 1980, where capitalism was subject to greater control (Luttwak 1999). The features of turbo-capitalism are:

- deregulation and privatization;
- globalization;
- the retreat of the state;
- the victory of the computer;
- the untrammelled acceptance and dominance of the American model.

Luttwak is no apologist for turbo-capitalism, unlike some of the new economy disciples. He points to an uncontrolled and possibly uncontrollable version of development. He rightly indicates the resulting consequences: rising inequality, poverty and crime. Luttwak refers to the Microsoft mirage. He argues that the rise in demand for high-level, high-tech labour within informational technology sectors is very limited, generating jobless growth. Even for a critic of this mode of development, he tends to swallow wholeheartedly the ideology of the 'new'. In the section entitled 'The victory of the computer', he states: 'A seemingly narrower, ultimately more important cause of accelerated structural change is the sudden arrival of the long-awaited, much delayed *big* increases in the productivity of offices that computers and other electronics were supposed to bring long ago' (ibid.: 46).

Luttwak contrasts the new Titans of the Information Age (Intel, Sun Systems, Cisco, Microsoft) with the old Titans (General Motors, Boeing), on the basis of employment totals, but more importantly stock market valuations. Unfortunately, Luttwak bases these assertions on the very short period of the new economy productivity *miracle* of the 1990s. As the subsequent bursting of the high-tech stock market bubble and the following analysis shows, reality is a little less simple. The other issue is the false distinction between the old and the new, as the case study below indicates.

In the UK, one of the most notable proponents of the new economy is Charles Leadbeater. His first foray into new economy territory was *Living on Thin Air: The New Economy* (Leadbeater 1999):

- The evolution of knowledge capitalism, which creates the modern economy of a 'system of distributed intelligence' (ibid.) whose dynamism is developing new products and the foundations of competitive advantage.
- The scrapping of the demarcation between consumption and production.
- Organizations are akin to neural networks (like a brain) rather than hierarchies.
- Knowledge society is the fulcrum of economic and social progress. The prospect of knowledge society is radical and ensures emancipation for its citizens. The three weightless components of the modern economy are finance, knowledge and social capital.[5]
- A new narrative and constitution for the New Economy. The latter consists of inclusiveness and promoting a knowledge-rich culture in the political sphere, demonstrating how inclusive knowledge and social capital would govern society.

Case study:
OLD OR NEW TITAN? THE GENERAL ELECTRIC COMPANY (GEC)

The General Electric Company of the US was consistently voted the most respected company by the world's financial press throughout the 1990s. Much of the hype surrounding the company was generated by the then Chief Executive Officer (CEO) Jack Welch. He had taken over a company at a difficult time and apparently transformed it for the global age. Notwithstanding the personal nature of the CEO, the key question is whether GEC is an old Titan or a new Titan. Its business is composed of:

- the manufacture of aircraft engines;
- the manufacture of medical equipment;

- the provision of financial services;
- the leasing of aircraft.

In the late 1990s, conforming to the rhetoric of the new economy and the knowledge economy, GEC considered turning itself into a 'new service company'. That is, franchising its manufacturing businesses, badged under the GEC name, with GEC providing maintenance services for medical equipment and aero engines. The change to a 'new service company' was afforded by using the Internet to manage the relationship between the franchised and service components of the business. The objective was to reduce transactions costs and enhance the value chain at each stage of production and service. The rhetoric of shifting its business into the new Titan territory ran into the buffers of business reality in the form of falling stock markets, global economic downturn and perhaps more importantly, the *increased* transactions costs of supply chain management and its associated value chains. Does the failure of this venture make GEC an old Titan? The reader can make his or her own mind up, on the basis of the following information:

- In 2002 GEC was the largest company in the world, with a market value of $372 billion; the same position as in 2001, according to the Dow-Jones 500 by market value.
- By comparison, the 'new Titan' Cisco Systems, was the second largest company in the world in 2001, by 2002 it was twentieth. On 27 March 2000, Cisco's market value was $555 billion. In May 2002, Cisco market value was $124 billion.
- According to the Fortune 500 ranking by revenues of the largest 500 companies, GEC was the second largest company in the world in 2003 with revenues of $187 billion, compared with the top company Wal-Mart Stores whose revenues were $247 billion. Cisco Systems position was 95th with revenues of $19 billion.
- GEC was the second most admired company in the world in 2003, according to Fortune, with Wal-Mart Stores in first position, Cisco's position was 22nd.
- In September 2003, GEC employed 315,000, had a profit margin of 11 per cent and had a market capitalization of $320 billion.
- In October 2003, Cisco Systems employed 34,000, revenues were $18.9 billion and a profit margin of 19 per cent and a market capitalization of $147 billion (http://yahoo.finance 2003).

Leadbeater approvingly quotes the British philosopher Bertrand Russell to explain that work in the past was a physical burden, whereas in the knowledge economy everything is 'thin-air' business that is potentially liberating. Leadbeater's inductive approach means that he fails the Gottdiener Test: there is no theory, little evidence and no data.

His other book of note is *Up the Down Escalator: Why the Global Pessimists are Wrong.* This begins with a much more measured approach, reviewing the events around the turn of the millennium and subsequent market downturns. He cannot resist the impulses of his previous book as he outlines the dreams of 'digitopia', 'innovation rules', 'the age of self-rule', 'the personalized society' and 'the end of capitalism' (Leadbeater 2002). However good his impressions are, his constant return to his personal experience, in an apparent search for evidence, renders Leadbeater into the rhetorical realm of all 'New Agers' and not the business reality of large monopolistic, bureaucratic and hierarchical corporations of the last two centuries. Many of these corporations die or are merged but this appears to be part of the normal cycle of creative destruction.

A less breathless account is that of Diana Coyle's *The Weightless World: Thriving in the Digital Age* (Coyle 2000). Coyle has the advantage of advancing evidence, data and quoting theory to support her arguments. Coyle, however, is too tied to the narrative of the 'new' to have sceptical distance from the changes she proclaims are universally transformative. To be in love with the 'new' appears to be part of the human condition throughout history. The speed and take-up of the new orthodoxies of the Information Age have been as rapid and universal as the capacities and capabilities of ICT itself. To challenge this orthodoxy is to invite charges of witchcraft for the unbelievers, as the economist John Kay nicely put it in drawing on Arthur Miller's play *The Crucible* to survey the performance of the stocks of new economy companies (Kay 2001). The high priest of the believers is Manual Castells, the urban sociologist at the University of California at Berkeley. His trilogy comprising *The Information Age*, *The Rise of Network Society*, *The Power of Identity* is certainly a *tour de force*, but again like others, Castells falls for the seductively transformative power of technology. Castells hardly lets evidence or data get in the way of his thesis and introduces concepts that are not fully explained, in language that invites confusion rather than clarity. His basic proposition is that society is now organized and developed by networks: a series of interconnected nodes. These nodes include the socio-organizing institutions of society, including the global financial system, national government, the European Commission (EC), entertainment and media systems, as well as including the network of drug trafficking around the world. The degree to which nodes are included in and their distance from organizing networks is 'The inclusion/exclusion in networks, and the architecture of relationships between networks, enacted by light-speed operating information technologies, configure dominant processes and functions in our societies' (Castells 1996: 470).

In the second volume of the trilogy, Castells explores the relationship between identity and network society, in the context of the challenges to the family and the state, under the rubric of the *Net and the Self* (Castells 1997). In the final volume, Castells sets out the transformation of society at the end of the second millennium. He summarizes this as:

> A new world is taking shape in this end of millennium. It originated in the historical coincidence, around the late 1960s, and mid 1970s, of three *independent* processes:

the information technology revolution; the economic crisis of both capitalism and statism, and their subsequent restructuring; and the blooming of cultural social movements. . . . The interaction between these processes, and the reactions they triggered, brought in a new dominant social structure, the network society; a new economy, the informational/global economy; and a new culture, the culture of virtual reality.

(Castells 1998: 336)

The reader is invited to compare this statement by Péguy, quoted above, made nearly a century before.

A less theological and more realistic view of the new economy can be found. The US Department of Commerce defines the new economy as: 'an economy in which IT and related investments drive higher rates of productivity'. One former Treasury secretary of the Clinton administration, Larry Summers, defines the new economy in a manner that could also apply to the e-Economy:

We are moving towards an economy in which the canonical source of value is gene value, a line of computer code or a logo, As Chairman Greenspan has often emphasized, in such a world, goods are increasingly valued not for their physical mass or other physical properties but for their weightless ideas (Coyle). In such an economy what you know matters more than how much you can lift.

(De Long and Summers 2000: 35)

If one wants to go beyond rhetoric, then one has to look at the **macroeconomics** and **microeconomics** of the new economy. The macroeconomics of the new economy hardly makes surprising reading. Table 1.1 sets out the growth and productivity performance of the world's largest economy. An economy, moreover, that is apparently in the forefront of the new economy;

Table 1.1 demonstrates that the rate of growth is returning to trend, although subsequent evidence after 2001 indicates that in the US at least there is above trend productivity growth. Whether this improvement is cyclical or structural will become clearer in time. The productivity performance of the 1990s was little different from that of the 1980s (ibid.). There is clear evidence that labour productivity increased rapidly

Table 1.1 Growth and productivity in the US, 1950–2001 (% annual change)

	Real GDP growth (%)	Productivity growth (%)
1950–72	3.9	2.7
1973–95	2.9	1.4
1996–2001	3.5	2.4

Source: Temple (2002).

13

in the durable manufacturing sector (Hansen 2001). Although the total amount of fixed capital investment as a proportion of national income in the US rose only slightly over the 1990s, the composition of investment changed rapidly. Investment in real equipment rose by 11.2 per cent a year between 1992 and 1998. This out-turn represents a faster rate than all previous 7-year periods in the post-war period (Tevlin and Wheeler 2000). A process of **capital deepening** possibly provides the main explanation. That is, the composition of the US economy's capital had shifted towards ICT, which would, as subsequent work has shown, create a more innovative environment for a superior productivity and growth performance to be sustained in the future (Gordon 2003). The investment in equipment surge in the 1990s, however, was not particularly related to the Internet. At its peak, the Internet sector only represented a small share of the total stock market capitalization in the US.[6] Much of the hype surrounding the dotcom phenomenon was associated with speculation in companies related to the Internet, not their underlying performance.

One of the issues that is central to a discussion of the macroeconomics of the new economy is whether the changes were cyclical or structural. For the stage theorists and New Agers, whose views are described above, the new economy represents a structural break with the past. The evidence appears to present a more prosaic picture. Outside the manufacturing sector, the productivity performance of the US economy improved in the 1990s, but not above the long-term trend set out in Table 1.1. However, if the new economy and the role of ICT in advancing this economy represents a break with the past, then why isn't the productivity performance outside manufacturing better? Output in the US non-manufacturing sector grew by about 1 per cent per annum between 1972 and 1995. In the mid-1990s, it grew by about 2 per cent. There may be two explanations. First, the significant investment in real equipment, incurred significant transition costs that depressed final output and thus rising productivity. Second, significant over-investment in telecommunications networks had taken place that had not generated greater final output (ibid.).

The contribution of ICT to greater overall productivity is a way of investigating the macroeconomics of the new economy in respect of inflation, unemployment and stability. The detailed issue of productivity is dealt with in the next section. However, unscrambling the impact of the new economy from a period of relatively long run price stability and declining unemployment in the advanced economies is the key issue. Is there a causal relationship or is it merely correlated? The period of the new economy coincided with external supply shocks, for example lower energy costs, more efficacious monetary policy with authorities acting quickly to head off potential crises, wider diffusion of globalization through the opening up of international markets and financial bull markets that generated 'irrational exuberance'.[7] In this deflationary environment, that is, where there is a tendency of the prices of all goods to decline, financial institutions look for higher returns on investments which implies greater risk.

The plethora of dotcoms becoming public companies, by issuing shares, created frenzied trading in these shares which drove up company valuations. The vast majority of dotcoms, however, made no money. The prospect of significant capital gains created the conditions for the 'greater fool' theory of investment. As these investments become riskier with the prospect of collapse in the share prices of these kinds of companies, investors sell on to the next fool. This kind of environment has been a feature of financial history for over 400 years and is not unique to the new economy. Even the cheerleaders of the new economy, for example De Long and Summers, are wary of making too significant claims for the macroeconomic impact of the new economy. Their claims rest primarily on microeconomic impacts.

THINK POINT AND LEARNING JUNCTURE

Has our analysis so far allowed us to answer the Gottdiener Test: where is the theory of the new economy, where is the evidence, where are the data?

- The theory appears to rest on the assertion that we now live in an Information Society and Knowledge Economy, yet the networked nature of the e-Economy lends itself to a transaction cost economics (TCE) approach resting on the analysis of organizational nature of firms, markets and hierarchies and contracting aspects of economic transactions.
- But have not all ages been ones in which information and knowledge are in the forefront of the development of economy and society?
- The information society and the knowledge economy are founded on the universal adoption and use of ICT.
- But, the growth in use of new technology has been a feature of the last four centuries, as Adam Smith and Karl Marx demonstrated.
- We seem to be living in the era of the new informational enterprise, driven by rapid improvements in and use of ICT.
- But, this claim does not seem to be borne out by the evidence. The largest and most respected companies in the world appear to be large old-style firms.
- The new economy has created a structural break with the past, leading to permanently higher levels of economic growth and productivity increases.
- But, Table 1.1 shows that for the US, its performance has returned to trend.

Overall, none of the accounts, even the more realistic ones, examine the particular characteristics of e-Economy closely, rather the generalities of the new economy.

Analysis of the microeconomic changes, particularly the implications for organizations, is undertaken in the final section of this chapter, set within a TCE framework. The overall macroeconomic impact of ICT in the medium term may rest

15

with how its use creates a new bout of creative destruction in the innovation process: that is, the degree to which human ingenuity adapts the technology in producing old and new goods and services more efficiently. However, we find that the rhetoric of the new economy and e-Economy is found wanting because business reality does not include making false distinctions between the old and new economies, as the GEC case study above demonstrates.

THE PARADOX OF PRODUCTIVITY IN THE NEW ECONOMY

Nearly all the claims for the path-breaking utility of the new economy and its component e-Economy rest on the role of ICT and its organization in producing step-change and permanent increases in productivity. Productivity is conventionally measured as output per worker or output per worker per hour worked. There are two concepts underlying these measures: total factor productivity (TFP) and multi-factor productivity (MFP).[8] Much of the debate about the role of the new economy in dramatically improving productivity concerns the relationship between TFP, MFP and labour productivity. As briefly described above, the ability of the new economy to develop and sustain unprecedented levels of productivity creates some interesting paradoxes.

The 'productivity miracle' creates a number of paradoxes and puzzles. Gordon asks the question of why productivity growth in the US between 2000 and 2003 has been much faster than during the boom years of 1995 to 2000? In order to answer this question he sets out five puzzles. These puzzles and their explanation are set out in Table 1.2.

International comparisons of economic performance are riddled with methodological difficulties. Comparing the Old and New World's institutional and cultural explanations beyond ICT investment, as shown in Table 1.3, may be more powerful in explaining the relative failure of the new economy to take off in Europe. We are back in the realm of creative destruction and the organizational implications of the e-Economy, which we explore in the next section.

The assertion that the only new economy is the US does not actually stand up to scrutiny if one compares it with the other leading economies, which are members of the Organization for Economic Co-Operation and Development (OECD). There are a number of studies that indicate that there is a strong positive correlation between MFP and ICT intensity.[9] The findings of these studies state that:

- During the 1990s, Australia, Canada, Denmark, Finland, Ireland, Norway and Sweden all achieved higher MFP growth rates than the US (Schreyer 2000).
- The role of human capital is important in explaining differences in productivity growth within the OECD and between the US and the EU.
- In the US, Australia, Ireland and the Netherlands, increased labour utilization and the upgrading of the skills of the workforce was accompanied by an acceleration in the growth of GDP per capita.

Table 1.2 *Gordon's five productivity puzzles*

Puzzle	Explanation
1 Why was the cyclical effect less prominent from 2000 onwards, when the post-1995 revival was part normal upturn of the economic cycle?	Compared with three periods 1975–6, 1982–3 and 1991–2, when the economic cycle moved from recession, little of the initial productivity growth between 1995 and 2000 was cyclical. Technical progress tied to ICT investment drove structural change, but the productivity growth bubble of the 2001–2 economic recovery corresponded to cyclical recoveries in the previous periods. The difference with 1995–2005 is that it is above trend and that there may have been a step-change in the structure and performance of the US economy.
2 Why did productivity accelerate after 2000 when investment in ICT declined rapidly?	Classic studies suggest that a large part of the 1990s productivity boom was due to the increased production and use of ICT equipment and software, and in one case including semiconductors (Jorgensen and Stiroh 2000; Oliner and Sichel 2000). But why did productivity keep on growing after the collapse in the ICT investment boom, that saw Cisco System drop from being the world's second largest company, by market value, in 2001 to 20th in 2002? The rapid production and use of ICT after 1995 created imbalances in the contributions of different types of capital, compared with the 'Solow paradox' period, when the proportion of GDP accounted for by computers was slow and gradual. The rapid upsurge in ICT investment and use generated hidden capital whose benefit is still being felt after the collapse after the investment is one explanation.
3 Why did computers have so little impact before 1995 and so much afterwards despite price of computing power declining for a very long time?	Technical progress from ICT investment is tied to the continuing fall in the real price of computing power over a relatively long period. In earlier work, Gordon compared the invention of the electronic computer and the Internet with that of 'great inventions', particularly electricity (Gordon 2000). However, there are significant time lags before new inventions and innovations can be adapted in the reorganization of business practices (David and Wright 1999). The central role of hidden or intangible capital in adapting and absorbing new technological developments into mainstream business is crucial. Gordon draws on the example of the invention of the motor car and the time-lags before it became the universal mode of transport though the rapid and large growth in the inter-state highway system in the US. This puzzle reinforces the importance of non-ICT capital and non-ICT innovations in sustaining the 'productivity miracle'

17

■ **Table 1.2** *Continued*

4	What will the impact be on innovation in changing business productivity from investment collapse with only small improvements in consumer products but not major ones in IT business related products?	Could the rapid productivity growth between 1995 and 2003 be sustained without a renewal of investment in ICT? The solution to this puzzle lies in examining the role of capital deepening and multi-factor productivity (MFP) in sustaining productivity growth. The quality of capital is also important in technical change. Short-term assets like computers need to earn higher rates of return from investment in them, because they are quickly replaced by technically superior ones. The quality of capital therefore improves through this process of technical change. ICT investment and the e-Economy, however, do not escape the basic principles of economics. Diminishing returns[11] will set in so that innovations that stimulate business productivity are hardly likely to be sufficient to generate a new investment boom in ICT, like that of the late 1990s
5	What were the causes of the slowdown in Europe compared with the acceleration in the US?	Perhaps only the US is really the only new economy and e-Economy. Despite large ICT investment productivity gains in the European Union (EU) have been poor compared with the US, but the EU is a much more heterogeneous economy. The productivity differential is accounted for by three industries: retail, wholesale and securities trading (i.e., financial assets), explaining 55%, 24% and 20%, respectively, of the difference throughout the 1990s (van Ark *et al.* 2002). These sectors also face a more stringent regulatory regime in the EU.

■ **Table 1.3** *Changes in output, hours and output per hour for the EU and US (per cent p.a.)*

	1990–5	1995–2000	2000–2	1995–2002	1995–2002 versus 1990–5
EU output	1.61	2.63	1.28	2.24	0.63
EU hours	−0.85	1.21	0.40	0.98	1.83
EU output per hour	2.46	1.42	0.89	1.27	−1.19
US output	2.38	4.00	1.28	3.22	0.84
US hours	1.24	2.03	−1.24	1.10	−0.14
US output per hour	1.14	1.97	2.52	2.13	0.99

Source: Gordon (2003), adjusted from McGuikin and van Ark (2003).

- Those economies where employment declined or stagnated experienced a worsening of their growth performance (e.g. Germany and Italy) (Bassanini and Scarpetta 2002). There are also demographic differences between the leaders and laggards in the productivity game.

- It is apparent that extra ICT factors are important in explaining the relatively poor productivity performance of other OECD economies compared with the US, in spite of similar or larger ICT intensity and PC usage (Schreyer 2000).

These findings strengthen the view that the Schumpeterian process of 'creative destruction', invoking technological and human innovation, is at the centre of benefits of any new economy and e-Economy. The rhetoric of the transformative power of ICT is powerful but has to be read in a wider firm, industry and organizational context. The final section takes a brief look at the organizational implications of the new economy and e-Economy.

ORGANIZATIONAL IMPLICATIONS

Regardless of scepticism, the new economy and e-Economy do bring new benefits to economic and business development. These include network externalities and the lowering of transaction costs in markets, particularly the labour market. Externalities can either be in the form of costs or benefits that cannot be measured in terms of purely market prices. The recently deceased Concorde may have been a wonderful piece of technology, but it imposed external costs on the residents near the airports it served. The building of the Channel Tunnel and high-speed rail link has created external benefits. These include time savings to travellers, locational advantages to businesses in the form of better accessibility and higher property prices near to the stations.

The network benefits of the new economy and e-Economy include the creation and management of supply chains, the development of the 'networked firm', through firms engaging in strategic alliances, joint ventures and partnerships to exploit increasingly global opportunities. For example, Wal-Mart's investment in electronic data processing (EDP) systems gives it greater management control and flexibility over a much bigger networks of hyper-markets both in the US and abroad. ICT equipment and systems create the prospect of inter-firm innovation networks. One can distinguish between *strategic networks*: set up by a 'hub' firm to actively manage the network in order to gain advantage over the competition, and *business networks*: encompassing the relationships of exchange of business actors that control business activities (Jarillo 1988; Forsgren and Johanson 1992). There are also three distinct types of network (Monsted 1993):

1 *service and assistance networks*: borrowing access to equipment and the provision of technical services;
2 *information and structuring networks*: collection of information through formal and informal information channels and its evaluation;
3 *entrepreneurship and product networks*: jointly exploiting markets opportunities and maintaining existing market dominance.

19

These networks suggest a confirmation of Metcalfe's law; the possible number of connections of a network rise much more proportionately than the number of nodes that are connected to it. This is the basis of the claim of the greater utility of the new economy and e-Economy (De Long and Summers 2000). However, the set-up costs are high and there is considerable evidence that networked organizational forms are unstable. This instability is most marked in large–small firm networks, whose outcomes have been described as '*unnatural mating*' and '*accidental squashings*', when one of the parties in the network is significantly bigger than another (Oliver and Blakeborough 1998).

The central issue is the management and control of transactions and transaction costs in networks. Network management is more complex and not as economically viable as many new economy disciples claim. There is a difficulty in measuring transactions costs. This difficulty may be overcome by focusing on whether the organizational relations (contracting practices, governance structures) correspond to the characteristics of the transactions within the networks (Williamson 1985). If all organizational behaviour was governed by rules, then opportunism would be absent (ibid.). How opportunism, as the strongest form of self-interest seeking behaviour, can be managed to mutual advantage if *ex ante* (before) and *ex post* (after) contractual safeguards are put in place in order to assign the benefits from the externalities and spillovers generated by the networks. Network participants are therefore confronted by bounded rationality. They are also faced by a number of strategic games, some of which are laid out in Figure 1.1.

Once the instability of networks is admitted and the importance of negotiating opportunism and bounded rationality is recognized, then the benefits of networked activities are reduced. The setting up of contractual arrangements, in order to manage transactions, becomes part of the transaction's costs themselves. In combination with high set-up costs, it is more likely that large monopolistic old Titans, with hierarchical and

		CONDITIONS OF BOUNDED RATIONALITY	
		Absent	*Admitted*
CONDITIONS OF OPPORTUNISM	*Absent*	Bliss	'General clause contracting'
	Admitted	Comprehensive contracting	Serious contractual difficulties

Figure 1.1 *Strategic payoffs from transactions governance structures*

20

bureaucratic organizational forms, will be able to exploit the network advantages bestowed by ICT rather than the dynamic new Titans of popular e-Economy imagination.

NEW ECONOMY FIRM STRATEGIES

Many of the new economy companies known as Internet start-ups or dotcoms pursued get big fast (GBF) e-Commerce strategies, for example Amazon.Com. These strategies included

- using first mover advantage to build brands and revenues;
- relying on the low cost of capital to raise external funding from venture capital companies and then large investment banks through initial public offerings (IPO) (that is offering shares to the public);
- exploiting positive feedback from scale economies, learning processes, network effects and complementary assets.

Once there is a market leader who is exploiting these positive feedbacks there are difficulties for other market participants to succeed. These include:

- service quality falls as growth becomes rapid;
- rapid growth outstrips internal financial resources;
- the inability to sustain the overblown valuations of new economy and e-Economy companies (see case study above) in the face of long periods of financial losses driven by rapid growth and low prices.

Unhappily, the fall-out from GBF strategies in e-Commerce was aided and abetted by large investment banks who, often against their better judgement, found themselves locked into a game of prisoner's dilemma with their competitors. They feared pulling out of an ultimately no-win game for fear of letting new entrants into what had been a very remunerative activity.[10] The limits of the GBF strategy for many dotcoms were:

> Far too many dot coms pursued GBF strategies without understanding whether there were in fact many scale economies, learning processes, network effects or complementary assets that would favor the largest player. Second, even when such reinforcing feedbacks exist, firms must grow long enough for their loops to become important. Doing so requires substantial access to cheap capital, since the GBF strategy entails rapid growth and low prices so that operating profits and cash flow form are significantly negative. The strong dependence of the GBF strategy on positive feedbacks makes it highly vulnerable; the same loops that power the growth and success of the firm can quickly become vicious cycles leading to organizational collapse if low quality or inadequate infrastructure begin to constrain growth.
>
> (Olivia *et al.* 2003)

21

The contingent factors that permitted the development of GBF in e-Commerce included low cost of capital, venture capitalists and investment bankers seeking higher yielding, higher risk investments and a macroeconomic institutional setting where central bank policy encouraged new economy and e-Economy developments. It was not the new economy and e-Economy of itself that permitted GBF strategies. One successful example of a GBF strategy, where positive feedback loops have been realised, is the OnStar telematics system developed by that old Titan GEC (ibid.).

As set out in this and the previous section, the productivity arguments for the new economy, and its impact on the microeconomy, vary in explanatory power and include a number of cultural, environmental, organizational and institutional factors. It is also clear that the impact of the e-Economy on organizational forms and structures has not been as significant as claimed, nor will be for the foreseeable future. Changes in the labour market have been more complex. In markets where there are weightless services, for example, travel and consumer financial services, the e-Economy has had the greatest impact (Freeman 2000). Organizational and labour market change are two important aspects of the development of e-Economy and e-Society. They represent an important new research agenda. This agenda will have to take on board the fact that the economic laws of gravity are not so easily defied, even when faced with the transformative promise of ICT technology:

> However, if the lessons of the failure of the new economy to mature, the dotcom to dotbomb and the stock market madness are to be learned, then the Internet and associated media may be part of new business models. . . . Three and a half centuries after the claim that supply creates its own demand was firstly falsely mooted, technology does not create its own business model. This is the fundamental lesson to be derived from the business environment for e-Commerce.
>
> (Budd and Clear 2003)

CONCLUSION

Every new age embraces the 'new' and the potential of technology to liberate human society once and for all. The claims made by the disciples of the Information Age, Knowledge Economy and the new and e-Economies, at the end of the second millennium, are no different from those made by Adam Smith and Karl Marx in the eighteenth and nineteenth centuries or the proponents of modernity at the turn of the century or the adherents of the second Machine Age in the post-war period. Where the old ends and the new starts is one of the universal conundrums of economy and society. Technological progress, in isolation from human ingenuity, as embodied in creative destruction, will not ensure economic development and progress. In fact, each new age ends and its embrace ultimately decays.

Returning to the *Shock of the New*, we find:

22

That splendour of the new age would soon be less evident. After 1914, machinery was turned on its inventors and their children. After forty years of continuous peace in Europe, the worst war in history cancelled the faith in good technology, the benevolent machine. The myth of the Future went into shock, and European art moved into years of irony, disgust and protest.

(Hughes 1980: 56)

The emperor is dead, long live the emperor! In the case of the economy is it the new or the old one? The material realities still seem to prevail. The goods that people buy today seem no more weightless than when the first bicycle appeared on the streets of the world's major cities. The rhetoric of the new economy and the e-Economy and its virtual universe is enticing, but business inhabits a more grounded reality.

GLOSSARY

Bull market   Conditions in which investors buy stocks and shares at lower prices and sell them on at higher prices. The opposite is known as a 'bear' market.

Capital deepening   Involves increasing capital-labour ratios in production in order to increase labour productivity. However, continuously increasing investment in new forms of capital (for example, Internet systems), of itself, will not contribute to long-term productivity. It is the supporting investment in other forms of capital, including infrastructure, which increases economic growth through technical change

Creative destruction   Theory devised by Joseph Schumpeter to explain how the seeds of germination of entirely new industrial and business processes are sown from the remnants of the old ones.

Governance structures   Pertain to the contractual arrangements between firms and organizations engaged in co-operative relationships, for example, networks and strategic alliances.

Kondratieff waves   A series of significant technological developments, each spanning some 50 years, which offer entirely new and profitable opportunities for business growth.

Macroeconomics   Branch of economics that deals with national income, economic growth, investment, inflation, unemployment and international trade.

Microeconomics   Deals with pricing and investment decisions of consumers and producers, economic welfare and distribution, market structures and regulation.

Modernity   The period of history from the nineteenth century and lasting until today, in some accounts, structured by scientific and technological advance and a fundamental belief that rationality and reason in conjunction with science and technology will transform human society and ensure its progress.

Paradigm shift   A constellation of theories, beliefs, attitudes and orientations that comprise the body of knowledge within a scientific discourse, known as normal science.

Paradigms are overthrown when there is a scientific revolution and replaced by a new paradigm that describes the new science. A paradigm shift occurs when these discoveries are not powerful enough to overthrow the existing normal science (Kuhn 1970).

Supply and value chain management The management of a dedicated system of part and service suppliers either horizontally or vertically organized that is managed by central information systems to produce goods. A value chain is related to a supply chain in that at each stage of the supply chain, the value added is identified and attempts made to increase it through more efficient supply chain management. In the marketing literature both concepts are related to distribution and marketing channels.

Vertical integration A firm operates a range of activities that successively build on each other. For example, an oil company will be vertically integrated if it not only produces oil, but then refines it into petrol and associated products and then sells these products in service stations.

NOTES

1 The Gottdiener Test is named after the American urban sociologist, Mark Gottdiener, who conceived of it in a conversation with the author about globalization whilst walking over Tower Bridge at dusk in the autumn of 2000. I trust I do justice to Mark's original concept.
2 The Tulip Crisis occurred in the Netherlands between 1636 and 1637, when the Amsterdam Stock Market developed paper assets that were traded against the value of buying and selling tulip bulbs, leading to the creation of a large speculative trading bubble. The South Sea Bubble arose out of the trading rights granted to the South Sea Company in Latin America and its use as an intermediary vehicle for the issue of Spanish public debt, which could be exchanged for stock in the South Sea company and then sold on, along with exchange of debt. Speculation in the South Sea Company stock rapidly increased its price before the bubble burst.
3 The author was Karl Marx writing in 1867 in the section 'Machine and modern industry' of *Capital* vol 1 (Marx 1887: 475).
4 The most well-known proponent of the stage view of history is Auguste Comte, the French founder of sociology. For Comte there are three stages *Theological*, *Metaphysical* and *Positive*. The first suggests that knowledge comes from an appeal to some god. The second, that knowledge proceeds from an appeal to abstract reason. The third suggests that knowledge proceeds from the application and testing of positive philosophy. For Comte, positivism was the final advanced science of society from which he derived social physics: what we know today as sociology.
5 Social capital causes all kinds of definitional problems for academics, policy-makers and commentators. For Leadbeater it means that social relationships in the form of collaborative networks reduces the risks of living in a market economy through created institutions of social solidarity.
6 Market capitalization is measured by the number of share or stocks on offer in the market structures and regulation.

7 This term was made by the economist Robert Schiller I (Schiller 2000) and used by the President of the Federal Reserve (the US central bank), Alan Greenspan, to describe the behaviour of the stock markets in reaction to the new technology and Internet companies (dotcoms).

8 TFP measures output divided by the combination of both the labour and capital units used in production. This last measure is also occasionally referred to as multi-factor productivity in some countries. Increases in total factor productivity are mostly achieved through the application of new technologies, better training, improvements in the production process and better management techniques. MFP measures output per unit of a set of combined inputs. A change in MFP reflects the change in output that cannot be accounted for by the change in combined inputs. As a result, MFP measures reflect the joint effects of many factors including research and development (R&D), new technologies, economies of scale, managerial skill, and changes in the organization of production. Labour productivity is the ratio of the output of goods and services to the labour hours devoted to the production of that output. MFP relates output to a combination of inputs used in the production of that output, such as labour and capital or labour, capital, energy and materials. Capital includes equipment, structures, inventories and land.

9 ICT intensity is measured by ICT expenditure as a proportion of GDP or the change in PC intensity. (i.e. per cent of the population usage) per 100 inhabitants.

10 For a good account, see *DotCon* by John Cassidy (2001).

11 Diminishing returns occurs when a smaller and smaller increase in output as more and more investment.

BIBLIOGRAPHY

Arrow, K. (1969) 'The organization of economic activity: issues pertinent to the choice of market versus nonmarket allocation', in *The Analysis of Public Expenditure: The PPB System*, Vol 1 US Joint Economic Committee, 91st Congress, 1st Session, Washington DC: US Government Printing Office 59–73.

Banham, R. (1960) *Theory and Design in the First Machine Age*, London: The Architectural Press.

Bassanini, A. and Scarpetta, S. (2002) 'Growth, technological change and ICT diffusion: recent evidence from OECD countries.' *Oxford Economic Policy Review*, 18, 3: 324–44.

Buchanan, J. (1975) 'A contractarian paradigm for applying economic theory', *American Economic Review*, 65 (May): 89–105.

Budd, L. and Clear, F. (2003) 'The business environment for e-Commerce' in P. Jackson, L. Harris and P. M. Eckersley (eds) *e-Business Fundamentals*, London: Routledge.

Cassidy, J. (2001) *Dotcon*, Harmondsworth: Penguin.

Castells, M. (1996) *The Rise of Network Society*, Oxford: Blackwell.

Castells, M. (1997) *The Power of Identity*, Oxford: Blackwell.

Castells, M. (1998) *End of Millennium*, Oxford: Blackwell.

Coyle, D. (2000) *The Weightless World: Thriving in the Digital Age*, Oxford: Capstone.

David, P. and Wright, G. (1999) 'Early twentieth century productivity growth dynamics: an inquiry into the economic history of our ignorance', Stanford Institute for Economic Policy Research Discussion Paper, No. 98–3.

De Long, J. B. and Summers, L. H. (2000) 'The 'new economy' background, historical perspective, questions, and speculations', *Federal Reserve of Kansas Review*, Q4: 29–59.

du Gay, P. (2000) *In Praise of Bureaucracy*, London: Sage.

Drucker, P. (1998) 'From capitalism to knowledge society', in D. Neef (ed.) *The Knowledge Economy*, Boston: Butterworth Heinemann.

Freeman, R. B. (2000) 'The labour market in the new information economy', *Oxford Review of Economic Policy*, 18, 3: 288–305.

Forsgren, M. and Johanson, J. (1992) 'Managing internationalization in business networks', in M. Forsgren and J. Johanson (eds) *Managing Networks in International Business*, Philadelphia: Gordon and Breech.

Gordon, R. (2000) 'Does the "new economy" measure up to the great inventions of the past?', *Journal of Economic Perspectives*, 14, 4: 49–74.

Gordon, R. (2003) 'Five puzzles in the behavior of productivity, investment and innovation', mimeo.

Hall, P. (1998) *Cities in Civilization*, London: Wiedenfeld and Nicholson.

Hansen, B. E (2001) 'The new econometrics of structural change: dating breaks in US labour productivity', *Journal of Economic Perspectives*, 15 4: 117–28.

HMSO (1998) *Our Competitive Future Building the Knowledge Economy*, London: HMSO.

http://yahoo.finance (2003).

Hughes, R. (1980) *The Shock of the New: Art and the Century of Change*, London: Thames and Hudson.

IMF (2003) *World Economic Outlook*, Washington: International Monetary Fund.

Jarillo, C. (1988) 'On strategic networks', *Strategic Management Journal*, 9: 31–41.

Jorgenson, D. W. and Stiroh, K. J. (2002) 'Raiding the speed limit: US economic growth in the information age', *Brookings Papers on Economic Activity*, 1: 125–235.

Kay, J. (2001) 'What became of the new economy?', *National Institute Review*, 117: 56–59.

Kondratieff, N. (1935) 'The long waves in economic life', *Review of Economic Statistics*, 17: 105–15.

Kuhn, T. S. (1970) *The Structure of Scientific Revolutions*, Chicago: University of Chicago Press.

Leadbeater, C. (1999) *Living on Thin Air: The New Economy*, London: Viking.

Leadbeater, C. (2002) *Up the Down Escalator: Why the Global Pessimists are Wrong*, London: Viking.

Luttwak, E. (1999) *Turbo Capitalism: Winners and Losers in the Global Economy*, London: Orion Publishing.

McGuiken, R. H. and van Ark, B. (2003) *Performance 2002: Productivity, Employment and Income in the World's Economies*, New York: The Conference Board.

Marx, K. (1887) *Capital*, vol 1, London: Lawrence and Wishart.

Monsted, M. (1993) 'Regional network processes: networks for service sector or development of entrepreneurs', in C. Karlssson, B. Johannisson and D. Storey (eds) *Small Business Dynamics: International, National and Regional Perspectives*, London: Routledge.

Oliner, S. D. and Sichel, D. E. (2000) 'The resurgence of growth in the late 1990s. Is information technology the story?', *Journal of Economic Perspectives*, 14, 4: 2–22.

Oliva, R., Sterman, J. D. and Giese, M. (2003) 'Limits to growth in the new economy: exploring the "get big fast" strategy in e-Commerce', *System Dynamics Review*, 19, 2 (summer): 83–117.

Oliver N. and Blakeborough, M. (1998) 'Innovation networks: the view from the inside', in J. Michie and J. Grieve-Smith (eds) *Globalization, Growth and Governance: Creating an Innovative Economy*, Oxford: Oxford University Press.

Quah, D. (2001) 'The weightless economy in economic development' in M. Pohjola (ed.) *Information, Productivity and Economic Growth*, Oxford: Oxford University Press.

Schiller, R. (2000) *Irrational Exuberance*, Princeton: Princeton University Press.

Schreyer, P. (2000) 'The contribution of information and communication technology to output growth: a study of the G7 countries', *Directorate for Science, Technology and Industry Working Paper* DST/DOC (2000) 2, Paris: OECD.

Schumpeter, J. (1939) *Business Cycles*, New York: McGraw-Hill.

Schumpeter, J. (1942) *Capitalism, Socialism and Democracy*, New York: Harper.

Solow, R. (1987) 'We'd Better Watch Out', *New York Review of Books*, 12 July: 36.

Tapscott, D. (1996) *The Digital Economy: Promise and Peril in the Age of Networked Intelligence*, New York: McGraw-Hill.

Temple, J. (2002) 'The assessment: the new economy', *Oxford Review of Economic Policy*, 18, 3: 241–64.

Tevlin, S. and Wheeler, K. (2000) 'Explaining the investment boom of the 1990s', *Finance and Economics Discussion Series 2000–11*, Washington: Board of Governors of the Federal Reserve System.

van Ark, B. (2000) 'Measuring the new economy: an international comparative perspective', *Review of Income and Wealth*, 48, 1: 1–14.

Williamson, O. (1985) *The Economic Institutions of Capitalism*, New York: The Free Press.

Chapter 2

Entrepreneurial chaos, entrepreneurial order and the dotcom bubble

PATRICIA LEWIS

KEY LEARNING POINTS

After completing this chapter you should have an understanding of:

- The cultural origins of the dotcom bubble
- The importance of cultural factors in facilitating the emergence of the dotcom bubble
- How to locate the phenomenon of the dotcom bubble within the discourses of enterprise and the new economy
- How to appreciate the dotcom phenomenon as something more than the simple suspension of traditional business fundamentals

INTRODUCTION

Only yesterday so it seems, Wall Street equity analysts almost unanimously proclaimed a new economic paradigm. Out with these old equity valuation models, out with fusty concerns about earning (actual or predicted), out with the business cycle, in with network effects, burn rates and global scale. Forget, ugh, prudence: caution is the new recklessness. Nowadays, as one reputable member of the breed then put it, the only danger is to be out of the market. Well, for the shrewd advice (as NASDAQ tottered at around 5,000) many thanks. For all those 'busy', 'hold' and 'accumulate' recommendations on stocks that cost $100 last year, and now cost $1.50, thanks a lot.

(*The Economist* 2001)

This time next year we'll be millionaires, was the cry of a raft of individuals breaking out of their corporate shackles and starting a Web site. And if they didn't have their own dotcom idea, they could simply steal other people's, and then claim to be running an 'incubator'. 'Far too many people thought that they had the skills to become an entrepreneur. And every Tom, Dick and Harry was getting funding' says Julie Meyer, founder of First Tuesday, and queen of the Internet revolution in Europe.

(Islam 2001)

The collapse of the greatest bubble in the history of capitalism wiped 40 per cent off the value of London shares. There are good grounds for believing that more losses are on the way. The bubble's growth and collapse followed a classic pattern. As in every capitalist crisis, from the Dutch Tulip mania of the seventeenth century on, as soon as the bubble inflated it became sane to be insane, profitable to be profligate. Sensible investors such as Tony Dye, the manager of the Phillips & Drew fund, warned that shares in dotcoms, telecoms and media were fantastically overvalued. He refused to touch them. For being right he was ridiculed as 'Dr Doom'. In 1999 *The Times* said he was a 'laughing stock' and he was driven from his job a few months later.

(Cohen 2002)

Many assessments of the dotcom bubble (which peaked in March 2000) tend to describe this as a period of extreme madness, mania, delusion, hysteria, characterized by an intent belief in 'new economy' fantasies. Such 'fantasies' led governments such as that of New Labour in the UK to believe that manufacturing industry, the working class and trade unions were 'leftovers' from a bygone era which would all soon be consigned to the dustbin of history (Cohen 2002). Peter Mandelson, a former member of the New Labour government, boasted of creating a Britain which would provide the 'best environment in the world for electronic trading'. This view was supported by Tony Blair and Gordon Brown with an emphasis being placed by various government spokespersons on the coming of 'a weightless world in which the economy dematerialised and we lived on thin air, working for the new knowledge industries' (Cohen 2002).

Following the collapse of dotcom shares such views have been widely criticized and various culprits (ranging from Eddie George, former Governor of the Bank of England to financial analysts such as Henry Blodget of Merrill Lynch and Mary Meeker of Morgan Stanley) have been identified, as commentators and those who lost significant sums of money have sought explanations for how this situation could have emerged. Can we explain the dotcom disaster as simply an old-fashioned bubble? How much 'blame' lies with financial analysts who secretly wrote off technology stocks while actively encouraging investors into them (Connon 2003)? Was its emergence due to the suspension of economic common sense on the part of managers, who it now appears did not believe in what they were doing (Shiller 2000)? It will be argued below that the recent dotcom bubble was the manifestation of extreme **entrepreneurial chaos**, and its materialization must be understood within the context of the continuing promotion and evolution of the **enterprise culture**, and the juxtaposition of this phenomenon with the discourse of the new economy.

29

'Entrepreneurial chaos' can be defined as:

1 the occurrence of the unexpected in all entrepreneurial activity;
2 a powerlessness to definitively control entrepreneurial activity and achieve a defined or desired end;
3 an inability to eliminate happenings or events from entrepreneurial activity which are objectionable or deemed unnecessary, all of which creates much ambivalence and keeps the danger and excitement of entrepreneurship alive.

'Enterprise culture' can be defined as a business environment within which entrepreneurial activity is fostered and encouraged.

THE RELATIONSHIP BETWEEN ENTREPRENEURIAL CHAOS AND ENTREPRENEURIAL ORDER

Enterprise and entrepreneurial chaos

Though the term 'enterprise' has been around for a significant period of time, the contemporary usage, particularly in conjunction with other concepts such as discourse or culture is a relatively recent phenomenon. As a contemporary academic concept, enterprise has a historical life of a little over two decades and was originally associated with Margaret Thatcher in the UK and Ronald Reagan in the USA (Lewis 2003). Notions of enterprise culture emerged in political and academic discussion in both of these countries during the 1970s and the 1980s, gaining a similar relevance and momentum in the rest of Europe at a later time (Scase 2000). Over the course of its brief history, enterprise culture has been surrounded by a high level of conceptual ambiguity. This has led a number of commentators (e.g. Burrows 1991; Burrows and Ford 1998; Drakopoulou Dodd and Anderson 2001), particularly those writing in the small business area, to claim that enterprise culture has no independent effect on the material reality of organizational life in countries such as the UK. In contrast, analyses of enterprise (e.g. Miller and Rose 1990; du Gay 1996a; Carr 2000a, 2000b) which have adopted a **Foucauldian** approach, have sought to demonstrate how enterprise changes in the government of organizational and social life have impacted upon societal, organizational and personal identity. From this perspective, one of the defining features of the phenomenon of enterprise culture is the generalization of an enterprise form to all kinds of individuals and establishments – to the conduct of organizations previously characterized as non-economic, to the conduct of government and to the conduct of individuals. In addition, its success is heavily dependent on individuals' identification with and acceptance of the norms of enterprise (du Gay *et al.* 1996). Such analysis has highlighted how enterprise implies a particular rationality of government, a more or less coherent prescription of how society, organizations and individuals should be remade in ways that promote competition, energy, drive and initiative (Fournier and Grey 1999; Lewis 2003).

A Foucauldian conceptualization of enterprise culture concentrates on the links between the activities of government and the activities of individuals, and the means by which individuals are encouraged to take-up the identity of entrepreneur. This linkage can be understood in terms of the strategies and policies drawn upon by government, for the direction of the behaviour of individuals and business in enterprise culture. In other words, the focus is on the range of technologies, policies and initiatives which aim to mould and shape entrepreneurial behaviour in business, both large and small, and the response of individuals and business to this.

The attempt to create an enterprise culture in countries such as that of the UK cannot simply be understood as an attempt at economic revival. It is also an identity project which aims to reform the moral character of those who come within its ambit (du Gay 1996b). In particular, individuals are enticed to relate to and take up the new attributes, values and priorities (demonstrate initiative; take risks; be flexible; be creative; show independence; possess a daring spirit; hold a strong work ethic) which conventionally are believed to reside in the persona of the entrepreneur. According to Lewis (2003) the association between an enterprise rationality of government and the ethical character of the enterprise has been made by both popularist and more serious academic writers (e.g. Osborne and Gaebler 1992; Peters 1992; Gordon 1987; du Gay 1996a; Scott 1996). Enterprise theorists contend that the entrepreneur has become the driving identity in the new economy, creating a situation where the character of the entrepreneur 'can no longer be seen as just one amongst a plurality of ethical personalities *but rather must be seen as assuming an ontological priority*' (du Gay 1996a: 181, emphasis in original). The entrepreneur is thus viewed as the ultimate enterprising individual, with a key aim of enterprise culture being the creation of new entrepreneurs (Carr 2000a).

However, both historical and current accounts of the entrepreneur and the entrepreneurial activity s/he is involved in, tend to accentuate the chaos, fragmentation and destruction that surrounds this activity. Though Marx was certainly aware of the rational and orderly character of modern European capitalism, there is also in Marx a clear account of what Berman (1988) refers to as his 'melting visions' of modern life. Within *The Communist Manifesto* Marx evokes the furious pace and hectic movement that capitalism arouses in every sphere of our lives. We are, according to Berman (1982: 91) 'hurtled along with a reckless momentum, a breathless intensity'. The source of such frantic, chaotic activity is entrepreneurial projects, leaving in their wake a sense of fragmentation and destruction. According to Marx and Engels (1985) bourgeois (entrepreneurial) activity constantly revolutionizes the instruments of production, the relations of production and the whole relations of society:

> Constant revolutionizing of production, uninterrupted disturbance of all social conditions, everlasting uncertainty and agitation distinguish the (entrepreneurial) epoch from all earlier ones. All fixed, fast-frozen relations, with their train of ancient

and venerable prejudices and opinions are swept away, all new-formed ones become antiquated before they can ossify. All that is solid melts into air, all that is holy is profaned, and man is at last compelled to face with sober senses, his real conditions of life, and his relations with his kind. The need of a constantly expanding market for its products chases the (entrepreneur) over the whole surface of the globe. It must nestle everywhere, settle everywhere, establish connections everywhere.

(Marx and Engels 1985: 83)

Similarly, Schumpeter placed an emphasis on the tendency towards chaos inbuilt in the capitalist system. Though Schumpeter conceived of capitalism as the highest expression of rational thought with rationalism being the essential spirit of the capitalist drama, he also recognized the creative and chaotic nature of capitalism which he described as 'creative destruction':

that incessantly revolutionizes the economic structure from within incessantly destroying the old one, incessantly creating a new one. This process of Creative Destruction is the essential fact about capitalism. It is what capitalism consists in and what every capitalist concern has got to live in. A perennial gale of creative destruction is going through capitalism.

(Schumpeter 1976: 84)

Contemporary studies of entrepreneurial activity also place an emphasis on the lack of certainty and constant change which small business entrepreneurs are subject to as the following quote taken from a recent study illustrates:

If you take a very small business like ourselves you know we're really being tossed around from wave to wave on the stormy seas of commerce . . . you just really have to reanalyse, basically reinvent yourself every morning. You've got to look at the whole thing afresh and make fresh assumptions. The assumptions you made yesterday morning aren't necessarily going to be quite as valid this morning. So it's very confusing and it's very hard to give definite answers but that's the way you have to be.

(Carr 2000b)

Entrepreneurs cannot exist without constantly revolutionizing production and constantly innovating. The never-ending struggle to enhance and maintain profitability requires that the entrepreneur is continually searching for new openings and exploring all kinds of possibilities. Enterprising activity ensures that capitalism is a permanently revolutionary and disruptive force, a perpetually unfinished project, a constantly mutating entity (Thrift 2002a; Carr 2003). Capitalist businesses run by entrepreneurs may be able to utilize resources to secure their objectives, but they are always operating in an uncertain future, unsure of what is around the corner, be it a potential oil crisis, a financial downturn, a threat to their brand or markets or the more mundane problem of a cash flow crisis (Thrift 2002a).

Enterprise and entrepreneurial order

Given the chaos outlined here, a key question to pose is whether a market can ever be 'left to itself'? Those in favour of the market have argued 'yes', placing an emphasis on the need for less state intervention, more deregulation, lower protection, the suppression of unions and the dismantling of the welfare state. However, to bring about the kind of transformation that those in favour of an enterprise culture desire requires a more interventionist not less interventionist state, as:

> the reformation of society along free market lines entails more than a mixture of legislative restrictions and a successful hegemonic project; it entails a bringing into line not merely of institutions but also of the way in which actors orientate their actions . . . institutions and the everyday orientation of social actors are brought into line with the principles of the market: individualism, competition, self-interest.
>
> (Scott 1996: 92–7)

The enterprise culture project is involved in the creation of areas of 'wild capitalism' which reproduces in a controlled and regulated way, a situation analogous to the circumstances of early capitalism but without forfeiting the state's ability to regulate these processes (Scott 1996). For example, with regard to the enterprising activity of the establishment and running of a small business, the state is interested in ordering this so as to get the greatest economic payback for both the individual and the economy in general. This is achieved through the implementation of small business policies which aim to develop elements constitutive of individuals' lives in such a way that their development also cultivates the strength of the state (Carr 1998; Carr 2003).

Thus promotion of enterprise and the creation of a market order is not simply about the removal of ordering mechanisms such as the state in favour of 'letting the market decide' through the 'chaotic' activities of numerous entrepreneurs. Rather it is about deciding on the balance between the order of regulation and the chaos of entrepreneurial activity, determining how order and chaos should co-exist. Recognizing this reveals the essential paradox that exists at the heart of enterprise culture where individuals and organizations are expected to be daring risk-takers, yet they are also expected to adopt this persona in a rational, organized manner, so that a significant material gain (profits, value added, employment, etc.) will emerge from their entrepreneurial activity. Thus the dialectic contradiction at the heart of enterprise culture can be defined as: 'The free unfolding of desire for capitalist accumulation and the need for a rational ordering of this' (Carr 2000a: 22).

This contradiction is internal to organizations as well as being external to them. Within a business individuals are required to be entrepreneurially chaotic (taking risks, continually seeking opportunities, working in a state of permanent emergency, etc.) as well as rationally ordered. The need for a co-existence of order and chaos within a business is not simply a theoretical claim. It is also recognized by individuals actively involved in developing a company, as the following quote from a contemporary case study of a business woman making the transition from employment as a senior manager in a large organization to independent business ownership demonstrates:

> It's taken me a year to realize that I'm a business woman and what I did was swing right out into the entrepreneurial way and I built my business in a real entrepreneurial way, really loose and it didn't work for me. So what I've done is bring in some of the corporate structure which you probably wouldn't find in a lot of entrepreneurs . . . because there are things from the corporate world that do make a lot of sense.
>
> (Lewis 2004)

This business woman recognizes the need for both enterprise in the form of entrepreneurship, and structure in the form of management in her business. She is aware of the need to maintain both without letting one dominate over the other. She constantly seeks a balance between structure and enterprise. In the wider business environment within which companies have to operate, this contradiction can be understood as an attempt on the part of government to align the enterprising abilities of individuals and businesses with the aims and objectives of the market order within which they are located (Carr 2000a).

It is suggested that the balance in countries like the UK and the USA is one which leans towards chaos, with conflicts around levels of regulation and deregulation being about the *degree* of control exercised by the state, rather than about absolute absence or absolute presence. According to Scott (1996: 106) 'capitalism was never either fully organized or disorganized, but always some mix of the two, and that it is the state which determines this mix'. Nevertheless, though the state may succeed in imposing some form of order on entrepreneurial chaos, the stability achieved is never permanent (Carr 2003). The dialectic nature of the relationship between entrepreneurial order and entrepreneurial chaos implies a continual fluctuation of their proximity and penetration of one another. The demand for an entrepreneurial order in the face of entrepreneurial chaos is insatiable and never-ending. Such ordering begets ordering in a never-ending spiral. Rather than decreasing, the level of chaos increases exponentially (Bauman 1991).

Within this theoretical framework, how should we then understand the phenomenon of the **dotcom bubble**? Though it is clear that we can represent the dotcom bubble as extreme entrepreneurial chaos, what is its relationship to state attempts to establish an entrepreneurial order, a relationship which we have suggested above is central to a Foucauldian understanding of enterprise culture? We might propose that the entrepreneurial chaos of the dotcom bubble is simply an unavoidable consequence of attempts on the part of the state to order entrepreneurial activity in general, or alternatively we could claim that it is a simple leaning towards chaos within the context of a market order. However, these explanations are problematic in that they conceal a significant shift in the contemporary treatment of new business within a country such as the UK. A key feature of the development of an enterprise culture in the UK over the past two decades is the promotion and development of the small business sector. As part of this development numerous policies and strategies (at significant financial cost) have been put in place to manage and order the expansion of this sector. What is significant about the dotcom bubble is that the normal ordering of new entrepreneurial activity which is characteristic of the small business sector was suspended. Instead, what occurred was the active promotion of entrepreneurial chaos over entrepreneurial order by various sources (including government) who either perceived this as 'the future' as discussed in the introduction to this chapter, or had a stake (often financial) in allowing this chaos to manifest itself.

THE PUSH FOR CHAOS

The shift in the business and organizational world away from a situation where order is the norm and chaos is the exception, to one where chaos is the rule and order unusual, provides the background to the emergence of the new economy and the dotcom bubble. Beginning in the 1940s and 1950s and gaining in intensity in the 1980s and 1990s, the dominant emphasis on order and rationality, central organization combined with rigid and impenetrable boundaries, gave way to a form of thinking which challenges the supremacy of reason. From this perspective the world is fundamentally chaotic, borders are less important, and territorial, ideological and issue boundaries are intensified, unclear and perplexing (Thrift 1998). It is suggested that:

> firms now live in a permanent stage of emergency, always bordering on the edge of chaos. So firms must no longer be so concerned to exercise bureaucratic control. Indeed, through a variety of devices – cultivating knowledge workers, valuing teams, organization through projects, better use of information technology, flattened hierarchies – they will generate just enough organizational stability to change in an orderly fashion and sufficient hair-trigger responsiveness to adapt to the expectedly unexpected. Firms will therefore become faster, more agile. They will be able to live life in a blur of change.
>
> (Thrift 2002b: 201)

Nevertheless, despite the emergence of a new discourse which heavily accentuates the dominance of chaos in contemporary business and social life, there is still a question mark over how realistic this is in the 'real world' of business. In other words, if we explore how businesses *actually* organize, the ethos which informs organizations and the individuals who populate these entities, the empirical evidence indicates that for 'all we read about bold companies managing in new ways, most enterprises continue to operate with functionally organized many-tiered hierarchies, the mechanistic model of a century

35

ago' (Colvin 2000 cited in Thrift 2002b: 201). It would seem then that the notion that 'chaos rules' is nothing more than rhetoric and does not have a material reality to match this discourse. However, despite recognizing the rhetorical nature of the contemporary emphasis on chaos in business life, the prominence given to turmoil and anarchy, increasingly forms the background to how business is practised, penetrating deeper and deeper into how individuals understand the world of business, acting as a justification for decisions taken, as well as future decisions to be made (Thrift 1998). If businesses appear to act (or are encouraged to act) as if chaos and permanent emergency is what drives them, then new regularities emerge which 'have the obduracy of the real' (Callon 1998: 47).

It is within this context that we must understand the emergence of the dotcom bubble. The rhetoric of turmoil and anarchy provided the background for the manifestation of the dotcom bubble. Situations such as the Internet incubator company, Oxygen Holdings, whose share price increased by 2,775 per cent on its first day of trading on the market, and whose share price crashed by an unprecedented 95 per cent the day after, can be understood as material manifestations of this rhetoric. However, where did this rhetoric emerge from and how did it manage to exert such a powerful influence?

According to Thrift (2001) a key source for this rhetoric is the 'cultural circuit of capital', made up of three knowledge producers, i.e. business schools, management consultants and management gurus. In the main all of these entities date from the twentieth century with business schools and management consultants being strong sources of executive education and business knowledge from the 1950s and 1960s onwards. Today, business schools are involved in an executive education market worth in excess of $12 billion a year, of which they generate one quarter of the value (Thrift 2001). Management gurus gained a strong position in the production and dissemination of business knowledge from the 1980s onwards. These three sources produce a range of different kinds of business knowledge and are involved in 'a process of endless, relentless and continuous critique of the status quo' (Thrift 2001: 416).

In recent years this cultural circuit of capital has produced a discourse of management practice built around an emphasis on chaos and the promotion of a new economic form, the **new economy**. The notion of the new economy emerged first in the 1980s and gained some analytical solidity in the 1990s through the development of an economic model which the label 'new economy' represented. It was symbolized by geographical areas such as Silicon Valley and what is referred to as the 'Technopolis' of the Austin/ San Antonio corridor in the USA (Armstrong 2001). In general, the new economy is characterized by: non-inflationary growth; the development of small high-tech firms; an increased importance assigned to information and communications technology; a strong emphasis on highly mobile and skilled employees; and the aggressive promotion of entrepreneurship (Thrift 2001). Both the discourse of enterprise and the discourse of the new economy place a strong emphasis on the importance of entrepreneurship, with various policy documents in the UK, such as the 1998 White Paper on Competitiveness suggesting that the UK:

will only succeed in building the knowledge-driven economy on the back of more dynamic innovation and more vigorous entrepreneurialism. . . . Entrepreneurship and innovation are central to the creative process in the economy and to promoting growth, increasing productivity and creating jobs. . . . We also need entrepreneurial individuals with the vision to turn new ideas into winning products and processes. Entrepreneurship is the lifeblood of the new British economy.

(DTI 1998: 2–6 cited in Armstrong 2001: 533)

This juxtaposition of the discourse of enterprise and the discourse of the new economy contributed to the mass motivation of individuals, with more individuals than ever believing that they had the potential to be entrepreneurs. Originally the project of the enterprise culture aimed to entice individuals to embark on entrepreneurship and business ownership by promoting an image of the entrepreneur as a rugged individual who possessed in large quantities the qualities of battle, struggle and rebelliousness. However, such a positive image of the entrepreneur has co-existed with more negative assessments, creating a situation where the moral character of the entrepreneur is ambiguous (Lewis 2003). While management consultants and management gurus tend to write glowing, highly positive accounts of the entrepreneur, such assessments tend to sit along side other contemporary accounts which warn of the darker side of the entrepreneur, his/her troubling characteristics and the dangers the entrepreneurial qualities of self-interest, risk-taking and rule-breaking pose for democratic governance (Terry 1998 cited in Lewis 2003). This kind of ambiguity and the association that is often made between entrepreneurship and rule-breaking (illegal?) activity, may create a disinclination to take-up this identity.

However, the combining of the enterprise and new economy discourses can assuage this type of reluctance in two ways. First, it reduces such ambiguity by appearing to establish a significant break with the past and allowing individuals to perceive entrepreneurship, particularly Internet entrepreneurship, only in positive terms. Second, whereas the project of the enterprise culture had attempted to entice people to set up their own businesses, the union of enterprise with the discourse of the new economy made this prospect seem possible and more attractive for larger numbers of people. Possible in that the information and communications technology which forms a central core of the new economy, was available to people in their own homes through the arrival of the personal computer, followed by the Internet and the World Wide Web. Attractive because setting up an Internet business seemed a far more glamorous prospect, with greater potential, than the establishment of a conventional small business, even if the latter had strong growth potential. Through the Internet and the World Wide Web, businesses run in an individual's back bedroom no longer seem so 'amateurish' or 'local' because the technology underlying them enabled the one-person business to 'act global' from the day it was set up. It also redressed the power imbalance conventionally felt by small organizations when put beside large organizations in the old economy. There was a strong feeling that new economy small organizations could quite easily go up against the 'big boys' as demonstrated by new media company Pacific Century Cyberworks when it demolished attempts by Singapore Telecom (which was being helped by Rupert Murdoch) to take control of Hong Kong Telecom (Islam 2001). The discourse of the new economy also painted a very clear picture of the type of individual it required. This person had to work exceptionally hard, be extremely adaptable and be passionate in the sense of continually pursuing their vision and overcoming any barriers in their way. According to Griffith (2000 cited in Thrift 2001: 422):

> The media has mythologized stories of entrepreneurs sleeping in dingy motel rooms, or on the office floor, slaving away at the computer until the early hours, sometimes forgetting to eat or to take a shower. They wear rumpled clothes, drink beer and play in their few free hours. Eventually they become billionaires. Just how much of this is reality and how much is myth is irrelevant. The point is that it has become the industry's image.

Overall the Internet, which symbolises the new economy, is an active technology. It provides individuals with a sense of mastery in their everyday life (Thrift 2001) and entices them to take up an entrepreneurial identity and embark on the risk of running their own business.

The notion of the new economy could not have developed without the rhetoric put forward by the cultural circuit of capital. However, it is also important to recognize that the rhetoric of chaos and the new economy was supported by two very significant sources, i.e. government and the financial sector. According to Thrift (2001), governments around the world articulated a commitment to the new economy with efforts being made to make this economic model specific to their country as demonstrated by New Labour boasts that Britain would create the best environment for e-Trading. From the perspective of government the notion of the new economy appeared to hold out the prospect that capitalism could enter a new phase which would bring benefits for large numbers of individuals. In particular in the UK context there was a perception that the new economy would provide the basis for enterprise with a more human and caring face, in contrast to the 'greedy' image which often attached to enterprise in the 1980s. In terms of economic organization, Britain has always maintained a type of dual-track policy in which some economic areas remain organized and others are disorganized (Scott 1996). Policy which promotes enterprise and entrepreneurship in areas such as the conventional 'old economy' small business sector has tended to be quite tightly circumscribed (Carr 2000a). However, for Internet business any type of regulation was believed to be destructive of the new economy creativity. An emphasis was placed on new economy businesses as creative institutions and spaces for personal expression and artistry and not just financial entities. However, according to Thrift (2001) finance became the ruling passion of the new economy and dotcom businesses.

The idea that Internet businesses and related information industries were a revolution in the way businesses and sectors organized themselves played very well to financial audiences. Dotcom business was not just the emergence of a new stand alone industry, it was believed to be a 'disruptive technology' which would lead to substantial cost reductions and profit growth (Islam 2001). Such interest is what one is likely to expect from those working in the financial sphere. However, one significant difference is that demand and interest in financial shares of economic assets expanded considerably during the last two decades of the twentieth century. This increase in the number of shareholders (both institutional and individual) and the interest they expressed in the new economy was compounded by a massive expansion in business reporting. The sports-style coverage of business issues by ordinary news programmes and dedicated business channels produced a more or less uninterrupted stream of business news which contributed to the hype around dotcom shares (Thrift 2001). The new economy story spread extensively 'and worked to the extent that it began to re-describe market fundamentals' (Thrift 2001: 425). It persuaded many individuals and institutions to take more risks with their investments despite evidence of faulty business plans and inexperienced management, which can be understood as the fostering of innovations that would otherwise not have taken place. A less positive interpretation is that the new economy discourse drew investors into taking on substantial levels of debt, leaving individuals and institutions in possession of little better than junk bonds (Thrift 2001).

CONCLUSION: AFTER THE 'GOLD RUSH'

So what's left since venture capitalist companies 'pulled the plug' on companies such as Boo.com which through its behaviour (wild launch parties, opening in 20 countries simultaneously, relaxed financial controls, extravagant tastes on the part of the founders, etc.) typified the chaos of the dotcom period? Does the apparent shift back to a form of entrepreneurial order epitomized by an emphasis on getting back to business basics such as sustainable business, good management, implementation of controls, etc. mean that entrepreneurial chaos has been 'put back in its box' and its effects have been well and truly neutered? According to Thrift (2001) it is important that we do not simply dismiss the notion of the new economy and the experience of the dotcom bubble. Organizations have experienced a general speed-up in the conduct of business, largely, although not only due to the increasing use of information technology, a trend which has been reinforced by the emergence of the new economy discourse and its juxtaposition with enterprise. According to those involved in the dotcom phenomenon, one year by the Julian calendar is equivalent to four years Internet time (Islam 2001). This sense that everything is constantly changing and at ever greater speeds, means that companies are obliged to launch more new products more frequently, compress product development cycles and react speedily to competitors, suppliers and customers. In such an environment all advantage is temporary and speed of reaction is crucial (Thrift 2002b).

At the same time the reassertion of entrepreneurial order means that individuals, particularly managers, must react swiftly in all circumstances, while also being subject to a constant monitoring and checking of their performance. Measures such as the share price of a company have become crucial determinants of business success and movements up or down can have a significant impact on future prospects as well as current remuneration. The renewed emphasis placed on the need for entrepreneurial order signals the re-emergence of the dialectic contradiction that exists at the heart of enterprise culture. Chaotic areas of economic activity will be restricted and constrained, with continuous efforts made to order and rationalize the perceived anarchy of entrepreneurial activity. The discourses of enterprise and the new economy may appear to have given rise to an uncontrolled and uncontrollable frenzy of entrepreneurial activity. However, it is important to remember that the 'road to the free market was opened and kept open by an enormous increase in continuous, centrally organized and controlled interventionism' (Polanyi 1955: 140 quoted in Scott 1996: 107). The dotcom bubble may have appeared to signal the triumph of the market over the state but it is important to remember Foucault's assertion that the development of a market economy and the promotion of entrepreneurial chaos is not the suspension of order, rather it is the emergence of a new form of state control which operates 'at a distance'.

QUESTIONS

Question 1
What characteristics of the dotcom bubble justify conceptualizing it as 'entrepreneurial chaos'?
Feedback
Entrepreneurial activity is historically characterized as chaotic, e.g. Schumpeter, Marx. The extreme energy and excitement surrounding the dotcom bubble; the interest expressed by various parties, e.g. government, financial sector, the business sector; the constant change surrounding e-Business; the large number of individuals willing to set up a dotcom company; the extreme highs and lows experienced by individual dotcom companies, are all factors which can lead us to characterize the dotcom bubble as 'entrepreneurial chaos'.

Question 2
In exploring the emergence of the dotcom bubble, how should we understand the relationship between 'entrepreneurial order' and 'entrepreneurial chaos'?
Feedback
An understanding of the relationship between entrepreneurial order and entrepreneurial chaos is central to a Foucauldian understanding of enterprise culture. The promotion of entrepreneurship over the past 20 years has occurred within a context of government attempts to manage and influence actively how individuals practise their enterprise. What stands out about the dotcom bubble is that the normal ordering and regulation of new business activity was suspended. This situation was supported by the cultural circuit of capital.

Question 3

How likely is it that something like the dotcom bubble will happen again?

Feedback

A question open to vibrant debate!

GLOSSARY

Dotcom bubble   The period from 1998 to 2000 (in the UK) when Internet stocks were rising, new businesses were bring started at a phenomenal rate and were assumed by many to be a passport to instant riches.

Enterprise culture   A business environment or ethos within which entrepreneurial activity is fostered and encouraged.

Entrepreneur   An individual prepared to take on the risk of establishing and actively developing a business which might be perceived to be an 'unknown quantity' or requiring action against received wisdom.

Entrepreneurial chaos   The occurrence of the unexpected in all entrepreneurial activity, powerlessness definitively to control entrepreneurial activity and an inability to eliminate happenings or events from entrepreneurial activity which are objectionable or deemed unnecessary, and keeps the danger and excitement of entrepreneurship alive.

Foucauldian   An approach which extends the concept of enterprise culture to all kinds of individuals and establishments – to the conduct of organizations previously characterized as non-economic, to the conduct of government and to the conduct of individuals. In addition, its success is heavily dependent on individuals' identification with and acceptance of the norms of enterprise.

New economy   An expression which evolved during the heady years of the 'dotcom bubble' to describe the high-tech, fast-moving environment within which Internet-based businesses could flourish – conditions which were once thought to render 'old' business principles obsolete.

BIBLIOGRAPHY

Armstrong, P. (2001) 'Science, enterprise and profit: ideology in the knowledge-driven economy', *Economy and Society*, 30, 4: 524–52.

Bauman, Z. (1991) *Modernity and Ambivalence*, Cambridge: Polity Press.

Berman, M. (1988) *All That Is Solid Melts into Air: The Experience of Modernity*, London: Penguin Books.

Burrows, R. (1991) 'The discourse of enterprise culture and the restructuring of Britain: a polemical contribution', in J. Curran and R. Blackburn (eds) *Paths of Enterprise: The Future of Small Business*, London: Routledge.

Burrows, R. and Ford, J. (1998) 'Self-employment and home ownership: after the enterprise culture', *Work, Employment and Society*, 12, 1: 97–119.

Callon, M. (ed.) (1998) *The Laws of the Market*, Oxford: Blackwell.

Carr, P. (1998) 'The cultured production of enterprise: understanding selectivity as cultural policy', *The Economic and Social Review*, 29, 2: 133–55.

Carr, P. (2000a) *The Age of Enterprise: The Emergence and Evolution of Entrepreneurial Management*, Dublin: Blackhall Press.

Carr, P. (2000b) 'Understanding enterprise culture: the "fashioning" of enterprise activity within small business', *Journal of Strategic Change*, 9, 7: 405–14.

Carr, P. (2003) 'Revisiting the Protestant ethic and the spirit of capitalism: understanding the relationship between ethics and enterprise', *Journal of Business Ethics*, 47, 1: 7–16.

Cohen, N. (2002) 'In the firetrap bubble', *The Observer*, 1 December.

Colvin, G. (2000) 'Managing in the Info Era', *Fortune*, 14. 5: 2–5.

Connon, H. (2003) 'Three years that shook the world', *The Observer*, 9 March.

The Economist (2001) 'Don't say "new economy"', 6 January: 75.

Drakopoulou Dodd, S. and Anderson, A. R. (2001) 'Understanding the enterprise culture: paradigm, paradox and policy', *The International Journal of Entrepreneurship and Innovation*, 2, 1: 13–25.

DTI (1998) *Our Competitive Future: Building the Knowledge Driven Economy*, London: Stationery Office.

du Gay, P. (1996a) *Consumption and Identity at Work*, London: Sage.

du Gay, P. (1996b) 'Organizing identity: entrepreneurial governance and public management', in S. Hall and P. du Gay (eds) *Questions of Cultural Identity*, London: Sage.

du Gay, P., Salaman, G. and Rees, B. (1996) 'The conduct of management and the management of conduct: contemporary managerial discourse and the constitution of the competent manager', *Journal of Management Studies*, 33, 3: 263–82.

Fournier, V. and Grey, C. (1999) 'Too much, too little and too often: a critique of du Gay's analysis of enterprise', *Organization*, 6, 1: 107–28.

Gordon, C. (1987) 'The soul of the citizen: Max Weber and Michel Foucault on rationality and government', in S. Whimster and S. Lash (eds) *Max Weber, Rationality and Modernity*, London: Allen and Unwin.

Griffith, S. (2000) 'It's a man's new economy', *Financial Times*, 25 August.

Islam, F. (2001) 'How dotcoms drowned in a tide of hype and hope', *The Observer*, 11 February.

Lewis, P. (2003) 'The making of an entrepreneur: enterprise and entrepreneurial identity', paper presented at 19th EGOS Colloquium, Organization Analysis Informing Social and Global Development, Copenhagen.

Lewis, P. (2004) 'Developing an entrepreneurial identity,' *The International Journal of Entrepreneurship and Innovation*, 5, 1: 59–65.

Marx, K. and Engels, F. (1888) [1985] *The Communist Manifesto*, London: Penguin Classics.

Miller, P. and Rose, N. (1990) 'Governing economic life', *Economy and Society*, 19, 1: 1–31.

Osborne, D. and Gaebler, T. (1992) *Reinventing Government*, Reading, MA: Addison-Wesley.

Peters, T. (1992) *Liberation Management*, Basingstoke: Macmillan.

Polanyi, K. (1955) *The Great Transformation*, Boston, MA: Beacon Press.

Scase, R. (2000) 'The enterprise culture: the socioeconomic context of small firms', in S. Carter and D. Jones-Evans (eds) *Enterprise and Small Business: Principles, Practice and Policy*, Harlow: Prentice Hall.

Schumpeter, J. A. (1943) [1976] *Capitalism, Socialism and Democracy*, fifth edn, London: Allen and Unwin.

Scott, A. (1996) 'Bureaucratic revolutions and free market utopias', *Economy and Society*, 25, 1: 89–110.

Shiller, R. (2000) *Irrational Exuberance*, Princeton, NJ: Princeton University Press.

Terry, L. D. (1998) 'Administrative leadership, neo-managerialism and the public management movement', *Public Administration Review*, 58, 3: 194–200.

Thrift, N. (1998) 'The rise of soft capitalism', in A. Herod, G. O'Tuathail and S. M. Roberts (eds) *An Unruly World?*, London: Routledge, pp. 25–71.

Thrift, N. (2001) 'It's the romance, not the finance, that makes the business worth pursuing: disclosing a new market culture', *Economy and Society*, 30, 4: 412–32.

Thrift, N. (2002a) 'Chasing capitalism', *New Political Economy*, 6, 3: 375–80.

Thrift, N. (2002b) 'Performing cultures in the new economy', in P. du Gay and M. Pryke (eds) *Cultural Economy*, London: Sage.

Chapter 3

Social shaping of government: what can be learned from the adoption of mobile-mediated communications?

JANE VINCENT

KEY LEARNING POINTS

After completing this chapter you should have an understanding of:

- Social shaping and what it might mean to future e-Citizens
- Social interaction with technology, and how they shape each other
- The influence of social relations and etiquettes on mediated communications
- The impact of social resistance to the adoption of new technologies

INTRODUCTION

This chapter discusses the social shaping of e-Government in the light of how everyday social practices have impacted on the adoption of new mobile-mediated communications. In so doing it separates the e-Economy reality from the rhetoric by highlighting some of the likely challenges that might affect the future adoption and use of e-Government services.

To contextualize this discussion: first consider the difference between the needs of the provider of the service, in this instance e-Government, and the needs of users of the service, the **e-Citizens**. Those who seek the introduction of e-Government tend to assume that people have a need to interact with their local government electronically, however, this might not be true for all. This chapter does demonstrate that people can change their daily practice with regard to using new technology, however, in practice, it is not the technology that people adopt but the means it affords of satisfying their needs, especially if in so doing it enhances their lives in some way.

A study of the social practices of users of mobile-mediated communications indicates that, despite the rhetoric, the recent technical domination of product design may have been less successful than existing devices or products which are continually adapted to meet personal needs, rather than technical developments (Vincent and Haddon 2003). There is a constant tension between old and new practices and, while people will accept the new they are reluctant to relinquish their use of known products or services when the benefits of changing are not obvious. Marvin argues that new communications technologies 'are always introduced into a pattern of tension created by the co-existence of old and new' (Marvin 1988) and Sacks, in explaining the failure of technocratic dreams with respect to new communications technologies, says that what in reality happens is that 'the object is made at home in the world that has whatever organization it already has' (Sacks 1992 cited in Cooper 2002).

In exploring the social shaping of e-Government this chapter draws on recent social sciences research into the social practices of mobile communications users, addressing in particular their needs for social relations, behavioural convergence and emotional attachment to mobile phones.

WHAT IS SOCIAL SHAPING?

There is a continuous interaction between humans and technology, however simple or complex that technology might be. This interaction has resulted in a continuing synthesis of ideas that in turn have been applied to the development of social practices and to advances in technology; this is what we mean when we use the expression 'social shaping'. Two recent examples of social shaping are the way users of mobile phones have developed a new argot in text messaging or **short message service** (SMS); and secondly in their unwillingness to adopt **WAP** (mobile Internet). It can be argued that social acceptance of WAP technology was not relevant because the technology was not able to deliver the promise offered by those marketing the technology. Had it worked the way it had been marketed, uptake may well have been quite different.

SMS was originally designed as a replacement for pagers and targeted at business users. However, its success in the market, despite early SMS-enabled mobile phones being cumbersome, was down to the way the public quickly learned how to 'text' each other directly between mobile handsets. In the UK alone, over 16 billion messages were sent in 2003 with teenagers being the most avid users. In no more than seven years, users of text messaging have transformed this product from a technologically designed concept to a mass-market user-driven service generating impressive, initially unplanned, revenues for the industry. Compared with the success of texting, WAP was a disaster for the mobile communications industry and its technology designers who had sold it as 'mobile Internet'. The increasing use and awareness of the WWW within society meant that people expected a similar experience on their mobile phone to that on their personal computer (PC) at home or in the office. The difficult interface and the small screen on the mobile phone meant that users quickly tired of trying to use this product to surf the net and despite extensive marketing the WAP technology continues to be underutilized today. However, this should be viewed in the light of the market conditions into which WAP was launched where everyone was on the hunt for 'killer-applications' and quick returns on investment – not a good environment for new, untested technology.

The social shaping of e-Government will come about as a result of many perturbations, but understanding the impact on society of the arrival of electronically mediated organizations such as e-Government is possibly simpler than one at first would think. Just because the delivery mechanism is complex, it does not mean that people will have to undergo a transformation of equal difficulty to become e-Citizens. After all, the apparently difficult technological interface for sending a text message is not a barrier when this is what someone wants to do. An e-Citizen does not have to be technologically literate – most important is that they must have a need for the information available through electronically mediated communications. If this need can be satisfied most easily in this way then they will probably persevere with the e-Interface to make it work for them. This is an example of how the arrival of a new technology demands the shaping or changes to existing user behaviours whilst at the same time the technology is being made to fit within a framework of current social practices. When information made available to users via this new medium is of no consequence to e-Citizens, as was the case with using WAP technology when accessing the same information via the Internet using their PC was better, then they are unlikely to adopt the newer technology. New technologies and frameworks do not tend to create a need just because of their existence, but rather that mobile-mediated communications technology is adopted when it satisfies existing needs better and faster than current technology or systems.

The mutual shaping of technology and society is a continuing and powerful process. Westrum (1991) argues that 'the very structure of our society is related to the kind of technologies we have' and he expresses concern that there is a gap between the technologies used by organizations and their ability to cope with them. He refers to high technology disasters such as Bhopal, Chernobyl and the NASA Space shuttle Challenger saying that 'in each of these cases there existed a conspicuous mismatch between the complexity of the technology and the capabilities of the human beings responsible for managing it'. These examples are cited to demonstrate that new technologies should not be introduced without a thorough knowledge of how to manage them not only in their planned use but also ways in which they might be used in the short and long term.

The way we do things and technologies we use to do them are constantly changing, but our reasons for doing things change less frequently. Some aspects of everyday life in society have remained constant throughout periods of technological change including the comforts of feeling safe, being near to loved ones, and shared moments. In addition, the need to be able to solve problems, conduct business and, for many people, it is also about being associated with the latest 'thing'. These needs lie at the heart of most things we do. If we can find ways of enhancing these needs using technologies such as text messaging to bring us closer together, then we will do so; thereby shaping the technology, or simply our use of it, to meet our own needs regardless of the original intentions of its designer or inventor.

THINK POINT

What are the implications of launching technologies developed according to deadlines, budget limits and other organizations' agendas before they have been fully tested? Testing is not only necessary to establish fitness for purpose, assuming this purpose has also been fully explored and understood, but also on what future users might choose to do with the technology, either by adapting it for a new purpose or simply using it in different ways. How might society shape technology and is the organization asking too much of society and itself to implement it in the first place?

CHOOSING THE RIGHT MOBILE-MEDIATED COMMUNICATION FOR E-GOVERNMENT

While the mobile phone was initially introduced for business users, it is now used more for personal use to maintain social relations than managing business affairs (Vincent and Harper 2003). There are a few exceptions to this as some companies, mainly those in the mobile communications industry and very small businesses with one or a few employees, have opted to use only mobile phones (but fixed lines for computers). However, this does not appear to be a trend, rather it is a choice made to suit the needs of that organization.

It is this choice of mediated communications available today that presents the biggest challenge to the e-Citizen. The range of mediated communications is expanding and there is no need to replace old systems with new as interoperability of technologies affords the opportunity to maintain the old systems and devices alongside the new (Vincent and Haddon 2003). This means that within groups of users, each can choose their preferred medium for communication. It is not only the technology and the device that they must choose but also whether they speak, write, type, text or send images, and whether they do this two-way in real time or one-way in some form of recorded message. Live conversations via instant messaging or text messaging can be conducted between participants who may be thousands of miles apart. The e-Citizen is becoming more aware of the choices on offer and more determined to use the mode that best suits them and the people with whom they communicate most. The adoption of any new communications media brings with it new or adapted etiquettes for its use. Initially users of a new service are not quite sure how to behave and question, for example, if it is acceptable to email or should a letter be used? Is a call to someone on their mobile

47

unacceptable – will it be too informal or intrusive? Users of camera phones who want to take and send pictures wherever they are have found resistance from people who feel threatened or concerned about misuse. Interestingly, these concerns were also expressed about fixed phones when they were first introduced (Lasen 2003). There was resistance to the adoption of the telephone because it was thought it might induce hysteria, cause aural over-pressure or raise hygiene issues through sharing handsets. Concerns were also raised about use of mobile phones. While it is not suggested that the introduction of e-Government will prompt a similar response, it does highlight the potential for irrational and emotional reactions to new technology.

Social shaping helps normalize new technologies by introducing ways of managing the new technology with accepted etiquettes which affects the rate at which new media are adopted and absorbed into society. For example, use of SMS grew exponentially once it became 'OK' to text and especially when texting was adopted by younger generations when texting became a new and private argot for their communications. Because providers had not anticipated their actual market, providers of text messaging services struggled to maintain service due to insufficient capacity planning. Another example of the public's actual versus anticipated demand for something outweighing expectations can be found on Web sites launched with little publicity which attracted the public's attention so much that they were closed down and rebuilt to accommodate unexpected demand. A good example of this was the UK Census site which provides useful historical data in a user-friendly format, unlike its unwieldy predecessor, microfilm.

THINK POINT

What do you think will be the etiquette used for the management of e-Government services? What type of mobile-mediated communication is most suitable for delivering the information made available, allowing e-Citizens to ask questions, and carry out any transactions that are likely to take place?

SOCIAL SHAPING OF MOBILE-MEDIATED COMMUNICATIONS

Recently, mobile-mediated communications have become omnipresent in many societies throughout the world. The construction of mobile phone infrastructure has provided a turning point for many nations, some of which have leap-frogged the development of fixed line telecommunications completely. In these circumstances mobile communications have been an enabling technology in the continued shaping of society and many have embraced the opportunity this affords to great effect. However, while there was the much publicized use of text messaging in the Philippines to mobilize people in the overthrow of their government in 2001 (Paragus 2003), or the use of the Internet and mobile phone in the process of political development in Korea (Kim 2003), this is not a revolution in social or technological shaping, it is merely another moment in the constant process of change. As Dányi and Sükösd (2003) point out when discussing these examples 'new communications technologies do not enter a social, economic, cultural and institutional vacuum, but are used in the context of pre-existing social organizations'. This holds true for the social shaping of e-Government in the UK and the emergence of the e-Citizen who will build on the social practices that already exist rather than starting from a clean sheet. So it seems that the reality of mobile communications may well be more prosaic than the rhetoric.

This section discusses three themes that describe the social practices of present-day mobile-mediated communications users, each of which is illustrated by a case study providing insights into the possible implications these social practices may have on the development of e-Government. The case studies are taken from research conducted during 2003 (Vincent and Haddon 2003) and describe the activities of groups of mobile communications users in the UK on a typical day in their lives.

KEEPING CONNECTED

The ecology of keeping connected is a complex one, where social relations, connections with family, friends and emotions combine to create a system of interdependencies that mobile-mediated communications can help foster and sustain. Indeed, in studies conducted in Europe and elsewhere, the importance of communication for keeping connected to one's peer group among teenagers is particularly noted. This is a period in life when the social network of young people is growing and when it is important to be available to peers (Vincent and Haddon 2003). The number of messages received, the number of times one teenager is rung up and the number of names in the dialling register have all been taken to be a sign of popularity (Ling and Yttri 2002). It is not only teenagers for whom the mobile phone has become a lifeline. In recent research it was noted that it is often the parents who are liberated by the availability of mobile communications as is demonstrated in the case study of the Burges family below. Here, three generations of the family use their mobile phones as part of their mediated communications repertoire to manage the processes of their daily life and in so doing perhaps pack more into their days. The needs of this family are typical. They negotiate the use of their communications media with each other, sharing mobile phones to make the best use of bundled tariffs. They have their mobiles with them at all times to keep connected with each other and with their friends, although they do not always use them. They like to avoid risk by texting and calling each other to ensure safe arrival or to inform of late running and they like the comfort of being able to contact each other wherever they are.

49

Case study:
BURGES FAMILY

It's a typical Saturday and the Burges family are organizing their day. Mum, Sue, is going to have her hair and her nails done because she is going out with her husband to celebrate a friend's birthday. Her sons are going round to a friend's house to play and to watch football and her husband has stuff to do around the house. Meanwhile at her house, Sue's mum, Mary, has shopping to do and is going out to friends for lunch. It's going to be a long day for Sue, she's going to have to take her sons places as well as get ready for the birthday party and so she has a cup of tea in bed and reads the papers. About 9.00am her Mum rings (using her fixed line) and she has a chat with her. Then her sister Paula rang her for a chat; she finished the newspaper and Sue got up around 10.00am to get breakfast for the family. While she made breakfast Sue called her Mum – she used the mobile to ring her because someone else in the family was on the cordless phone.

She went back upstairs – her mobile is in her dressing gown pocket. She showered and got dressed – her friend called her on the mobile about the evening. Her friends usually call her mobile and so she takes it around the house with her – they could call any time. She made the beds, got the boys together and, leaving her husband at home, they headed off in the car. There was much more traffic than expected and so she called her friend to say they were delayed and then rang the hairdresser to check her appointment time. She asked one of the boys to use WAP on his mobile (because it was free on his mobile but not on hers), she wanted the telephone number of a place she wanted to go to but he couldn't make it work. He tried later and was more successful but mostly he uses WAP to get football scores.

Leaving the boys at the friends she went to the hairdresser for a quick haircut. No one rang her while she was in there – respite for a while. On her way home she called in at her mum's who was out so she used her mum's fixed phone to call her on her mobile, (it was more expensive for Sue to use her own mobile), but she had switched it off. During lunch another friend rang her mobile about the evening. After lunch Sue did some cleaning, watching the television at the same time – her husband had it on to watch the football; afterwards she went to the beautician's by car, phoning her sister Paula again on the way. Returning home the traffic was bad again and so she called her husband to let him know and texted her friend to say she was late collecting the children; this meant less time to catch up and chat with her friends who'd had the boys all day. It was another half hour to get home and they stopped for petrol, lottery tickets and a take-away meal. Having spent more time than planned in traffic Sue was behind with things so she disappeared up to her bedroom and switched on the TV but she didn't have time to sit and watch it. She phoned her mum and her sister and then a friend called – she used her mobile. At 8.30pm she and her husband bid the boys farewell and went out in the car, going first to a restaurant they'd arranged to meet up at and later to a night club until the early hours – she had her mobile with her but she didn't use it at all and the boys didn't ring her. The next morning she texted her friend to say thank you.

THINK POINT

The link between the need for constant connectivity and the e-Citizen may at first appear to be tenuous and indeed it is unlikely that e-Government will ever form an integral part of the social relations of the average UK family. However, if we look at the social practices they use there are some lessons here for the way that the e-Citizen may or may not mediate their communications with e-Government?

It would appear that different generations although familiar with mobile-mediated communications do not all use it as a first choice. The appropriateness of the communication is not only about when and where it is made and received but also about what type of communications medium should be used. An intimate call on a mobile phone might be acceptable on a train but not on a fixed line phone in the living room with the rest of the family present. A call to a mobile might be preferred but if the recipient is uncomfortable with this the caller might make the call to a fixed phone. Similarly, a social arrangement can be made by text among friends but a formal invitation within the same group might be made by phone call or even using the postal service. The e-interface chosen by family members to communicate with e-Government will also be subject to negotiation. They will want to consider what is the most appropriate means of achieving it and how it can be done within the existing portfolio of services and at no extra cost. e-Government will not easily penetrate households if it chooses only one form of mediated communications.

BEHAVIOURAL CONVERGENCE

All types of technologies, especially digital ones, can be combined and managed by the user in some way that is unique to them and this is what has been called behavioural convergence (Vincent and Haddon 2003). This behaviour facilitates the multi-tasking activities that people seek to achieve in their day-to-day lives and because it is done in response to their particular needs or circumstances, the nature of the technologies that are combined is likely to vary from day to day. The advent of the digital age means that the opportunities for behavioural convergence are manifold. Everything from an espresso coffee-maker to a highly complex computer infrastructure can claim to be digital, and vending machines can dispense drinks in response not to money paid but to a text message

51

sent. These are just a few examples of the increasing numbers of technologies that use electronically mediated communications to function and with which the e-Citizen can have a direct interface. Behavioural convergence doesn't mean that people are busy building hybrid machines that dispense drinks whilst running a report off a database. What it does mean is that as each new layer of technology is added it is interwoven with previous technologies rather than used to replace them. In the business team case study described below a local government office has added each new system on to the next resulting in some prescribed systems that require staff to use their computers but other tasks can be completed in a variety of ways using paper or computerized systems or simply asking someone who knows.

Case study:
BUSINESS TEAM

Simon is a team leader in the local government office and is a keen user of the latest computing technologies; he is writing the IT strategy for the department. He leads a group of five and in common with the other 60 people in the department he is on the road for about half of his working day. The offices are set up as shared 'hot desks' but people have tended to adopt a routine of either coming in to the same desk everyday or working from home and only occasionally coming in. There are at least two people allocated to each desk and the fixed phone system and the PCs are password operated. Simon and his team have a mobile phone each supplied by their employer who has recently banned their use when driving cars. Their cars serve as an office when out on the road and this change in policy brought about by new legislation is causing a lot of problems. Simon is on emergency call out for which he has a pager and he uses a laptop for home working and a handheld tape recorder for letters that his administrator types (he cannot type accurately or fast). He doesn't have a PDA although he is excited that they will be trialling BlackBerrys soon so he'll be able to get his emails on the road – he currently uses an A4 diary for all appointments, records of meetings and for phone numbers and addresses. Simon's day starts early – he can work flexible hours and so he comes into the office at 7.30am to beat the traffic and have some peace and quiet so he can get on with his paperwork. He has to maintain records about his work on two databases as well as recording on another database how he spends his own time. His records are used from time to time in court for legal proceedings and thus must be accurate and withstand scrutiny at any time. When he has quite a lot of paperwork to catch up on he books the conference room to read up on files and dictate some letters. Although much of his work is on the PC, plans and letters from clients are on file and these must be checked against the computer database and his personal notes in his diary. He would be lost without his diary – his 'bible'. It not only has appointments and records of meetings but it is an industry diary and contains all the phone numbers of the other authorities he must deal with. The supplier of the diary does not offer this information on a CD or Web site and the diary is the only place that has it all together. Most of the things Simon and his team use their PCs for are record keeping in response to the new systems being introduced by their local government. This is additional to the jobs they have been doing in the same way since before they had the systems they now use. They all find that they are in the office much more now than before they had all these IT systems and so don't get around so many of their clients. They do find the intranet useful and Simon will check it when he is in the office to see if there is any news and to see details of training requirements. Although Simon is the team leader the focal point of contact on the team is their administrator and Simon will ask her for data or assistance with most new cases whilst at the same time she is taking calls on her fixed line from others on the team, and from the general public.

THINK POINT

Is there a risk that e-Government will not become the dominant system within its own organizational infrastructure despite its best intentions? Some mobile telecommunications companies only use their own products in their premises and have removed all fixed line telephones — should local government follow suit and conduct all its internal business electronically too?

The social practices within offices determine what equipment is purchased and how much it is used. This often means that old systems are not necessarily wholly replaced and people can continue to use the old alongside the new until one or other fails or becomes redundant. The same applies in households but budgetary constraints mean that more people may use less equipment to satisfy more needs. For example, computers are used as DVD players, televisions for computer games, and stereos are used to play music downloaded from the WWW from PCs.

EMOTIONAL ATTACHMENT TO MOBILE PHONES

The mobile phone affords a much more intimate and confidential relationship than other communications devices and it would appear that the owner of the mobile phone has a much more emotional relationship with their mobile than with any other computational device (Vincent 2003). A mobile phone somehow engenders strength of feeling about the content it carries and the connectivity it affords that cannot be surpassed — it is as if one's nearest and dearest are tethered via an invisible link to the mobile phone. This is not to say that people do not develop an emotional attachment to their laptop or PC and with the arrival of **wifi** and **Voice Over Internet Protocol (VOIP)** this attachment may increase. However, key factors in the use of mobile phones in preference to a multi-tasking PDA/mobile Internet device or laptop is their small size and long battery life. These two factors have been prominent in users' expectations since mobile phones came into general use in the 1980s. A small phone that can be carried on the person at all times, and a battery that doesn't fail at a critical moment is key to the emotional attachment as it enables it to be discrete and 'always on'. The experience of users is that games, multi-media messaging and WAP are all battery hungry and difficult to use on a small screen. An additional factor is that they are perceived as expensive whereas maintaining voice and text connectivity is accepted as essential whatever the cost (although the cheapest will do) (Vincent and Harper 2003). Person-to-person connectivity will always take priority over person to information connectivity unless price and battery life can be improved – factors that e-Government planners need to be cognisant of if they are thinking of accessing customers via mobile devices.

Case study:
TEENAGERS

Kelly is in her last year at school before she goes to university and in a steady relationship with her boyfriend Wayne. When they got together a few months ago Kelly changed her mobile phone number and contract to the same provider as Wayne so that they could text and call each other more cheaply. At the time they had treated themselves to camera phones so they could send pictures and video clips to each other but in the first month they spent over £250 which was much more than usual and the extra cost had gone on sending the images to each other – neither has anyone else they can send images to at the moment. They don't send pictures to each other using their mobiles now but download them to their PC using the Bluetooth capability on the mobile and send the pictures by email, or print them off. Alternatively, they just store them on their mobile and show them to each other and their friends. Recently, they went bowling with a youth group and Wayne took a picture of Kelly and her friend Jen. As soon as he had taken it (using Kelly's mobile) they all crowded round to look and laughed at their expressions; Kelly scrolled through the images showing everyone and then found one of Wayne – he didn't have much on and his head was out of the frame. They laughed as they remembered when it was taken; Wayne was quite happy for it to be shown to Kelly's friends.

On a typical day Kelly will have her mobile with her at all times and will text her friends and Wayne constantly. She is very adept at sending texts and can do so in seconds – a lot faster than her mum who texts her but she takes a few minutes just to send a short one. When she doesn't see Wayne they send each other texts much more and right through the night; the other night Kelly got really fed up about it as the phone was beeping every time she got to sleep and in the end she texted Wayne to ask him to stop texting her – she wouldn't have been happy if it had been the other way around. All of Kelly's friends have got mobiles and they exchange information about boyfriends, they arrange their social life and especially use them to call each other when they get to a place rather than arranging a specific time to meet up. What sort of mobile you have is important for creating the right impression and Kelly recently lent her old mobile to a friend for the evening; they were spending the evening together and she didn't want to be seen with someone who had an unfashionable mobile like the one her friend usually used!

Kelly keeps some of her text messages if they are special – like some of the ones between her and Wayne. The mobile phone has all her phone numbers in it and she wouldn't be without it. Recently, someone got hold of her number and started bothering her and so she had to change the number – this was irritating but because she had backed up her numbers she could easily transfer them to her new SIM. She knows her mum wouldn't allow her to stay out late nearly as much as she does if she didn't have the mobile phone and she likes to know where her mum is too as she relies on her for lifts. She really couldn't do without her mobile phone and will answer it wherever she is among friends but puts it on silent when she is in places where mobiles are banned or she'd be embarrassed to answer it – after all it's usually Wayne who's contacting her.

THINK POINT

What does emotional attachment mean to the e-Citizen? Will people have one inviolable device that serves as their emotional prop and others that meet more functional needs such as for conducting e-Business? Will e-Government services be made available like cash and banking services are from an ATM machine or will this be a step too far?

The impact of emotional attachment to mobile devices on e-Government and other organizations that seek to use the mobile phone as their medium of contact with their customers may be greater than these organizations realize. The mobile phone is carried about the person, is not turned off even at night (and usually put on silent rather than turned off when in mobile-free zones), and the phone number is not given out freely. Mobile phones have become an icon for all that they engender such as the invisible tethering to loved ones; the information about relationships and friendships and social engagements that they contain; and the way they can instantly connect you to someone – even if it is merely by way of an image on caller display silently received in a school lesson or business meeting to say 'I'm thinking of you'. The users who do not want their social relations violated might quickly squash aspirations of e-Government and other e-Organizations to communicate messages and conduct transactions over this same device. This is not to say that they do not want to be contacted electronically, and as has already been discussed, they will probably choose a preferred method from their own repertoire of electronically mediated communications which might, in time, include several mobile phones.

CONCLUSIONS

This chapter has examined the issue of the social shaping of e-Government. It has explored the topic by investigating how users have shaped mobile-mediated communications, and how the technology has in turn shaped the framework within which people conduct their day-to-day lives. It has examined the three themes of keeping connected, behavioural convergence and emotional attachment to mobile phones to highlight the social practices that will most likely continue regardless of technological advances. Social practices include keeping constantly connected with family, friends and business colleagues; choosing devices and services that best suits the user's own needs, and using past experiences to develop etiquettes for new media and interfaces. The e-Citizen of the future appears happy to embrace new technologies but only if they serve as a means of enhancing their satisfaction in the ways that they meet needs. Technology is recognized as being no barrier to social change, rather it is seen as an enabler. However, where there is no perceived need or added value achieved by the technology, however excellent and innovative it might be, it is unlikely to be adopted. There are important 'rhetoric versus reality' lessons here for policy-makers.

The intensifying of communications within social groups and the strategies people adopt to achieve constant connectivity with loved ones lies at the heart of mediated communications that deliver person-to-person connectivity. Business matters relating to personal or work life are frequently conducted using more traditional methods such as fixed telephony, email and even paper mail, and people need to have these as back-up even if they never use them. It would appear that this complex repertoire of mediated communications available to every e-Citizen and to every e-Organization offers both a cornucopia of choice and an opportunity for mismatched expectations. Suppliers of e-Government would do well to watch and listen to the preferred choices of their customers and their own employees as guidelines for the best choice mobile-mediated communications for the delivery of services to the e-Citizen.

QUESTIONS

Question 1

What examples of social shaping can you think of that might inform the development of e-Government?

Feedback

- The growth of text messaging as a new argot
- The rejection of the technologically inferior mobile Internet service WAP
- Using mobile phones for personal lives more than for business use
- Demand for retaining old equipment and technologies alongside the new.

Question 2

Which social practices will the e-Citizen most likely continue regardless of technological change?

Feedback

- Keeping connected with family, friends and business colleagues
- Choosing the device and service that best suits their own needs
- Using past experiences to develop etiquettes for new media and interfaces
- Person-to-person connectivity as a priority over person-to-information connectivity.

Question 3

How might people's need for social relations affect future use of mediated communications?

Feedback

- More intensive use of mobile communications for keeping connected at all times
- Allocating different media for business use and personal use
- Increasing demand for communications of all types
- Developing strategies for financial management that maximise use of tariff bundles.

GLOSSARY

e-Literate   Describes people able to use electronically mediated technology.

GSM   Global System for Mobile Communications – a mobile phone technology that enables its users to make and receive mobile mediated communications in almost any country in the world using their own phone.

SMS   Short Messaging Service – a mobile phone technology that enables text messaging.

Social practices   What people do in their everyday life.

Voice Over Internet Protocol (VOIP)   The technology which allows telephone conversations to be held via computers.

WAP   Wireless Application Protocol – a mobile phone technology that enables wireless access to the World Wide Web.

Wifi   Wireless local area networks that provide a wire-free interface to the World Wide Web for personal and laptop computers.

BIBLIOGRAPHY

Cooper, G. (2002) 'The mutable mobile: social theory in the wireless world', in B. Brown, N. Green and R. Harper (eds) *Wireless World Social and Interactional Aspects of the Mobile Age*, London: Springer-Verlag, pp. 19–31.

Dányi, E. and Sükösd, M. (2003) 'Who's in control? Viral politics and control crisis in mobile election campaigns', *Communications in the 21st Century Mobile Learning Essays on Philosophy, Psychology and Education*, Vienna: Passagen Verlag, pp. 285–315.

Kim, S. D. (2003) 'The shaping of new politics in the era of mobile and cyber communication, the Internet, mobile phone and political participation in Korea', *Mobile Learning: Essays on Philosophy, Psychology and Education*, Vienna: Passagen Verlag, pp. 317–26.

Lai, O. (2003) 'Mobile communicating for (e)-democracy beyond sovereign territorial boundaries', in *Mobile Learning: Essays on Philosophy, Psychology and Education*, Vienna:Passagen Verlag, pp. 327–37.

Lasen, A. (2003) 'History repeating? A comparison of the launch and uses of fixed and mobile phones' in Conference Proceedings: The Mobile Revolution – Retrospective Lessons in Social Shaping Digital World Research Centre, University of Surrey 17–18 July 2003.

Ling, R. and Yttri, B. (2002) 'Hyper-coordination via mobile phones in Norway', in J. E. Katz and M. Aakhus (eds) *Perpetual Contact – Mobile Communications, Private Talk, Public Performance*, Cambridge: Cambridge University Press.

Marvin, C. (1988) *When Old Technologies Were New*, Oxford: Oxford University Press.

Paragas, F. (2003) 'Drama*text*ism mobile telephony and people power in the Phillipines', in *Mobile Learning: Essays on Philosophy, Psychology and Education*, Vienna: Passagen Verlag, pp. 259–83.

Sacks, H. (1992) *Lectures on Conversation* vol. 2, Oxford: Blackwell.

Vincent, J. (2003)'Emotion and mobile phones', in K. Nyiri (ed.) *Mobile Learning: Essays on Philosophy, Psychology and Education*, Vienna: Passagen Verlag, pp. 210–24.

Vincent, J. and Haddon, L. (2004) 'Informing suppliers about user behaviours to better prepare them for their 3G/UMTS customers', UMTS Forum Report No. 34: www.umts-forum.org.

Vincent, J. and Harper, R. (2003) 'The social shaping of UMTS, educating the 3G/UMTS customer', UMTS Forum Report Number 26 www.umts-forum.org & in European Information Technology Observatory 2003, Frankfurt am Main: EITO–EEIG, pp. 246–67.

Westrum, R. (1991) *Technologies and Society: The Shaping of People and Things*, Belmont, CA: Wadsworth Publishing Company

Chapter 4

e-Leadership: challenges of new governance models

LEFKI PAPACHARALAMBOUS

KEY LEARNING POINTS

After completing this chapter you should have an understanding of:

- The basic principles of leadership
- The characteristics of 'virtual' and 'networked' organizations
- The challenges faced by leaders of such organizations in managing 'knowledge workers'
- The ways in which 'new economy' rhetoric is influencing leadership styles

INTRODUCTION

In the corporate world of today the rapid advancement of technology and its applications is challenging the legacy of business activities as new possibilities for business strategy emerge. The need for creativity and innovation in knowledge-intensive organizations creates new institutional demands, not only in the structural context of the organization but in the social arena as well. Skyrme (1999) and DeFillipi (2002) point out that leaders need to transform their mindsets to be able to enhance the predictability of relationships, and ensure consistency in behaviour and thinking across a number of project teams. At the same time, in order to be able to meet new organizational challenges effectively and fulfil their customers' needs for service, they typically have to maintain operational continuity during periods of change. In these circumstances it is suggested that effective team-working acts as a crucial driving force with a tremendous impact both on the individual's performance and the organization's productivity. In this chapter the principles of 'e-Leadership' will be examined to assess the extent to which such organizational arrangements actually reflect the reality as opposed to the rhetoric of working conditions in the 'e-Economy'.

THE HISTORY OF LEADERSHIP

From the mid-1970s until the mid-1980s Hewlett Packard implemented a five-step procedure called the Process of Management (POM):

1 Establish a purpose
3 Build a shared vision
4 Develop shared plans
5 Lead the action
6 Evaluate the results.

Following the five steps of POM as a continuous improvement exercise the top managers in the company could energize their talents and experience, and build up an 'outstanding organization'. From this perspective, environmental conditions are constant and leadership is a rational exercise whereby predictable results can be achieved according to the nature of the inputs made. During the 1980s attention was directed towards 'transformational leadership' (Burns 1978; Badham 1995) whereby the leader was expected to adapt, think creatively and avoid becoming bogged down in the detail of the 'how-to'. In the words of Rosabeth Kanter (1989) managers had to become 'business athletes'. She notes:

> You watch human resource policies now, move in British firms, from being sort of backwater, 'they're the people who do the paperwork', to being a much more significant piece of strategic thinking for the firm because everybody is going to compete for people in the 1990s. In fact the quality of people is going to make a bigger difference than the quality of products or the quality of services.

In the 1990s, survival in an environment characterized by continuous change and turbulence relied hugely on innovation. However, innovation is not only about putting together nuts and bolts in a game of technology; questions like 'are we doing the right things?' and 'how can we do things better?' are of primary importance. Adam Bricker, managing director of the global consulting firm Bearing Point (formerly KPMG Consulting) points out:

> Clients are really challenging proposed IT spending. No longer are we seeing clients buying IT that is faddish. Now they want to see how this expenditure will impact on the enterprise, and they are asking to see value within 12 to 18 months of many IT purchases.
>
> (McGarvey 2003: 52)

The next developmental phase in leadership priorities is typified by Barnatt (2001) who distinguished two transformational cycles, the *First Digital Revolution* and the *Second*

Digital Revolution. In the 1990s, the *First Digital Revolution* was characterized by a strategic shift; **business process re-engineering** stimulated the formulation of 'an atom-based economy' with communication and storage of electronic binary digits being the focus of attention. In the second *Digital Revolution*, deployed in this decade, a massive amount of digital content is pulled into the realm of daily routine business processes. Thus this radical shift from 'mass digitization' towards 'mass atomization' typifies the evolving language of e-Business rhetoric.

Myth links 'leadership' with top management positions; it is a profound assumption that as soon as one rises to the top of the hierarchical ladder one automatically becomes a leader. At this point the line needs to be drawn between managers and leaders in order to understand that differentiation goes beyond the contemporary labels of convenience. As Bennis and Nannus (1985: 21) stated in their celebrated phrase: 'Managers are people who do things right and leaders are people who do the right things'. Obviously, leadership is about *being* rather than *doing*. In this radical sense, change is vested in the individual rather than the structure or the process. On the one hand, leaders are exhorted to 'be first, be daring, and be different' (Carnall 1999: 68), while on the other, 'chase profits through virtue, through humanity, through love' (Harvey 2001: 37). Bridging the gap between these two rather controversial extremes is an immensely slippery process for today's leaders. If organizations now struggle to cope with the mountains of knowledge they own (McGarvey 2003) this begs questions about the leader's ability to unlock the knowledge kept within people's heads. For example, how easily can today's leaders create real conversations with their people, the aim of which is neither to command nor to convince, but instead to connect with them on equal terms?

Such a transformation of leadership style cannot happen overnight; it takes time and effort to reveal untapped talent. Bain (1998) identifies the problem when he notes that during the implementation of any change process social defences are built up against the anxiety created by the unknown. Organizational innovativeness as part and parcel of a change process is usually a painful experience for the people involved as 'a mini-death to a known way of being' (Bain 1998: 416). This is why people's natural reaction towards change follows Newton's first law of motion, which is to say that people 'tend to be at rest or in uniform motion unless compelled to change by the action of an external force' (Sawhney and Zabin 2001: 268).

THE ROLE OF TECHNOLOGICAL CHANGE

Now, with technological advancement being in the spotlight of e-Business strategy and applications, disruptive technologies can cut across time and spatial boundaries to bring together the power of different mindsets which collaborate in pursuit of technological innovation. In this context the trend for knowledge-based organizations has been to build up a sustainable competitive advantage using non-transparent and difficult to imitate core competences. Identifying the key attributes that can help a leader to succeed in such highly complex business environments is a daunting task, and developing the skills of potential leadership is neither simple nor straightforward. What makes this problematic situation even more difficult is that the leaders of many organizations are still heavily influenced by trends in the industrial era. This is why leaders preparing for the future need to understand that in order to thrive in 'messy' business situations they have to reinforce the development of a climate which will allow people to transcend their existing **cognitive barriers**. For example, Dotlich and Cairo (2002) recommend a **paradigm shift** which invites organizations to rethink the entire social context in which they operate.

Information and communication technologies have increasingly become a 'must-have' tool for many organizations to facilitate the exploitation of their knowledge assets; yet the burst bubble of 'dotcom' stocks reminds us that the road to success is full of hazards as well. The use of ICT opens up new vulnerabilities in the organization's ecosystem which can lead to massive damage. For example, tough questions like 'who has got the information?' or 'how can we track the information down?' or even 'where is this information kept?' are raised. Highly evolved structures for co-ordinating internal resources and decision-making are now emerging as part of a shared ownership over an organization's knowledge assets. In these conditions, entrepreneurship can become the focus of management practices. For example, 'virtual organizations' permit teams of employees located anywhere in the world to interact effectively through the use of technology, in an environment where specialist expertise, empowerment and autonomy are prevailing characteristics. In such circumstances there is an increasing need for new leadership styles to emerge in order to control and co-ordinate these **knowledge professionals**. This is not to suggest that employees do not need direction anymore; on the contrary, coordination and control are still needed but from a more 'therapeutic' perspective whereby leaders need to see their employees as partners rather than subordinates.

The catalyst for many recent changes in the leadership of organizations is, of course, information technology. When this critical feature is taken together with general business trends towards reduced management hierarchies, de-bureaucratization, team-based working and inter-organizational collaboration, then opportunities for entirely new ways of working across both time and space are created. One such innovation is teleworking, where employees may work from home or specialist regional centres rather than from a central office location. The Directory Enquiries service provides a good example of how callers can now be automatically routed to BT employees working from home who can access all the necessary data stored on a CD Rom.

Other examples of virtual organizations include software development companies that have considerably enhanced their productivity by creating new product development teams with representatives in the Far East, Middle East, Europe and America. Software development can thus be passed electronically around the world on a 24-hour basis; as the working day comes to an end in one particular centre, it will still be lunchtime in the next! Taking the degree of 'virtuality' to new extremes, some organizations now require no physical presence at all. A current example concerns a company set up under the control of one individual to provide data-warehousing and analysis services to retailers. The entrepreneurial owner out-sources all of the product development, marketing and administrative functions to different organizations as required. The organization therefore has no permanent staff, no geographic location and no expensive infrastructure. It can therefore compete effectively with the major market players on price.

Another enormously successful virtual organization is Edmunds.com which acts as a 'one-stop shop' for the automobile market. The firm has redrawn market boundaries by grouping together related services online such as spare parts, leasing facilities, insurance and car dealerships in 'seemless bundles' with a customer perspective. In the 'real' world, such organizations may inhabit different industry groups and sources of information are consequently fragmented. Edmunds collects referral fees from the connections made between customers and service providers, and with 80,000 'hits' per day, can provide a highly targeted audience for advertisers. The firm maintains its central position in the webs that it creates by broking connections between buyers (for example, by setting up special interest groups for classic cars) and also between sellers (for example, by linking finance companies with car dealerships). As such, it can also be regarded as a classic example of a 'networked' organization, which may in fact be a 'hybrid' of several firms working together for mutual benefit. The rationale for network formation is that synergies can be created by collaboration that would not be available to any one partner firm if acting alone. Networked structures permit organizational flexibility in the face of rapidly changing environmental conditions. In its most simple form, one party to a collaboration may obtain access to particular skills that it does not maintain in-house, while the other party is able to 'piggy-back' access to new markets that it would otherwise have found difficult to penetrate. In more complex cases, it may be difficult to ascertain the position of organizational boundaries, particularly if an organization is involved in a number of different networks that change composition and evolve over time. This flexibility raises a number of leadership issues.

LEADERSHIP ISSUES FOR THE E-BUSINESS ERA

Networked organizations do not just 'happen' by themselves. Even if a 'win-win' situation is evident, the relationship between the partners still has to be developed, nurtured and managed over time if the firms are to work together effectively. Formal legal agreements are often deemed necessary to set out the respective obligations of the partners, especially in the early stages of a relationship. Over time, formal arrangements may be relaxed as trust becomes established. On the other hand, the costs associated with managing the network may counteract the benefits of participation. A critical leadership role may be played by a 'network broker' who focuses upon finding suitable partners, reconciling vested interests within the network and negotiating how network benefits are to be shared between the participants. While IBM now talks of the need for 'triple hybrid' managers to manage collaborative relationships effectively, the skills of the network broker can extend even further to encompass those of an entrepreneur, technician, sociologist, businessman and politician!

Drucker (2002) suggests that the emergence of knowledge as a 'must-have' resource increasingly means specialization and mobility within specializations; however, since knowledge is not hierarchical in nature it has to be put in a form that will sustain its potential and upward mobility. There is a clear implication in this view that managers need to do more than simply provide employees with knowledge and information; they are expected to equip their co-participants with all the skills, qualities and methods they will need to apply their knowledge in situations characterized by ambiguity and complexity. In this era of interdependence, paternalistic authority gradually gives way to delegated power and coaching styles of management. Drucker also suggests that in most cases organizational restructuring has to be planned with collaborative, rather than individual, work conditions in mind.

It has been suggested that the most challenging task for leaders in knowledge-intensive organizations is the demand set by the external environment to downplay formal structures and achieve co-ordination through social norms and reward schemes rather than through hierarchical control (Starbuck 1992). To have any chance of winning this continuously accelerating race, it becomes vital that managers focus mainly on people's processes rather than on functional procedures; the anticipated outcome should be the creation of new knowledge by using the knowledge they own as a stock of shared expertise rather than merely as a flow of information. Clearly, the knowledge that underpins an organization's internal capabilities is a valuable asset but it might not reside in individual people; instead, it could be the outcome of shared knowledge among experts who build their own roles as part of a new social context where autonomous collegiality and structural flexibility prevail. This is why this asset is very often mismanaged or undermanaged; because leaders fail to acknowledge that the power of this knowledge is kept in their people's heads rather than in the technological capabilities at their disposal.

To summarize the arguments presented so far, at the micro-level within an individual organization 'reality versus rhetoric' scenarios for e-Business could look something like this:

- *Rhetoric*. Managers regard e-Business as a 'transformation' with technology being the major focus of radical change which needs to be achieved in order to meet e-Business targets. The social dynamics of change tend to be neglected in comparison.
- *Reality*. e-Business needs to be treated as a change management exercise in which technological change runs at a faster pace than organizational change. However, technology alone cannot drive organizational change unless it is embedded in a social context. Narrowing the gap between what technology can attain and what people can actually handle in a business transformation process is a big challenge

for today's managers, because transformational attitudes cannot just emerge overnight.

It is now an established fact that successful e-Business is not simply a matter of investing in digital technology. The most valuable commodity in a business today is the human capital: 'Companies that manage people right will outperform companies that don't by 30 to 40 per cent' (Chowdhury 2000: 10). An organization's performance does not relate so strongly to mathematical equations as it used to some years ago. According to Chowdhury, key metrics like return on investment (ROI) and return on assets (ROA) expressing the financial might of organizations are gradually being replaced by a new measurement, ROT (return on talent) which is expressed as follows:

$$\text{ROT} = \frac{\text{Knowledge generated}}{\text{Investment in talents}}$$

ROT measures the pay-off from investment in people. It can be measured on a qualitative or quantitative basis in order to assess management's ability to recruit the right workforce and exploit them to the best benefit of the business. Chowdhury's ratio is a clear indication of the fact that we are moving towards an unstructured world populated by creative workforces, continuous product improvements and costless communication. Knowledge generation in this context is highly valued and talented individuals have to be utilized as the key to the capitalization of opportunities. Adler and Docherty (1998) support this argument in their theory of 'dynamic effectiveness' which explicitly suggests that in an unstable, rapidly changing environment the key dynamics of change are: learning and innovativeness; availability of resources and how they can be exploited; how tolerant people are towards change and how easily they can improve their performance.

THINK POINT

'We want people who get up every morning with a passion about finding a better way: finding from their associate in the office, finding from another company. We're constantly on the search.' Jack Welch, the General Electric CEO.

How easy do you think it is for managers to always find new and better ways of using the disruptive power of information and communication technologies?

From a tradition of 'I've got to stay in control' to the point that leaders have the courage to set aside hierarchy and exercise self-criticism is a long journey to expect them to take. Owen (2000) suggests that one's behaviour manifests at the face of 'persona' and 'character', the former representing the mask behind which one's self seeks protection against personal fears and anxieties created by the external world, and the latter being one's real self that goes beyond what we do. Leaders have to know when they act in persona or in character; to maintain the balance between the two they have to go through the 'layers' and reveal the deepest personal self rather than try to reinvent themselves in processes or structures which keep them far away from integrity and self-actualization. As such, leaders need to find the courage, for example, to utter phrases like 'I don't know' or 'you know better than I do' as a way out of a natural competition process in which they are expected to know everything and do things better than anyone else (Dotlich and Cairo 2002).

In summary, leaders cannot easily avoid the strategic dilemmas presented by e-Business opportunities or delegate the issues thus raised to others. Strategic leadershipis multi-functional and involves effective exploitation of core competencies and human resources. This challenges many old myths underpinning traditional leadership paradigms.

Case study:
LEADERSHIP IN THE BUDGET AIRLINE INDUSTRY

The practical reality of effective leadership in the e-Business context will now be examined in a case study from the airline industry. Such professional service organizations rely heavily upon their human assets; as such they can be characterized as knowledge-intensive organizations. The name of the company has been disguised for reasons of confidentiality, so for the purposes of this case study we will call it Plane Co.

Plane Co is an adaptive organization in the sense that it has developed in a very fast-changing market where speed and flexibility are necessary for survival. In 2003 the organization was serving about 10 million passengers per year but its growth rate was very high.

The two keys to success were:

1 'state of the art' Internet-based marketing policy
2 the entrepreneurial leadership style adopted by the company's owner.

Nevertheless, the continuously increasing growth rate and the expansion of the internal communication network had generated issues regarding the manageability of the growing amount of knowledge held within the organization. Thus the main research questions that came up as a result of the first discussion with the company's managers were the following:

● How can team leaders can build 'virtual teams' that are capable of learning?
● How can team leaders maintain the climate of openness, trust and responsiveness in the team?

- How can members of virtual teams become members of 'learning teams'; that is how can they be motivated towards enhancing their knowledge sharing practices?
- How can team members be encouraged to build and enhance their social identity as a team, that is how do they:
  - develop and accomplish shared goals?
  - enhance their team's accountability?
  - develop sustainable relationships that are built on trust?

To gain a fundamental understanding of these issues two methods were followed when gathering the data: first observation of confidential meetings held with marketing managers and their top management team, and second, semi-structured interviews were conducted with individual managers. The research was mainly focused on the ways leadership and team membership are developed with regard to knowledge-sharing practices during processes of change, so the study of action, interactions and reactions was important. Nevertheless, it was naturally quite impossible to capture the entire developmental process that takes place in human interrelationships over a period of time. In practice we are only able to observe fragments of extremely complicated processes.

'There are no secrets in the company' was the leader's outspoken belief giving emphasis to openness, commitment and sharing with regard to internal communication practices. His leadership style incorporated a pioneering employee-driven system which allowed freedom for the individual team members to make their own choices which were based on their personal mindsets. However, they had to conform to the company's basic rules. As a result, employees operated in an environment that mixed conformity and autonomy, allowing creativity to flourish in conditions of continuous change. This adaptive leadership was described by the leader as follows: 'coaching, facilitating and delegating procedures are used in a different manner to accommodate great human, and consequently, cultural diversity'.

The marketing managers in the team were enthusiastic, autonomous decision-makers, who were always quick to use their own local knowledge, energy and creativity towards the accomplishment of the organization's goals. Being part of a linear organizational structure, bureaucracy played the least important role in their working practices, and decision-making processes were always related to two fundamental attributes of the organization's policy, 'autonomy' and 'shared responsibility'. As one manager stressed: 'There is not one single action for which one specific person is responsible for'. Another one reinforced this view noticing that 'it's not only one person in charge of everything; everybody plays their part and everybody's contribution is of utmost importance'.

Working in an atmosphere of openness, responsiveness and trust, people were able to build strong collaborative bonds; the only barrier they had to confront was the accelerating rate of the organization's growth, which seemed to enrich the team's knowledge repository on the one hand, but on the other led to expressed concerns that very soon they might not be able to manage it any more. To cope with this daunting challenge of creating sustainable growth within a climate of instability and continuous change in the external environment,

67

the marketing managers worked hard to develop a collaborative network of virtual teams. The use of 'disruptive' technologies underpinned this process to a great extent but paradoxically they also relied heavily on interpersonal, face-to-face communication.

The paramount importance of information sharing and knowledge management was acknowledged by the managers in the marketing team of the airline company. Although they had been given no formal training, active learning evolved as part of their daily routine; people worked hard to acquire capabilities and much needed human capital, although finding the right people required a great deal of time and energy. With knowledge sharing being a central activity, the organization aimed to exploit shared practice to enable individual team members to develop a shared world-view while using the organization as the central locus of shared identity. The company aimed to develop strong ties with its customers in the long run and there was a continuous effort to realize this perception in day-to-day processes. Everybody in the organization admitted that it was the leader's unique style that inspired them to develop cohesiveness and collegiality in order to attain company goals, regardless of how they had to struggle with the instability of continuous change and a highly competitive business environment.

BRIDGING THE GAP BETWEEN RHETORIC AND REALITY

The case study provides an example of a company that has been able to translate the rhetoric of e-Business into practical success. So what lessons can be learned from this that may be more widely applicable? One word from the ancient Greek language is particularly relevant, and that is 'metanoia' meaning a shift of mind. Champy (1995) more explicitly describes the concept of 'metanoia' when he claims:

> Everyone must change. The change will go deeper than technique. It touches not merely what managers do, but who they are. Not just their sense of task, but their sense of themselves. Not just what they know, but how they think. Not just their way of seeing the world, but their way of living the world.
>
> (Owen 2000: 31)

In this context, there is an urgent call for managers to transform themselves into adaptive leaders whose job will be not to know everything and make decisions on everything, but instead to inspire their people and create a climate that will encourage people to share their knowledge and act on their own initiative. From the leader's perspective new norms have to be reinforced which will link people's expectations with their actions rather than with their words simply because 'knowing comes from doing and teaching others how' (Ahmed *et al.* 2002: 120).

An adaptive style of leadership will make it easier for leaders to accept the unpredictability of the future and better able to inspire individuals to work well within teams in a non-stop learning process. They will also be able to embrace the discomfort created by conflict and openness and use technology in an inclusive rather than exclusive way in order to fulfil people's needs for inclusion, control and affection.

Adopting the adaptive leadership style basically requires new leaders to be willing to expose their vulnerabilities and challenge conventional wisdom.

CONCLUSION

In this chapter a contemporary case study of the airline industry has been drawn upon to examine ways in which the role of leadership is evolving in networked organizations where e-Business plays a central role. Based on this example, it is suggested that leaders of such organizations need to focus upon synthesizing the diversity of mindsets at their disposal within the organization in creative and flexible ways. At the same time, bearing in mind that the nature of their business means that they are heavily dependent on communication technologies, they need to ensure that their customers' needs are met by providing operational continuity of service. In these circumstances it is suggested that effective team-working acts as a crucial driving force with a tremendous impact both upon individual employee performance and organizational productivity. However, it is clear that truly 'networked' organizations are still rare in practice despite early 'new economy' rhetoric which proclaimed that this was the way of the future for many types of business. Leaders of such organizations who are prepared to manage their staff in the semi-anarchistic ways detailed here are even harder to find. Further research needs to be carried out to investigate the issues raised in this chapter.

QUESTIONS

Question 1
What types of businesses would you classify as 'virtual organizations'?
Feedback
For example, a business that needs no physical presence in order to trade, a software company can both accept and deliver customer orders online.

Question 2
What types of businesses would you classify as 'networked organizations'?
Feedback
Amazon, for example, which operates in conjunction with a number of business partners in a virtual environment.

Question 3

Why do you think these new technology-based business models have been slow to catch on?

Feedback

Not all types of business are suited to 'virtual' operation. In many cases, customers prefer to deal face to face with their suppliers.

Question 4

Why might leaders be reluctant to try out the new styles of leadership discussed here?

Feedback

A leader may feel that adaptive leadership requires too much trust, power and influence to be vested in key employees rather than kept directly under his/her own control.

GLOSSARY

Business process re-engineering   A re-thinking and re-framing of the fundamental ways in which business systems are co-ordinated.

Cognitive barriers   A limitation of the brain to overcome certain problems, for example, an inability to comprehend how a new technology can be implemented or used.

Knowledge professionals   Employees whose key skills reside in their particular expertise which may well be tacit in nature and hence difficult to store or transfer for the benefit of the organization as a whole.

Paradigm shift   A fundamental change in approach or philosophy.

BIBLIOGRAPHY

Adler, N. and Docherty, P. (1998) 'Bringing business into socio-technical theory and practice', *Human Relations*, 51, 3: 320–45.

Ahmed, P., Kok, K. L. and Loh, A. (2002) *Learning through Knowledge Management*, London: Butterworth-Heinemann.

Badham, R. (1995) 'Managing sociotechnical change' in J. Benders, J. de Haan and D. Bennet (eds) *The Symbiosis of Work and Technology*, London: Frances Pinter, pp. 45–8.

Bain, A. (1998) 'Social defences against organizational learning' *Human Relations*, 51, 3: 413–17.

Barnatt, C. (2001) 'The second digital revolution', *Journal of General Management*, 27, 2 (Winter): 1–16.

Bennis, W. and Nanus, B. (1985) *Leaders: The Strategies for Taking Charge*, New York: Harper and Row.

Burns, J. M. (1978) *Leadership*, New York: Harper and Row.

Carnall, A. C. (2000) 'Managing Change in Organizations', *Financial Times*.

Champy, J. (1995) *Re-engineering Management: The Mandate for New Leadership*, New York: Harper Business.

Chowdhury, S. (2000) 'Management 21st century – the future of business will be different: whose version are you reading', *Financial Times*.

DeFillipi, R. (2002) 'Organizational models for collaboration in the new economy', *Human Resource Planning*, 25, 4: 7.

Dotlich, T. and Cairo, D. (2002) *Unnatural Leadership: Going against Intuition and Experience to Develop Ten Leadership Instincts*, New York: Jossey Bass.

Drucker, P.F. (2002) *Managing in the Next Society*, London: Butterworth-Heinemann.

Hammer, M. and Champy, J. (2001) *Reengineering the Corporation: A Manifesto for Business Revolution*, New York: Nicholas Brealey Publishing.

Harvey, M. (2001) 'The hidden force: a critique of normative approaches to business leadership', *SAM Advanced Management Journal*, 66, 4 (Autumn): 36–48.

Kanter, R. M. (1989) *When Giants Learn to Dance: Mastering the Challenges of Strategy, Management and Careers in the 1990s*, London: Unwin.

McGarvey, R. (2003) 'What do CIOs know – keeping up with the hottest IT trends for building better businesses', *Harvard Business Review*, January: 52–7.

Owen, H. (2000) *In Search Of Leaders*, London: Wiley.

Sawhney, M. and Zabin, J. (2001) *The Seven Steps to Nirvana: Strategic Insight into eBusiness Transformation*, New York: McGraw Hill.

Skyrme, D. J. (1999) *Knowledge Networking: Creating the Collaborative Enterprise*, London: Butterworth-Heinemann.

Starbuck, W. H. (1992) 'Learning by knowledge-intensive firms', *Journal of Management Studies*, 29, 6: 713–40.

Chapter 5

e-Management and workforce diversity

NELARINE CORNELIUS

KEY LEARNING POINTS

After completing this chapter you should have an understanding of:

- How e-Business is extending the role of the traditional call centre
- The globalization of the labour market through developments in information technology
- Tensions between 'work' and 'home' environments in e-Business settings
- The relevance of 'capabilities theory' in e-Business settings such as call centres

INTRODUCTION

It has been argued that managing a workforce within an e-Business context requires new ways of thinking about the interaction between the customer service provider/employee interface. However, a narrow focus on this part of the work of employees in much of the literature potentially masks many important issues, including the limited amount of research that captures the diversity of experience of such employees in the developing and developed world. For researchers and practitioners, corporate governance and organizational ethical issues could form the basis for creating new perspectives on how to balance commercial needs and employee vulnerabilities. Little is known about the breadth of experience of employees engaged in e-Business from a reflective or empirical standpoint, and this chapter is an attempt to create a conceptual framework for such considerations. Drawing from employment management disciplines including human resource management, employment relations, organizational studies, emotional labour and applied philosophy and ethics, an attempt will be made to create a tentative framework through the application of capabilities theory (Sen 1992, 1999; Nussbaum 1999) and the outline of a tentative agenda for future research and practice in this area.

e-Business can be thought of as 'any business conducted in whole, or in part, through a digital infrastructure (Coltman *et al.* 2001), and in practice, it is likely to be a combination of telephone and computer technologies. A simple description of an e-Business might be that of an organization that conducts key aspects of its business operations electronically, be it business-to-business or business-to-customer transactions. Many inter- and intra-company financial transactions have taken place electronically for years before the term e-Business became popular. It is the lead taken in these sectors that has stimulated other business activities. The global phenomenon of the growth of e-Business has created the opportunities for businesses to draw their staff from labour markets around the world. The classic example is the call centre organization or the global virtual team, that is able to deliver 24/7 service, by locating outlets that enable companies to 'follow the sun'.

Much has been said about the benefits of such working for companies, but what are the problems that might be facing workers coping in a 24/7 environment? The international literature has often focused on the need to manage across borders, and to manage employment has focused on cross-cultural teams and the advantages that new technology affords this group. But typically this literature focuses on professional knowledge workers from the primary labour market who generally enjoy the benefits of reasonable contracts and terms and conditions of employment Ironically, because of their privilege it could be argued that the problems of such groups are even more neglected than those in lower skilled, low wage work.

At the other extreme, there have been concerns about the globalization and the impact on the less fortunate, those from the secondary 'flexible' part of the labour market, who may be exposed to poor pay, hazardous working conditions and little job security, in both the developed and the developing worlds.

THINK POINT

What do you think might be the sources of work pressure for 'e-Employees'?

THE HUMAN SIDE OF E-BUSINESS: THE DIVERSITY OF E-BUSINESS WORK AND ITS WORKERS

Interest in e-Business centres changes significantly depending on the way in which goods and services are sold. In particular, e-Business has created a move away from more traditional high street operations, especially those in areas like financial, travel and retail services, and has changed the way important interactions take place both within companies, and also between companies and their customers. In the service industry,

73

face-to-face transactions that predominated (and indeed continue to predominate) this interface are now often subjected to competition with electronic alternatives, for a variety of commercial reasons, that include 24/7 'follow the sun' service delivery, lower cost bases (with the store being replaced by Web sites or Web stores). Today, employees can be located in any town or country, or indeed the world, to provide the services needed to support service delivery. Such strategies have an additional attraction to employers, as they shift the transaction costs of service delivery to the consumer, not just the lower labour operating costs in new locations.

Whether public or private, the shape of these organizations is typically less 'virtual' than the term e-Business might suggest. The virtual dimension refers to the lack of face-to-face interaction between service providers intra-organizationally and between the customer and the organization's service providers, which is mediated technologically. However, even in those e-Business organizations which are heavily virtual, the terminology employed – e-Business, **virtual business**, **virtual teams**, and so on – refers more to changing relationships across time and space and the mutual 'invisibility' of the service provider or recipient than to the absence of people. Organizations such as Amazon that are regarded as a 'purely' online business and are largely about order collection, warehousing and distribution still require traditional kinds of human resources (HR) operations to deliver their services.

Many e-Businesses are in fact arms of well-established bricks and mortar operations: indeed, some of the most successful e-Businesses, such as Tesco Online in the UK, actively capitalize on their traditional bricks and mortar infrastructure and reputation in order to run their home delivery grocery service. It could be argued that gaining customer confidence depends on long-established brand familiarity where e-Business success is built on customer acquaintance with and confidence in products and services of the bricks and mortar business operation.

There are important differences with more traditional and familiar kinds of business. The invisibility of what happens 'behind the scenes' is not only invisible to the customer. Many e-Businesses are also unlikely to be unionized (Dietz and Brosseau 2001) although call centres are more likely to be so, with up to half of those in Scotland, for example, unionized (Taylor and Bain 2001). It has been suggested that such organizations are often actively resistant to the idea of unionization, and create organizational arrangements and conditions that makes their presence less likely. Consequently, the conditions under which employees in e-Businesses operate are less likely to be open to third-party scrutiny. The terms and conditions for e-Business are particularly important if important parts of the e-Business are subcontracted to centralized bureaux. The nature of the work undertaken by call centre staff in particular is continually coming under critical scrutiny, with some observers suggesting that they are the new factories, 'bright satanic offices' (Baldry et al. 1998), modern **electronic panopticons** (Fernie and Metcalfe 1997; Bain and Taylor 2000), in which staff are constantly monitored. There is also a tendency for the formal contract of employment to be even more tenuous in the developed world (Bain and Taylor 2000), while there are concerns that the growth of e-Business in the developing world with skilled workers with lower cost bases, such as India and China, are in effect, social dumping into labour markets within which employees enjoy significantly fewer legal protections (Anon 2003a, 2003b).

However, there are also suggestions that different kinds of tight controls operate for those employed at the more professional end of the spectrum. High salary and status are likely to come with the proviso that access to employees is round the clock (Kunda 1993). The contrast with *constant surveillance and tight formal control* is increased autonomy but *constant access and tight informal controls*: with staff available to the company at its behest. The consequences for life outside of work are compromises or a diminution of the privacy and intensity of home life or a reallocation of attention to work as the primary source of social as well as work commitments, with home regarded more as where laborious and unfulfilling home commitments are undertaken reluctantly (Hochschild 1997). Opportunities to balance work and home are compromised. Among the implications of such developments is the impact on employer–employee relationships, in particular in relation to trust, as will be discussed further in Chapter 11. The shift to low trust/greater centralized control despite the appearance of autonomy among such portfolio workers may result in poorer organizational performance caused by the stress of failing to achieve a healthy work–life balance.

WHAT DO WE KNOW ABOUT E-BUSINESS EMPLOYMENT MANAGEMENT PRACTICE?

e-Business literature contains many examples of what could be done in relation to employment management policy and practice for e-Business employees, but much less in terms of hard evidence about what is actually happening. Some work is beginning to be carried out on the importance of factors like workplace design (Bagnara and Marti 2001), team structure and culture (Jackson and Harris 2003) and HR policies and strategies (Dietz and Brosseau 2001) but these tend to be small studies or think pieces for conceptual development.

For example, in a survey of HR strategies of 37 dotcom companies, Dietz and Brosseau (2001) found enormous variation in the character undertaken. e-Business start-ups rather than as e-Business ventures of bricks and mortar establishments, were far more likely to adopt more fluid and organic working structures but also less likely to have employee representation, and operated largely as non-unionized firms. Established firms that had set up e-Business operations were more likely to utilize in-house HR professionals to design policy and practice, but often struggled to appreciate what was distinctive about HR in an e-Business context, as well as what might be regarded as 'universal' needs and issues for employees.

However, these companies were not archetypal SMEs. Dietz and Brousseau compared their findings with averages for SMEs based on the Workplace Employment Relations Survey (WERS) (whose questionnaire they used – Cully *et al.* 1999). For the majority

75

of the firms surveyed, it was found that employee feedback, decisions about future plans and consultation about decisions likely to effect staff were more likely to be engaged with in dotcoms than in more traditional bricks and mortar SMEs. Consultation was also fairly common, with 48 per cent of these firms using team and departmental meetings for staff feedback. However, employee welfare issues were more contentious; only half were appraised regularly, there was high staff turnover, long working hours and low unionization.

In part, this is because only a limited amount of work has been conducted on job analysis and thus employee needs. Bagnara and Marti's (2001) study on call centre work where people did business by telephone, usually in a computer-automated environment (Merchants Limited 1998), led them to argue that such organizations can be thought of as centres of distributed knowledge, where knowledge is distributed within and between workers, organizational structures, cognitive artefacts of the organization, and clients, and that this knowledge needs to be accessed in order to get the job done. However, their analysis identified a number of general problems that included first, culture, as the operator did not trust the client and was frustrated by limited supervisor support, with the employee having to manage the problem in isolation. Second, employees were confused about distribution of roles in the organization, and third, employees typically had to abandon their work position to sort out problems, leaving the client waiting on the phone.

Kunda's (1993) seminal anthropological study of virtual workers in the technology industry suggests that the shadow side of high status, high salary work is also weakly understood by companies, albeit deeply felt by professional staff. The technological links that generate a 24/7 portable office create limited opportunities for absence from the company, at work or at home. The outer appearance of autonomy and self-management of a working day masked the deeper reality of constant connection with colleagues and the organization. This blurring of barriers created a state of constant alertness to the needs of the company, to an unhealthy degree, with often a deleterious impact on relationships between family and friends, and limited opportunities to express a non-work-centred identity. As mentioned earlier, organizational performance may have been lowered.

This failure to know how to undertake work and address problems suggests that there are issues around learning strategies, with some scholars arguing that such environments are more behavioural control centres permeated by tight measurement and surveillance that create climates of resistance and resentment, rather than learning sites that under-mine capacity to learn (Houlihan 2000). Indeed, it has been suggested that the real growth in e-Business employment will be in low-level service jobs with an emphasis on social and aesthetic skills rather than technical ones; this is more commonly thought of as knowledge work, and consequently, workers need to: 'Develop an understanding of themselves that allows them to consciously use their emotions and corporeality to influence the quality of service' (2001: 1).

Thus, this kind of work has more of the characteristics of emotional labour-based service work (Hochschild 1979, 2003) than more autonomous, professional knowledge work. **Emotional labour** can be thought of as the kind of work where employees' ability to control their mood and influence the mood of others is central to their work. Hochschild's original work was conducted on flight attendants, but other examples of emotional labourers include call centre workers, nurses, doctors, debt collectors and police officers. This might also explain concern about stress in such environments.

Deery *et al.*'s (2002) study of call centre workers in Australia suggests workers were expected to interact extensively with customers, had high workloads and a lack of variety in their work. These factors characterize what is often seen as necessary for getting operations in line in order to maximize e-Business value creation by aligning processes and stakeholder needs (Barua *et al.* 2001), though of course, high commitment strategies need not be associated with high employee discretion. Kinnie *et al.*'s (2000) research suggests that high-commitment, high control HR strategies characterized the call centres they studied, but that tension existed for employees between the high degree of autonomy afforded for employee customer transactions and the tight monitoring and control environment that they operated in.

Case study:
UK CALL CENTRES BRANDED 'SATANIC'

Some UK call centres deserve to be compared with the Victorian 'satanic' mills, a study has said. Low wages, poor working conditions and repetitive tasks were common gripes, according to research by the Health and Safety executive. 'People are very depressed and demoralized,' stated Christine Sprigg, the report's author. Workers in telecoms and IT call centres showed the poorest job satisfaction and highest levels of depression.

The work, carried out by the Health and Safety Executive Laboratory based in Sheffield, concluded that employees in the worst UK call centres felt powerless and tied to their desks – a familiar story according to the union Unifi. 'Automated systems mean workers only have a couple of seconds between calls. This isn't long enough, particularly if they have just been sworn at by a frustrated customer,' said Liam Groves, a Unifi spokesperson. 'Workers should be able to choose when they are ready to receive a call – it is no surprise people working in the industry only stay in it for just two years on average,' she added.

Call Centre Association chief executive Anne Marie Forsyth said the industry – which employs an estimated 790,000 people in the UK – was misunderstood. 'The comparison with satanic mills is very disappointing,' she said. 'Most of our members are trying to empower their workers and create career paths for them. However, there are bad employers in all parts of UK industry.'

The boom in UK call centre employment has come under threat, with some firms moving their operations to countries such as India where labour costs are substantially lower.

Source: Anon (2003a) http://bbc.co.uk/1/hi/business/3376803.stm

Case study:
LEARNING TO IMPROVE JOB DESIGN IN UK CALL CENTRES

Call centres are attractive to organizations seeking to improve their customer services in a cost-effective way; however, they find they have to balance carefully the needs of customers and employees. Achieving this balance is especially difficult in these organizations because of the direct exposure which employees have to customers for long periods. Two organizations are considered, one a vehicle emergency breakdown company, the other a call centre operation of a major high street bank. In both companies, employers sought to manage staff through a mixture of control and commitment strategies. Although controls were tight in some areas of their work (for example, attendance records, performance targets), it was difficult to argue that it was the 'electronic panoptican' that writers such as Fernie and Metcalfe (1997) have suggested, as the effects of the controls varies depending on the detail of the scripting, the nature, frequency and relevance of the measures used and the penalties for non-adherence. There was a lack of alignment between the high quality customer interactions expected, the close control systems and the HR practices adopted. Among the consequences were high staff turnover (35 per cent at the emergency breakdown and 25 per cent at the high street bank e-Operation). Gradually work practices were introduced that were better aligned with high quality customer inter-actions and to some extent, with customer needs. These changes resulted in a reduction in staff turnover in both services (down to 8 per cent and 10 per cent respectively).

Source: Abridged from Kinnie *et al.* (2000).

HOW TRANSPARENT ARE HR PRACTICES IN E-BUSINESS?

The perceived efficiency gains and service potential in a commercial context has caught the attention of non-commercial organizations, with local and central government providing an increasing number of services electronically (Anon 2003c). The latter is important, because it is in this sector that public financing demands public scrutiny of how effective service provision in this form is. A report by government auditors in the UK suggests that the organization of e-Services requires improvement in a number of ways, including the technology employed, staff training, employee management, and so on.

It should not be assumed that these shortcomings have come about largely as a result of a less efficient public sector relative to the private sector. Limited experience with such approaches is likely to affect the quality, efficiency and effectiveness of e-services.

However, it is worth pondering that the requirement to evaluate performance and make such an evaluation available in the public domain, creates a degree of accountability and transparency for both the hard and soft side of e-Business operations that often does not occur in commercial operations. Importantly, given that, for example, government has a specific responsibility as a public organization to be a 'good employer', and that the workforce is also unionized, is likely to put many more employee safeguards in place relative to the private sector. One example of where there was a lack of appreciation of the importance of front-line staff is illustrated by the attempt to offer a virtual housing benefit system in the UK. The contractor tasked with introducing the change, Capita, underestimated the impact of the absence of face-to-face, client–employee contact on the quality of the service. The anticipated efficiency gains were undermined by rapid deterioration in service.

People abound in, and are the 'soft systems' of, e-Business and its transactions. Although much of the debate in the field has been lead by hard systems, technological advancement and interest, far less attention has been paid to the experiences of employees and how they are managed in such enterprises (though this is slowly changing). This is all the more remarkable given the impact of e-Business on the labour market. For example, if one takes an important part of e-Business, the call centre, this sector alone accounted for 4 per cent of GDP in 2002 in the UK labour market (Anon 2002).

However, irrespective of how pure or hybrid the e-Business operation, there remain few critical accounts of how human resourcing issues are addressed in such organizations. Granted there are many accounts of what might constitute best practice but there is less in the way of empirical and reflective research-based evaluation outside of call centres.

Of particular concern is that the focus of much of the non-call centre-based research is regarding whether it is compliance based, concerned with efficiency gains or the 'motivational' gilt on the gingerbread of what might otherwise be regarded as highly stressful and de-motivating work for employees. Also in practice, much of the work undertaken in e-Business is gender segregated, undertaken by women, often as part-timers, on flexible contracts, with less favourable contracts of employment than their contemporaries in full-time employment (Bain and Taylor 2000; Fernie and Metcalfe 1997).

MOVING JOBS FROM THE DEVELOPED TO THE DEVELOPING WORLD

Although much call centre work originated in Western Europe and North America, such work is increasingly being transferred to lower cost, high skill economies such as India. As suggested earlier, with the growth of e-Businesses (in both the pure and hybrid form) the demand for labour, for employees – and at the 'right price' beyond their national labour markets has grown. Increasingly, companies are seeking to set up part or all of their operations in high skill, low wage economies. The globalization of these business operations places additional demands on the management of a globalized labour force. The concerns here are numerous, for instance: the 'social dumping' of e-Business work into areas which are economically depressed, often through short-term government inducements, with jobs moving on when the inducements run out; the export of e-Business jobs overseas with potential in the medium to long term; the contraction of jobs in this sector and contractual and working conditions of those in the developing countries where many of these jobs have been relocated.

The characteristics of business vary greatly. Within a European context, it is known that different approaches have been adopted towards the running of call centres. For example, in the UK, many writers have raised concerns about the fairness of treatment of call centre employees. As noted earlier, these concerns are represented by the notion of the call centre as modern sweatshops, organizations where employee actions are controlled extensively through tight managerial and electronic surveillance. Work is continuously de-skilled, control over how work is undertaken is minimal, and levels of surveillance (managerial and electronic), high. Other research has suggested that in many UK call centres, employees are subject to intense supervisory power, are selected on the basis of their ability to have their social competencies moulded (Callaghan and Thompson 2002), there is little opportunity for creativity and autonomy, generating low employee commitment (Rose 2002). These organizations are, essentially, highly controlled, scripted emotional labour (Rose 2002) environments and often, gender segregated work largely undertaken by women. Employee turnover can be high, particularly in areas of low unemployment (Grimes 2000). It is very much secondary labour market work and consequently, the service provision is likely to be grudging. Further, professional workers in primary labour markets often enjoy high salaries and wages but also face the challenge of constant and persistent connection and interaction with work, mediated electronically, thus encroaching on private and personal non-work time and space.

In contrast, much call centre work in Scandinavia and India's 'Silicon Valley' of Bangalore is undertaken by graduates who have more control over how they conduct their work. In such organizations, enterprising attitudes and self-management of work is expected, working conditions are good and service delivery more likely to be spontaneous rather than scripted, terms and conditions of employment are good, and the work is seen more as senior administrative or professional (see Grieg 2001 on e-Centres). However, even in these environments, overseas locations are part of an economy drive, with organizations seeking out high skill, low wage economies such as India, with much of the work conducted on less favourable contractual agreements than could be negotiated in the West. Further, there is some debate regarding the long-term impact on developing economies.

Case study:
INDIA'S BURGEONING CALL CENTRES

The biggest insurance firm in the UK, Norwich Union, has announced it is to cut 2,350 jobs in Britain and export the work to India. It is the latest in the tens of thousands of British call centre jobs lost to India in the past 5 years. Industry experts in India say that more will inevitably follow as employees in Britain find that satellite communication has given British companies access to a highly qualified, motivated and cheap workforce. The call centre industry in India is in its infancy, but is maturing very fast. Five years ago there were just a handful of offices. There are now more than 300 employing about 180,000 people. With the industry growing at over 20 per cent a year, it is expected two million Indians will be working in out-sourcing in 5 years time. Thousands of jobs are coming to India from the UK. The reason is simple – India offers a better product and it comes at a fraction of the cost.

The workforce undercuts the competition in almost every respect. 'I think that basically there are two things that India offers in this industry,' says Padmaja Krishnan, director of business development at Xansa, an international business process and IT services company working in India. 'One is the quality of the manpower, the other is the cost-quality advantage.' This is the cream of India's educated workforce. Indian call centres only recruit college graduates and competition for jobs is intense. New recruits start work after 6 weeks of training. They will be paid the equivalent of about $150 (£87) per month. This is less than one-tenth of what a call centre worker in the UK earns, but in India this is good pay – more than a newly qualified doctor earns. The hours may be long, but the recruits have not signed up to sweatshop work and promotion to management comes quickly. It is the legacy of spoken English left behind after India gained independence from Britain nearly 50 years ago which also gives India the edge in the global jobs' market.

Source: Mynott http://news.bbc.co.uk/1/world/south_asia/3258080.stm

Case study:
CALL CENTRES 'BAD FOR INDIA'

The mass transfer of call centre jobs from Europe and North America to India is bad for the subcontinent, a leading Indian newspaper writer has warned.

The huge growth in India's call centre industry was highlighted again as the British company Norwich Union announced they would be cutting 2,350 jobs and relocating them.

But author Praful Bidwai said that in effect the centres reduced young Indian under-graduates to 'cyber-coolies'. 'They work extremely long hours, badly paid, in extremely stressful conditions, and most have absolutely no opportunities for any advancement in their careers. It's a dead-end, it's a complete cul-de-sac. It's a perfect sweatshop scenario, except that you're working with computers and electronic equipment rather than looms or whatever.'

In just 3 years, the number of centres has risen from 50 to 800 as Western companies have sought to take advantage of cheaper operating costs – estimated to be about 30–40 per cent lower than in the UK. Average call centre salaries in the UK are about £12,500 ($22,000) a year, compared with £1,200 ($2,100) in India.

But Mr Bidwai said that call centres were exploiting young English-speaking Indians who have 'an undergraduate degree and nowhere else to go'. The tragic thing about India and the Indian economy is that in the last couple of decades, the GDP growth rate has actually improved, but joblessness has actually grown. The call centre industry is seen as a vital part of India's economic development. But Mr Bidwai said it added little value to India's wider economy. 'It's a couple of billion dollars a year at the moment, which isn't a hell of a lot, even by Indian standards.' The criticisms were acknowledged by Assim Hander, recruitment manager at Excel, a Delhi call centre, which includes Dell computers among its clients. But Mr Hander said that it was also important to stress the benefits that the centres brought. 'You have to look at the positives. Let's take the scenario where there was no call centre industry in India. What would these people be doing? Today, there is a demand for 150,000 graduates to be employed in an industry which was non-existent five years back. Because of the fact that the demand for call centre executives is increasing day by day, the supply from Delhi is getting lower and lower. What we have done is to move into smaller towns. Over the last three months, almost 60 per cent of our total hiring has been done through these outstation offices.'

Source: Anon (2003a) http://news.bbc.co.uk/1/hi/world/south_asia/3292619.stm

---

A CAPABILITIES APPROACH TO ADDRESSING THE DIVERSITY OF E-BUSINESS WORK AND WORKERS

There are many issues, challenges and potential vulnerabilities facing companies, government, law-makers and employees with regards to e-Business within national borders and globally. There are also important cross-border cultural differences that are ignored by the hype of e-Business and the e-Economy. **Capabilities theory** might provide one way of dealing with a range of choices that various stakeholders face in the management of e-Business-based employees. Capabilities theory is concerned with inequality, quality of life and life chances that people have, and with equality of opportunity but also with freedom of opportunity. Developed by Amartya Sen (1992, 1999) and Martha Nussbaum (1999, 2000), at the heart of capabilities theory is a focus on human capacity, development, and the opportunity *to be able to be or do what one has reason to value, to fully function, and to flourish*. Further, Sen argues that human diversity is paradoxical: it is not only a potential source of strength for communities but also generates different kinds of inequality in different arenas or equality spaces.

Capabilities theory was developed primarily in the context of regional development. However, the importance of this work is that it has in part been developed in an international context, and comparisons and measures of human dignity and quality of life can be made across as well as within borders. However, there is evidence that work organizations in general, not just communities in particular, benefits from scrutiny from a capabilities perspective (Gagnon and Cornelius 2000, 2003; Cornelius 2002).

Organizations are voluntaristic and additionally, even modern traditions of ethical and philosophical development when applied to work have largely left the family out of the equation (Nussbaum 2000). At the more neo-Tayloristic end of the spectrum, in the secondary labour market or the constantly wired professional virtual worker, such organizations are likely to see employees as a cost, desire flexibility, 'ethically neutral' (Fisher and Rice 1999) low wages and limited employee voices, and transactional leadership is preferred. The likelihood of 'worker sympathetic', pluralistic management and transformational leadership is questionable in this context (Bassett-Jones 2002), and so ensuring entitlements is most likely to be delivered through the legislative framework guided by a floor of entitlements (Nussbaum 2000). In a less exploitative and more empowering and ethically aware context, companies are likely to see the law as a minimal position (Bassett-Jones 2003) and seek to go beyond it to allow employees fully to function and flourish.

The challenge of applying capabilities thinking is that it arguably sets the fence higher than other approaches to managing difference fairly. It demands attention not only to whether the gifts and talents that employees have (basic capabilities) are enabled and developed so that potential is converted into readiness to act (internal capabilities), but that the meso- and macro-environments within which workers operate, created by organizations, the law and government, are enabling and work in concert and are supportive of community members (combined capabilities).

Although capabilities theory was developed in a regional development context, it has been further elaborated for work settings (see Gagnon and Cornelius 2000; Cornelius 2002). The challenge is particularly substantial in the globalized company, as many are likely to have a keener sense of diversity and inequality issues at home in their parent company than in their overseas satellites. Paradoxically, there is emerging evidence that effectiveness in an international context deepens the depth and breadth of knowledge, often resulting in a higher level of awareness and competence relative to a mainly local configuration of what it is to address inequality and difference (Arroba and Pritchett 2003).

The highlighting of the potential technological, strategic and market benefits has tended to push more critical accounts of the soft side of enterprise, from an employee perspective, into the shadows. Given the limited empirical research that has guided much thinking about e-Business and employees, it is suggested that both corporate social responsibility, company policy and practice and research projects in relation to the management of employees in an e-Business context need to pay attention to the following in particular:

- Employee protections, particularly in terms of physical and mental health and safety.
- The emotion of work and emotional labour aspects, which tend to be problematical in terms of stress at work rather than more fully understood in terms of labour process, merit greater scrutiny.
- Terms and conditions of employment with regards to segmentation of the labour market into knowledge worker and service worker sectors – that enjoy very different terms and conditions of employment and development opportunities (albeit that there is diversity within the field). Psychological contracts merit scrutiny also.
- There is a need to address the issue of safety work systems, and also the consequences of poor job and workplace design.
- The potential for marginalization of issues of equity and equality should be explored.
- Legal and corporate social responsibility as vehicles for promoting employer obligations for employees located locally or globally, particularly for multinationals.
- Vulnerabilities of 'new' organizations and especially e-Business sheds, where HR professionals may not be employed or there is no pluralistic tradition/memory to draw upon, so that the potential of unionized labour is less well understood.
- Exploration of whether companies are moving into e-Business as a means of reducing employee representation, including opportunities for unionization.
- There is a need to identify frameworks that ensure that the socially responsible organization considers its obligations to its entire workforce and demonstrably so, and that a clear ethical structure is needed if such an approach is to take root.
- The positive aspects of e-Business, particularly that appear to manifest themselves in the dotcoms, merit scrutiny in terms of their genesis and likely sustainability.

CONCLUSION

There has been much talk about the benefits that can arise from e-Business. However, it could be argued that e-Business constitutes a logical extension of the mechanization that has driven enterprise since the nineteenth century and the first Industrial Revolution. Work continues to be speeded up and the degree of surveillance wrests control from the worker and shifts it towards the employer. Further, the employee protections often available to such workers in bricks and mortar establishments are less likely to be available: indeed, it would appear that some companies are using e-Business as a means of side-stepping traditional employee protections. However, it is not just the shop floor or its modern equivalents where employees are subject to such changes. Increasingly, professional, high wage, high skill employees are also subject to tighter organizational control, albeit of a more subtle hue. There may not be electronic surveillance of keyboard activity, but there is an increasing expectation that work blurs into home. Teleworking no longer means just working away from the office, but also remote access means that your email inbox can be dealt with from home, not just as an option but as an expectation. Thus, employers increasingly encroach into private space and private time. The down-sizing so prevalent in the 1980s has been followed up by systematic work intensification, facilitated by computer technology.

The globalization of work processes means that jobs can ebb and flow as they follow the lower labour market costs around the world. It is argued by some that countries such as India that are currently benefiting from the influx of e-Jobs into their economies remain nervous about the potential efflux into high skill, lower cost economies such as China. However, in these countries, there is an emerging debate on the sustainability of the value added to their economies. In spite of the differences in the skills, wages and nationalities of those employed around the world, there is a common thread of the transient nature of such work, as 'follow the sun' not only applies to service provision, but moving on to the next most 'economic' location in the wake of a trail of job losses.

GLOSSARY

Capabilities theory   A philosophical approach that seeks to understand how to understand inequality and diversity. Developed by Amartya Sen and Martha Nussbaum, the focus is on individuals and groups freedom to pursue what they have reason to value, to fully function and flourish. Are they able to make full use of their potential, or to what extent do social or cultural factors limit life chances?

Emotional labour   The kind of work where employees' ability to control their mood and influence the mood of others is central to their work.

Electronic panopticon   The original panopticon was a glass-sided prison which allowed inmates to be covertly viewed at all times. An electronic equivalent could be software which monitors how long call centre employees take for breaks.

Virtual business   Business that can be conducted electronically either within or between organizations without the need for physical form.

Virtual teams   A group of employees who may be widely dispersed geographically but that work together on a specific project communicating through IT.

QUESTIONS

Question 1
What are the arguments for and against call centre work from the perspective of (a) the employee and (b) the organization?

Question 2
Who benefits from relocation of call centre work from Western Europe and the UK to low cost, high skill economies such as India?

Question 3
How might responsible companies improve call centre work?

BIBLIOGRAPHY

Anonymous (2003a) 'Protests over call centre moves', BBC News Online. Available http://www.news.bbc.co.uk

Anonymous (2003b) 'China predicts e-business boom', BBC News Online. Available http://www.news.bbc.co.uk

Anonymous (2003c) 'New technology and service reference'. Available http://www.hmso.gov.uk

Arroba, T. and Pritchett, P. (2003) 'Globalization versus local practice'. Paper presented at the ESRC Seminar, *Diversity under Globalization: Ideas into Action*, Brunel and Cranfield Universities, March.

Bagnara, S. and Marti, P. (2001) 'Human work in call centres: a challenge for cognitive ergonomics', *Theoretical Issues in Ergonomic Science*, 2, 3: 223–37.

Bain, B. and Taylor, P. (2000) 'Entrapped by the "electronic panopticon"? Worker resistance in the call centre', *New Technology, Work and Employment*, 17, 3: 170–85.

Baldry, C., Bain, P. and Taylor, P. (1998) '"Bright, satanic offices": intensification, control and team Taylorism', in C. Warhurst and P. Thompson (eds) *The New Workplace*, London: Macmillan.

Barua, A., Prabhuder, K., Whinston, A. B. and Yu, F. (2001) 'Doing e-business excellence', *MIT Sloan Management Review*, 43, 1: 36–45.

Bassett-Jones, N. (2003) 'Evaluating organizational readiness for change', in N. Cornelius (ed.) (2002) *Building Workplace Equality: Ethics, Diversity and Inclusion*, London: Thomson.

Callaghan, G. and Thompson, P. (2002) 'We recruit attitude: The selection and shaping of routine call centre labour', *Journal of Management Studies*, 39, 2: 233–54.

Coltman, T., Devinney, T. M., Latukefu, A. and Midgley, D. F. (2001) 'E-business: revolution, evolution or hype?', *California Management Review*, 44, 1: 57–89.

Cornelius, N. (ed.) (2002) *Building Workplace Equality: Ethics, Diversity and Inclusion*, London: Thomson.

Cornelius, N. and Gagnon, S. (2004) 'Still bearing the mark of Cain? Ethics, diversity and inequality measurement', *Business Ethics: A European Review*, 13, 1: 27–40.

Cully, M., Woodland, S., O'Reilly, A. and Dix, G. (1999) *Britain at work: As Depicted by the 1998 Workplace Employment Relations Survey*, London: Routledge.

Deery, S., Iverson, R. and Walsh, J. (2002) 'Work relationships in telephone call centres: understanding emotional exhaustion and employee withdrawal', *Journal of Management Studies*, 39, 4: 471–96.

Dietz, G. and Brousseau, J. (2001) *HR Strategy in the New Economy*, London: Involvement and Participation Association/Equity Incentives Limited.

Fernie, S. and Metcalf, D. (1997) '(Not) hanging on the telephone: payment systems in new sweatshops', *Centrepiece*, London: London School of Economics.

Fisher, C. M. and Rice, C. (1999) 'Managing messy moral matters', in J. Leopold, L. Harris and T. Watson (eds) *Strategic Human Resourcing*, London: Pitman.

Gagnon, S. and Cornelius, N. (2000) 'Re-examining workplace inequality: the capabilities approach', *Human Resource Management Journal*, 10, 4: 68–87.

Gagnon, S. and Cornelius, N. (2003) 'From equal opportunities to managing diversity to capabilities: a new theory of workplace inequality?', in N. Cornelius (ed.) *Building Workplace Equality: Ethics, Diversity and Inclusion*, London: Thomson.

Grieg, E. (2001) 'From call centres to "eCentres": managing change in the new technology centres' *British Journal of Administrative Management*, 16–17.

Grimes, C. (2000) 'Software giant strives to stem exodus of staff', *Financial Times*, 30 June.

Hochschild, A. R. (1979) 'Emotion work, feeling rules and social structure', *American Journal of Sociology*, 85: 551–75.

Hochschild, A. R. (1983) *The Managed Heart: The Commercialization of Human Feeling*, Berkeley: University of California Press.

Hochschild, A. R. (1997) *The Time Bind: When Work Becomes Home and Home Becomes Work*, New York: Henry Holt and Company.

Hochschild, A. R. (2003) *The Managed Heart: The Commercialisation of Human Feeling* (2nd edn), Berkeley: University of California Press.

Houlihan, M. (2000) 'Eyes wide shut? Querying the depth of call centre learning', *Journal of European and Industrial Training*, 25, 2/3/4: 228–40.

Jackson, P., Eckersley, P. and Harris, L. (2003) *E-Business Fundamentals*, London: Routledge.

Kinnie, N., Hutchinson, S. and Purcell, J. (2000) '"Fun and surveillance": the paradox of high commitment management in call centres', *International Journal of Human Resource Management*, 11, 5: 967–85.

Kunda, G. (1993) *Engineering Culture: Control and Commitment in a High Tech Corporation*, Philadelphia: Temple University Press.

Nussbaum, M. (1999) 'Women and equality: the capabilities approach', *International Labour Review*, 138, 3: 227–45.

Nussbaum, M. (2000) *Women and Human Development: The Capabilities Approach*, Cambridge: Cambridge University Press.

Rose, E. (2002) 'The labour process and union commitment within a banking service call centre' *Journal of Industrial Relations*, 44, 1: 40–61.

Sen, A. (1992) *Inequality Re-examined*, Cambridge, MA: Harvard University Press.

Sen, A (1999) *Development and Freedom*, Oxford: Oxford University Press.

Taylor, P. and Bain, P. (2001) Trade unions, workers rights and the frontiers of control in UK call centres', *Economic and Industrial Democracy*, 22, 1: 39–66.

Taylor, P. and Bain, P. (2002) 'An assembly line in the head: work and employee relations in the call centre', *Industrial Relations Journal*, 30, 2: 101–17.

Chapter 6

ICT and institutional change at the British Library

MARTIN HARRIS

KEY LEARNING POINTS

After completing this chapter you will have an understanding of:

- The role of traditional learning institutions in the e-Economy
- Challenges posed to such institutions by developments in IT
- The growth of public/private partnerships to best exploit the potential of IT

INTRODUCTION

The new information and communications technologies (ICTs) are currently playing a major role in redefining the public role of libraries in the information society. The growth and spread of networked technologies and associated organizational forms suggest that large public bureaucracies engaged in the provision of knowledge will wither away (Castells 2000). These technologies also create the prospect of globalized private education companies usurping the role of public institutions in the creation and dissemination of knowledge in the sphere of education. This chapter examines these prospects by investigating the digitization of the services provided by the British Library: one of the leading global brands in knowledge provision.

As a library of legal deposit, the British Library (BL) is responsible for the integrity of the national published archive, and the library has been the single most influential body in lobbying for the principle of legal deposit to be extended to electronic resources in the UK.[1] Digitization is central to the BL mission of providing 'Access to the world's knowledge' and features heavily in maintaining the BL's position as the largest provider in the UK national research infrastructure. A recent report from the House of Commons Education and Skills Select Committee identified the British Library as a national resource for the UK higher education (HE) sector (House of Commons Education and Skills

Committee 2002). Although sponsored by the Department of Culture, Media and Sport, more than 50 per cent of BL activity is aimed at supporting HE. A further 25 per cent is directed towards support for industry and business. A White Paper on 'The future of higher education' (DfES 2003) argues that the BL should focus its efforts in three main areas: its contribution to the effectiveness of the UK HE sector as a provider of knowledge and information services; its contribution to excellence in teaching through digital and other resources; and its role as a provider of resources for corporate and business users.

This chapter presents findings on three major aspects of the digitization now underway within the library:

1 It examines the application of network publishing technology to the library's long established document supply service.
2 It investigates the ways in which the BL is using new Web content to bring the resources of the library to lifelong learners and schools.
3 It examines the ways in which new developments in integrated discovery tools, portals and digital preservation are bound up with plans for the BL to assume the role of a 'hub' institution within a reconfigured UK research infrastructure.

The key question this chapter engages with is whether the rhetoric of global borderless education, delivered through increasingly privately controlled networked information technologies, will actually impact on the business reality of managing the knowledge services of a large public educative institution. The chapter is based on interviews carried out with a range of library personnel including e-Learning specialists, project managers and senior curators. It also draws on published reports, policy statements, Web sources and internal documentation provided by the BL.

ACADEMIC DEBATE ON DIGITAL LEARNING AND ITS IMPLICATIONS FOR HE

Changes in the role of public and university libraries have preoccupied academics concerned with changing status of knowledge in the public sphere.[2] Empirical investigations of how libraries or other HE institutions are responding to challenges of the digital age are still comparatively rare – but senior decision-makers and policy-makers within the UK higher education sector have become increasingly concerned with the 'business of borderless education' (Committee for Vice Chancellors and Principals (CVCP) Higher Education Funding Council for England and Wales (HEFCE) 2000) and this has added to the debate on ICTs and their implications for institutions of learning. Academic comment and debate has been sharply divided between the belief that the Internet will transform the landscape of higher education (Hague 1996; Handy 1995; Negroponte 1995) and more critical work which regards virtual learning as synonymous with **marketization**, **commodification** and the **delocalization** of knowledge

(Noble 1998; Schiller 1999; Garnham 2000). Recent commentary reflects the widely held belief that access to knowledge through global networks will decisively undermine established institutions of learning. Thus, Robins and Webster cite Readings (1996) to the effect that global information networks may have triggered a 'dereferentialization of knowledge' which detaches learning from its institutional and national context (Robins and Webster 2002: 5), whilst Delanty (2002) notes that global information networks may act to undermine the autonomy of learning institutions as their public service remit 'becomes diffused in a new set of social relations' (Delanty 2002: 42).

LEARNING JUNCTURE

The new information and communications technologies (ICTs) have stimulated a wide-ranging debate on the future of learning institutions in the age of the 'network society' (Castells 2000). Senior decision-makers in the UK higher education sector are increasingly concerned with 'the business of borderless education' (CVCP/ HEFCE 2000), whilst recent academic commentary equates global information networks with commodification and the delocalization of learning, with consequent threats to the public service traditions of higher education (Robins and Webster 2002). The evidence presented in this chapter does little to support the view that the spread of global information networks will necessarily act to undermine the public sector role of large knowledge providers such as the BL. The findings suggest, rather, that these institutions are becoming more connected to other players in the digital environment and that this interconnectedness has complex, and sometimes highly ambiguous, implications for the production of knowledge in the emergent 'network society'.

Much of the above discussion turns on the belief that both global markets and ICT are transforming the world of HE – however, the debate has been short on empirical investigation of specific cases and institutional choices. The existing empirical work on ICT and HE reflects the diversity and complexity of the choices now facing learning institutions (see, for example, Dutton and Loader 2002) – and it is far from clear that the changes underway are as simple as those depicted by either proponents of virtu-alization or critics of globalization.[3] While it is clear that there are market and technological pressures for change, some commentators have argued that learning institutions have been more active in responding to and shaping the new environment than has previously been acknowledged. Thus, Robins and Webster point to the rise of 'academic capitalism' (Slaughter and Leslie 1997) whilst others suggest that the HE sector is playing a central role in the economies of information-based capitalism (Etzkowitz and Leydesdorff 1997; Curie and Newson 1998).

The above controversies notwithstanding, Robins and Webster point out that much of the comment on ICT and HE has been based on a highly abstract contrast between 'a past we must lose and a present/future we find "progressive"' (Robins and Webster 2002). Research and analysis of ICT in higher education should, in this view, reject abstract notions of 'the virtual organization' and move towards 'investigations of concrete institutions . . . understood as historically variable sets of practices' (Robins and Webster 2002: 101). There is a need for research which can show the ways in which ICTs are implicated in the changing dynamics of knowledge production, shifts in the public sector remit of HE institutions, and new services delivered online. It is with these aspects in mind that this chapter investigates the use of digital technology in furthering the BL's mission of providing 'Access to the world's knowledge'.

NEW FORMS OF SCHOLARLY COMMUNICATION

The current price of journals and forms of information and knowledge tends to rise, and combined with the fast growth in the number of journals has meant that major UK research libraries (including the BL) are experiencing difficulties in maintaining historic levels of coverage. This is the starting point for the discussion of how new electronic formats can facilitate innovation in scholarly communication. The BL is prominently represented on a high level advisory body known as the Research Libraries Support Group (RLSG).[4] The RLSG final report, published in 2003 (www.rlsg.ac.uk) (based on surveys designed to assess the needs of researchers over a 10-year planning horizon), provides an authoritative view of some major developments which are germane to the present study of ICT and institutional change at the BL. The report states:

> As prices rise and research providers are forced to cut subscriptions and thus reduce access, scholarly discourse and the wide communication of research, on the one hand, and formal publication in media of recognized status on the other have become increasingly divergent goals. The interests of authors and readers, who are often effectively the same people, are not aligned.
>
> (RLSG 2003: para. 149)

The report argues that the UK HE sector could use ICTs to circumvent the crisis in the cost and volume of resources, creating an alternative to established publishing channels.[5]

Many scholars within the e-Science community already use the Internet to share provisional and interim research findings. As specialized software becomes more generally available, this will offer wholly new ways of presenting and sharing research information. There has been increased debate within the academic community on the management of intellectual property rights, leading to calls for authors in some disciplines to avoid assigning exclusive copyright to commercial publishers (ibid.: para. 32). The report also notes increasing support for the development of 'open access'

91

publication and new pricing models – notably the Budapest Open Access Initiative (ibid.: para. 31) and the new titles set up with the support of the Scholarly Publication and Academic Resources Coalition (SPARC). A significant UK development is the JISC-sponsored SHERPA project, which is currently exploring the use of new electronic forms for the self-archiving of scholarly output. The RLSG envisages that new electronic formats may reduce the research community's dependence on academic publishers and also resolve some of the issues surrounding the digital archiving of electronic materials.

ELECTRONIC DOCUMENT DELIVERY (EDD)

The BL is one of the world's largest repositories of intellectual property and has long been recognized as a leading supplier of documents to academic and business users in the UK and abroad. The introduction of electronic document delivery (EDD) via the Web has allowed the BL to commercialize one of its most highly regarded services. Customers can choose from a range of delivery options and have documents delivered within 2 hours of ordering if required. Seventy per cent of the BL document supply transactions remain paper-based, but operators now convert documents held as hard copy using scanners equipped with specially customized software which allows files to be emailed direct to customers. The existing paper-based document supply was free to university users – the dissemination of published material (notably journal articles) via the Web has involved the BL in extensive discussions over issues of security and copyright compliance with leading publishers, and the library is currently using digital rights management (DRM) software (developed jointly with Adobe Systems) to charge users for documents

Box 6.1:
THE RESOURCE BASE

Holdings at the library's Boston Spa repository include an estimated 283,000 journal titles, 3 million books, 433,000 conference proceedings, 5 million reports, 150,000 UK theses and 47 million patents. The BL estimates that its document supply service is used by 90 per cent of the UK's top R&D scoreboard companies. EDD is also aimed at the growing number of small and medium-sized enterprises (SMEs) who use the library.

Electronic files supplied to users are scanned from material held as hard copy by the library. The Adobe Reader software contains an encryption algorithm which creates a PDF file, 'wrapping' the original document in a secure package rendering it immune to unauthorized copying, or further file transfer. The BL now supplies PDF files of journal articles from over 2,500 titles.

supplied. The introduction of EDD has created a new revenue stream in document supply and there are plans to develop a range of new commercial services for corporate clients – but it should be noted that approximately 80 per cent of the basic charges made to users are levied on behalf of publishers who hold the copyright on the material supplied.

The BL has also consolidated its position as a leading document supplier through its collaboration with Elsevier, a leading global publisher of scientific and medical journals. Access to Elsevier material has been negotiated on the basis of the library's position as one of the largest and best known repositories of intellectual property, and on its reputation for maintaining copyright compliance. The library is currently adding more publishers to the service and EDD is helping to establish the BL-Adobe DRM software as the industry standard for the research market and is thus acting as a broker between the interests of publishers and BL users.

DIGITAL PRESERVATION

The BL has been a prime mover in efforts to extend the principle of legal deposit to electronic resources. The BL is also involved in a number of digital preservation initiatives including the Digital Preservation Coalition of national libraries which fosters collaboration in preservation strategies and tools. The senior curators responsible for long-term thinking about digital preservation at the BL regard the Web as a more or less unstable medium which is inherently unsuited to the task of retaining and preserving electronic content in perpetuity. A particular problem is that much commercial electronic publishing ceases to be regarded as viable when its income-generating value declines. Individual Web sites hosting material of research significance may cease to be maintained making the material impossible to track down once the link is lost. The Joint Information Systems Committee (JISC)[6] has proposed establishing a Digital Curation Centre as a central repository of file formats, preservation software and archiving tools. Early assessments of the resource and cost implications of the above developments provide some indication of how national digital memory might be organized. The RLSG report suggests that 'some cost elements might be initially high but achieve economies of scale later, some may increase, and others are likely to decline with the development of common standards and tools and effective collaboration (particularly with creators)'. (ibid.: para. 140).

The report also states that:

> The preservation and access costs associated with content held as hard copy are distributed across the whole library system whilst the costs of maintaining holdings in an electronic environment may be aggregated over time in a smaller number of repositories serving others and sharing preservation tools, thus delivering economies of scale but potentially requiring a large spend by a few providers.
>
> (ibid.: para. 142)

93

One way of assessing the cogency of the RLSG analysis is to consider the report's assumptions about how the proposed reforms might be implemented. The report takes a highly directive line on the need for close co-ordination of the changes envisaged whilst acknowledging that both the implementation of the structural reforms envisaged, and the take-up of new technology will be the responsibility of the individual libraries and academic user groups. The scale of the integration envisaged is such that the actual form taken by the proposed Research Libraries Network will almost certainly be determined by a protracted process of negotiation and constituency-building among a wide range of stakeholders (UK research councils, the four UK Higher Education Funding Councils and their specialist committees such as JISC, university vice-chancellors and academic user groups). The complexity of the changes envisaged, and the number of players involved suggests that the process will unfold incrementally with the overall pattern of change that will only become apparent in the longer term. Whether the passage of time will create a new business reality or a digital rhetoric for the collection and dissemination of information and knowledge remains a key issue.

DIGITIZING THE BL COLLECTION: FROM TURNING THE PAGES TO 'COLLECT BRITAIN'

The BL is a recognized innovator in the use of digital media in the display of rare manuscripts. Table 6.1 shows the ways in which three different types of digital technology are related to changes in service delivery and the library's engagement with its core users. The British Library began the Electronic Beowulf project in 1993, as one of a

Table 6.1 ICT and institutional change at the British Library 2001–4

ICT applications	Changes in organization and delivery of services	BL engagement with user constituencies
Information utilities: Electronic document delivery	Redefinition of BL document supply service	Commercialized services aimed at HE and business users
Knowledge media: virtual exhibitions e-Learning	Public access to digitized Web content	Widening of BL audiences to include lifelong learners, schoolchildren and teachers
Knowledge infrastructures: Integrated search tools Subject specific portals Scholarly communications Digital preservation initiatives	Collaboration on 'deep sharing' of library resources Rationalization of UK national research infrastructure	BL role as knowledge provider facilitates efficiency/ effectiveness of UK HE sector BL as knowledge provider to business users

94

number of initiatives to increase access to its collections using digital imaging and network technology. Selected images from the project were among the first pictures of medieval manuscripts to be mounted on the Internet. In April 1998 the library launched 'Turning the Pages'. This project created virtual objects from four of the library's greatest treasures: the Lindisfarne Gospels, the Diamond Sutra, the Sforza Hours and the Leonardo Notebook. The current version of 'Turning the Pages' was developed using 3D software and is displayed to the public on a 37-inch touchscreen designed to give the sensation of leafing through a rare volume.

The first attempt to provide more comprehensive online access to BL collections was closely bound up with the library's response to policies aimed at fostering an inclusive 'learning society'. In 1999 the National Lottery New Opportunities Fund (NOF) (www.nof-digitise.org) launched a £50 million programme aimed at reducing social exclusion by providing public access to new digital content and learning media. In 2001 the BL won NOF funding of £3.5 million to provide online access to its collections. This initiative, which became known as 'Collect Britain' (CB), was aimed specifically at lifelong learners, teachers and schoolchildren. The project incorporates themed tours and virtual exhibitions of historic maps, ephemera, manuscripts, photographs, music scores, prints and drawings. The BL has also collaborated with the Office for National Statistics (ONS) and the Public Records Office (PRO) on '21st Century Citizen', an online resource for 11–16 year olds. This became a statutory part of the UK schools curriculum from September 2002.

'Collect Britain' is the largest digital media project ever undertaken by the BL. The project aims to digitize a target of 100,000 artefacts between early 2001 and 2004, with Web resources to remain available online until 2007. A large volume of the content available on the project Web site is of local and regional interest. The project was also shaped by broader definitions of Britishness – the content includes material from the home countries of UK citizens from south Asia and the Caribbean. One senior member of staff interviewed noted that the project was designed around the need for a regional appeal which would help to overcome the perception of the BL as an 'elitist' 'metropolitan' institution. Another interviewee stated that the project provided a way of 'making the national library fully national'.

As noted above, the CB initiative reflected the BL intention to adopt socially inclusive 'learning society' policies aimed at widening access to BL material. However, the curators who were responsible for initiating CB were uncertain about the needs and assumptions of the lifelong learners at whom the project was directed. As production of digitized objects continued through 2002/3, curators were faced with the question of how the large volume of material was to be interpreted and presented in ways which would engage with the needs of lifelong learners and schoolchildren. The head of the BL education service saw the initiative as an opportunity to experiment with different modes of engagement with schoolchildren and teachers, arguing that using the Web to reach a wider audience was dependent not on the volume of material digitized or on the functionality of the Web site, but on the library's ability to develop new forms of outreach and interpretive content. This included the recruitment of specially appointed creative research fellows (funded by Pearson Education, the global information provider) and close engagement between the BL education service and teachers in creating interpretative content and courseware. This approach was in accord with plans for the BL to become a supporting partner to the DfES in specific areas of innovative pedagogy. Plans to extend the CB initiative beyond the 3-year NOF funding anticipated the creation of new digital environments for individuals and groups to make formal or informal 'learning journeys' through BL Web resources.

The impetus for the project was that digital media would allow interaction and engagement with high quality content – but it later became clear that developing the Web site as a learning tool would require considerable investment in specialized online learning expertise and a corresponding shift of emphasis away from the production of newly digitized content towards the interpretation of this content. The senior curators responsible for the project took the view that the BL is essentially a content provider (rather than educational service provider); the library's commitment to core HE and business users is such that efforts to embark on new educational activities were 'inevitably underresourced'. Funding on the scale provided by the original NOF grant is not currently available and the short-term project-based funding is seen as a major constraint on longer-term prospects for further digitization. 'Collect Britain' began as a discrete project which is separate from mainstream collections – but the BL director of scholarship and collections made it clear that the library has moved to a more centralized and systemized approach to collection management. The collection management system developed for CB has allowed the BL to create a standardized template for new media which can be added to as required. There are plans for Web content currently available on the CB site to be migrated to the new Explore Web site – this will allow it to be repurposed and become more integrated into the digital library system

The '21st Century Citizen' initiative offers a contrasting example of digitization – although much less ambitious in terms of the volume of images digitized, this initiative provides Web content and activities which support enquiry-based learning. The development of this learning tool for the UK schools curriculum drew on the skills of three content providers and a specialized interactive media agency. This squares with the view that the successful management of innovation often depends on the ability to manage complementary intellectual and creative assets in innovative projects (Quinn 1992; Star and Ruhleder 1996; OECD 2001).

THE BL AND ITS ROLE IN THE RESEARCH LIBRARIES SUPPORT GROUP (RLSG)

The BL is the largest and most heavily used research library in the UK and it provides a critical mass of content and services for the research information network. This network has four major components:

THINK POINT

Knowledge infrastructures: the British Library and the UK Research Libraries Network

The chapter has so far examined the introduction of new information utilities and knowledge media at the British Library, relating these technologies to changes in the services offered to the library's core users. The BL is currently involved in a number of technological developments which have significant implications for the UK national research infrastructure. Understanding these developments requires a broad view of the BL and its recent involvement in collaborations and strategic alliances.

By investigating the case of the global public brand of the BL, we have discovered that e-Learning strategies and their implementation in an e-Economy is complex. Furthermore, the idea that networked technologies of themselves can replace large bureaucratic knowledge institutions, that are part of a public resource and public history, is not borne out in practice. The appeal of this particular case study is that it provides important insights of how the rhetoric of the e-Economy is confronted by the business reality of a well-known public institution.

1 the university libraries (with dual function of research and teaching);
2 the national libraries including the British Library and the national libraries of Scotland and Wales;
3 dedicated research libraries and archives;
4 material made available online from a range of sources including the Information environment managed by JISC.

Its role on the RLSG has been set out above. One of the crucial roles of the RLSG, to date, has been the publication of a 2003 report, assessing the potential of ICT in learning environments. The report begins by highlighting the 'double crisis' in the price and volume of research periodicals, arguing that the UK research infrastructure is faced with resource shortfalls whose scale is such that individual research libraries cannot meet them. The report also presents evidence on the current use of emerging technologies (integrated discovery tools, subject-mediated gateways, new forms of scholarly communication, and new developments in digital preservation) and it assesses the adoption of these by UK research libraries and academic research communities. The RSLG report ends by calling for the formation of a new public body, the Research Libraries Network (RLN), which will form the core of a reconfigured national research infrastructure. A key feature of the latter is that the BL, together with other large providers, would become 'hub' institutions whose public remit would be to serve smaller libraries within the proposed network. One striking feature is the emphasis on the institutional means to these ends – the RSLG makes it clear that the vision of a reconfigured national research infrastructure will be realized not simply by adopting the requisite information technologies, but by means of collaboration between a range of players including the UK Higher Education Funding Councils, the British Library, the Joint Information Systems Committee (JISC) and other UK research libraries.

The RLSG report contains two major strands of analysis:

- The first of these is the need to address the 'double crisis' of steadily rising costs and the consequent shortfall in library resources by implementing a programme of structural reform.
- The second is the need to support the latter by encouraging the take-up of new technologies by libraries and academic user groups.

The report highlights the rises in the volume and cost of scholarly journals over the last decade. The RLSG estimates that between 1990 and 2000, purchasers of research publications in the UK saw the number of journal titles increase by 34 per cent (from 117,000 to 157,000). The average cost of each title rose by 210 per cent over the same period – six times the increase in the Retail Price Index – and access to research material provided by UK providers is declining in terms of what is globally available. In one of its key passages the report argues that:

> Maintaining the service that researchers have come to expect will require concerted and collaborative action to improve the resource efficiency of the system. . . . We strongly urge, therefore, a concerted shift from the comparatively loose network of providers, each serving its own user group, to a more coherently managed network in which providers work together to develop and deliver an agreed national agenda.
>
> (RLSG 2003: para. 82–3)

Another way in which the RLSG is seeking to mitigate the current resource shortfalls being experienced by particular libraries is by encouraging collaboration on the acquisition of research resources. The RLSG reports some progress being made in negotiations at national level[7] but states that support for collaborative acquisition or rationalization between individual libraries is very limited. Turning to the longer-term process of 'deep resource sharing' and collaborative management of collections the report states that:

> strong constraints exist upon deeper resource sharing. These include concerns about loss of control by an institution over resources for its own staff and students; and about what would happen if a scheme collapsed or a participating institution changed its policies.
>
> (ibid.: para. 76)

The RLSG case for a more directive approach to the co-ordination and rationalization of library resources has been made on the assumption that the BL will retain its position as the largest UK provider of information to academic and business researchers. A careful reading of the report and interviews carried out at the BL suggests that implementing the RLSG proposals on the redistribution of library resources may result in an enhanced role for a group of large 'hub' institutions (the British Library, the national libraries of Scotland and Wales and the larger university libraries) to provide for the entire HE sector. The report also argues, in a second strand of analysis, that the benefits of ICTs can only be realized through a process of 'managed innovation'. The RSLG has reported on a number of significant developments and these are outlined below.

MANAGED INNOVATION IN THE AGE OF THE HYBRID LIBRARY

The RLSG analysis of innovation in the UK library system is based on extensive research into current practice of providers and academic researchers with regard to electronic media. All libraries now spend a significant proportion of their budgets on acquiring or accessing electronic material[8] but a survey of researchers contained in the report shows that hard copy forms an important part of the information resource for most researchers and that this will be a central feature of research and scholarship for the foreseeable future

LEARNING JUNCTURE

Different horses for different courses

The RSLG survey findings show significant differences in patterns of information use among researchers working in different disciplines. Sixty per cent of medical and biological science researchers and 77 per cent in physical science and engineering regard printed books as essential resources. Some 92 per cent of researchers in the arts, humanities and social sciences regard printed books as essential resources. Ninety-five per cent of all researchers perceive access to printed refereed journals as essential. Seventy-five per cent of researchers in the sciences now view electronic access to e-Journals and electronic full text services as essential, compared with 57 per cent in social sciences and 22 per cent in the humanities. However, almost 60 per cent of the third group expect their use of electronic journals to increase in the next 10 years. However, RSLG reports that 'even in those disciplines where electronic resources have made a heavy impact, there is no sign of hard copy resources being abandoned' (RSLG 2003: para. 29).

Research libraries have thus far provided electronic resources alongside those held as hard copy – but the boundaries between electronic and hard copy resources are blurred in so far as libraries now have to manage resources held as hard copy; material which has been 'born digital' and material which is digitized retrospectively. The concept of the 'hybrid library' (RLSG 2003: paras 54–6) has emerged from the recognition that the key issue facing those tasked with providing research resources for the UK academic community is not simply the addition of new electronic formats, but the use of these formats in the management of existing collections held as hard copy. The RLSG reports that there is no complete catalogue of holdings for the major UK research providers, and also notes that a considerable volume of hard copy remains uncatalogued, or catalogued only in manual form, rendering this material invisible to online searches (ibid.: paras 64–6). The RLSG expects that the task of rationalizing national resources will require very considerable efforts in the mapping, assessment and management of collections which are at present dispersed throughout the UK's research libraries. The RLSG supports efforts by JISC and others to develop integrated resource discovery tools. These tools will use the Internet to identify, list and describe materials in a range of formats and to provide an online catalogue accessible through a single user interface.[9]

CONCLUSIONS

In the glitzy world of global information society, the relationship between knowledge and information and their dissemination by digital means is a complex one. Where large public institutions are the major providers of knowledge and educative services, their role is likely to be questioned by the development of 'borderless education' by powerful global corporations. The rhetoric of the e-Economy reinforces this questioning. Whether borderless education will be a business reality is a far bigger and long-term issue.

Table 6.2 provides an overview of the findings of this chapter and shows the ways in which the three main types of digital technology were related to changes in services offered to various user constituencies. The table also shows the role of the BL in shaping the utilization of these technologies.

The introduction of EDD has provided the BL document supply operation with a range of new commercial services, reflecting the shift to more consumer-oriented provision of services from 2001 onwards. However, a more significant aspect of EDD is that this has allowed the BL to enhance its role as a broker of intellectual property, mediating between the strategic interests of publishers and library users in the UK and abroad. The strategic agreements with Adobe and Elsevier have been crucial in the digitization of the BL document supply operation. Strategic collaboration between content providers and an interactive media specialist appears to have been the key element in the success of the '21st Century Citizen' project – and it can reasonably be argued that the lack of such collaboration explains the relative lack of success in developing e-Learning material within the 'Collect Britain' project. Extensive collaboration

Table 6.2 The British Library and the institutional shaping of digital media 2001–4

ICT applications	Changes in organization and delivery of services	BL engagement with user constituencies	BL role in shaping digital media
Information utilities: electronic document delivery	Redefinition of BL document supply service	Commercialized services aimed at HE and business users worldwide. Marketization of information utilities	BL as 'knowledge broker' Leveraging of intellectual assets held by BL
Knowledge media: virtual exhibitions e-Learning	Public access to digitized Web content	Widening of BL audience to include lifelong learners, teachers and schoolchildren	Emergence of new public interfaces shaped by organizational and resource constraints
Knowledge infra-structures: integrated search tools Portals Scholarly communications Digital preservation	Collaboration on 'deep sharing' of hybrid resources Rationalization of UK national research infrastructure	BL role as knowledge provider facilitates efficiency/ effectiveness of UK HE sector BL as knowledge provider to business users	Strategic collaborations with HEFCE and others BL as 'hub' institution within UK research libraries network

and reciprocal agreements between libraries are also seen as critical to the rationalization of national resources proposed by the RSLG, and to the implementation of integrated discovery tools being developed by the SUNCAT project.

As noted above, one of the main themes in discussions of virtualization in HE has been the concern with the commodification of learning. The BL has used its position as one of the world's largest knowledge providers to align itself with a range of private sector partners, using new technologies to supply documents online. The BL has certainly become more responsive to commercial factors – but a more nuanced view of developments in EDD is that the library has itself been a decisive agent of transformation within this environment (Child 1972, 1997). The BL is, nevertheless, using private sector means to further its public mission of providing 'access to the world's knowledge' and this supports the view that the public sector remit of the UK's largest knowledge provider may indeed have become 'diffused in a wider set of social relations' (Delanty 2002). The proliferation of 'networked' technologies and organizational forms across the whole spectrum of BL activities documented in this chapter would, moreover, seem to support Castells' argument that we are seeing the demise of large institutions based on the bureaucratic form (Castells 2000). However, this view assumes that ICTs can necessarily be equated with the disaggregation and dispersal of knowledge provision – and is contradicted by the findings on the role of the BL in shaping the digital environment and on the emergent new structures being proposed by the RSLG. The BL has been the single most influential player in securing historic legislation on legal deposit of digital material in the UK and the indications are that responsibility for preserving digital memory in perpetuity is being organized by large institutions on a national basis.

The BL is operating in a highly interventionist policy milieu which is far removed from the atomized visions of the virtual campus (Hague 1996). Moves to develop a more integrated research infrastructure in the UK are being underwritten by state-sponsored bodies (such as HEFCE). The impetus for this integration derives not from the roll-back of the state but from the fact that the state has now assumed the role of regulator rather than sole provider. Current developments in both research infrastructure (for example, new discovery tools, portals and electronic formats) and in the new field of digital preservation suggest that the BL will be able to expand and merge its operations with those of the other research libraries. Like other global suppliers of digitized content, the BL is consolidating its position as a major provider, using ICTs to expand its operations to achieve the economies of scale in reaching large audiences (Daniel 1999; Harris 2002). This squares with the RSLG view that the BL, together with a small number of other large providers, should become a 'hub' institution which will serve smaller libraries as part of an expanded public sector remit. The use of network technology in UK HE research libraries is thus linked to the emergence of more centralized organizational structures than has been acknowledged by most discussions of virtuality (Harris 1998). The evidence presented by this chapter does little to support the view that the spread of global information networks will necessarily act to undermine the public sector role of large institutional knowledge providers. The findings suggest, rather, that these institutions are becoming more connected to other players in the digital environment and that this interconnectedness has complex, and sometimes highly ambiguous, implications for the production of knowledge in the emergent 'network society'.

What have we learned? This chapter began with a brief review of the debate on ICT and learning institutions. Much of this debate has turned on the notion that learning institutions are being subjected to new forms of commodification and disaggregation in the age of the global information networks. The review noted that the debate has failed to get analytic and substantive purchase on the organizational choices which shape the actual form taken by ICT in higher education settings, and it was with this in mind that the chapter has examined the digitization now underway at the BL.

102

GLOSSARY

Commodification   The transformation of goods and services which may have certain wider-society benefits into a commodity to be bought and sold, like any other, in the marketplace; for example, higher education.

Delocalization   Has a specific and geographical meaning. In the first instance, it refers to operations or undertakings being done for a general purpose at no specific time. In the second, it means that operations or undertakings no longer take place in a particular place.

Marketization   The creation of markets for goods and services and consumer choice, that had previously been supplied collectively, publicly, or both. For example, the creation in private markets in certain types of health care, where the consumer has a choice over the timings, price and location of treatments.

NOTES

1   The principle of 'last resort' access through legal deposit libraries, available for printed publications, was extended to electronic resources by the legal Deposit Libraries Act of 2003 as this paper was being drafted.

2   For an overview, see Hand (2003).

3   An important distinction to emerge from debate in the last few years is that between entirely new entities (for example, Jones International University) and existing institutions (Baer 2002; Cornford 2002; Harris 2002).

4   The RLSG was established in 2001 by the four UK HE funding councils, the BL and the national libraries of Scotland and Wales.

5   These tools will allow access to resources held outside the UK, including those being developed for the e-Science community. The RLSG anticipates that subject-specific portals will eventually incorporate additional value-added services which meet the specific discovery needs of researchers.

6   The JISC is responsible for the Joint Academic Network (JANET) and for delivering the national electronic research network.

7   The shared licensing of electronic resources has been achieved through the National Electronic Site Licensing Initiative (NESLI). This has apparently met with some success in leveraging lower prices and reducing the burden on individual university libraries to negotiate licences.

8   The Society for College, National and University Libraries (SCONUL) estimates that spending on electronic resources has rise from close to zero to more than 10 per cent of information provision expenditure.

9   The report anticipates that the recently developed Serials Union National Catalogue (SUNCAT) will provide both a comprehensive national catalogue of serials holdings and an electronic mapping device.

BIBLIOGRAPHY

Baer, W.S. (2002) 'Competition and collaborating in online distance learning', in W.H. Dutton and B.D. Loader (eds) *Digital Academe*, London: Routledge.

Castells, M. (2000) *The Rise of the Network Society*, Vol 1, Oxford: Blackwell.

Child, J. (1972) 'Organization structure, environment and performance: the role of strategic choice', *Sociology*, 6, 1: 1–22.

Child, J. (1997) 'Strategic choice and the analysis of action, structure, organizations and environment', *Organization Studies*, 18, 1: 43–76.

Cornford, J. (2002) 'The virtual university is . . . the university made concrete?', *Information, Communication and Society*, 3, 4: 494–507.

Curie, J. and Newson, J. (eds) (1998) *Universities and Globalization: Critical Perspectives*, London: Sage.

CVCP/HEFCE (2000) *The Business of Borderless Education: UK Perspectives*, London: CVCP/HEFCE.

Daniel, J. S. (1999) *The Mega-Universities and Knowledge Media: Technology Strategies for Higher Education*, London: Kogan Page.

Delanty, G. (1998) 'The idea of the university in the global era: From knowledge as end to the end of knowledge?', *Social Epistemology*, 12, 1: 3–25.

Delanty, G. (2002) 'The university and modernity', in K. Robins and F. Webster (2002) (eds) *The Virtual University?*, Oxford: Oxford University Press.

DfES (Department for Education and Skills) (2003) *The Future of Higher Education*, White Paper, cmnd No. 5735 London: The Stationery Office. Available at www.dfes.gov.uk/highereducation/hestrategy.

Dutton, W.H. and Loader, B.D. (eds) (2002) *Digital Academe*, London: Routledge.

Etzkowitz, H. and Leydesdorff, L. (eds) 1997) *Universities in the Global Economy: A Triple Helix of University Industry Government Relations*, London: Cassell Academic.

Garnham, N. (2000) '"Information Society" as theory or ideology: a critical perspective on technology, education and employment in the information age', *Information, Communication and Society*, 3, 2: 139–52.

Gibbons, M., Limoges, C., Novotny, H., Schwartzman, S., Scott, P. and Trow, M. (1994) *The New Production of Knowledge*, London: Sage.

Hague, D. (1996) 'The firm as a university', *Demos Quarterly*, issue 8.

Hand, M. (2003) 'The people's network? Self education and empowerment in public libraries.' Paper presented to the Information, Communication and Society Research Symposium 17–20 September 2003.

Handy, C. (1995) 'Trust and the virtual organization', *Harvard Business Review*, May–June: 40–50.

Harris, M. (1998) 'Rethinking the virtual organization', in P. Jackson and J. Van der Weilen (eds) *Teleworking: International Perspectives*, London: Routledge.

Harris, M. (2000) 'Virtual learning and the network society', *Information, Communication and Society* 3, 4: 580–96.

Harris, M. (2002) 'Virtual learning and the network society', in W.H. Dutton and B.D. Loader (eds) *Digital Academe*, London: Routledge.

House of Commons Education and Skills Committee (2002) *Library Resources for Higher Education*, Fifth report of Session 2001–02. Available at www.publications.parliament.uk/pa/com200102/cmselect/cmedusk/804/80402.htm

Howells, J. and Hine, J. (eds) (1993) *Innovative Banking: Competition and the Management of a New Network Technology*, London: Routledge.

Molina, A. (1990) 'Transputers and transputer-based parallel computers: socio-technical constituencies and the build-up of British-European capabilities in information technologies', *Research Policy*, 19: 309–33.

Negroponte, N. (1995) *Being Digital*, London: Hodder and Stoughton.

Office of Science and Technology (1995) *Leisure and Learning*, Technology Foresight Panel report number 14.

Noble, D. (1998) 'Digital diploma mills: the automation of higher education', *Science as Culture*, 7, 3: 355–68.

Organization for Economic Co-operation and Development (2001) *E-Learning: The Partnership Challenge*, Paris: OECD, Centre for Educational Research and Innovation.

Quinn, J. B. (1992) *Intelligent Enterprise*, New York: The Free Press.

Readings, W. (1996) *The University in Ruins*, Cambridge, MA: Harvard University Press.

Research Libraries Support Group (2003) *Final Report of the Research Libraries Support Group*. Available at www.rslg.ac.uk/final.final.pdf

Robins, K. and Webster, F. (eds) (2002) *The Virtual University?* Oxford: Oxford University Press.

Schiller, D. (1999) *Digital Capitalism: Networking in the Global Market System*, Cambridge, MA: MIT Press.

Slaughter, L. and Leslie, L. L. (1997) *Academic Capitalism: Politics, Policies and the Entrepreneurial University*, Baltimore, MD: Johns Hopkins University Press.

Star, S. L. and Ruhleder, K. (1996) 'Steps towards an ecology of infrastructure: design and access for large information spaces', *Information Systems Research*, 7, 1: 111–34.

Chapter 7

Coerced evolution: a study of the integration of e-Mediated learning into a traditional university

SIMRAN K. GREWAL

KEY LEARNING POINTS

After completing this chapter you will have an understanding of:

- The scope of e-Learning initiatives
- The role of e-Learning in higher education
- The challenges inherent in integrating 'old' and 'new' learning systems
- The importance of training and resourcing in the effective management of change

INTRODUCTION

This chapter provides an account of the preliminary findings of a study into the integration of e-Mediated learning technologies into traditional campus-based universities. It argues that the changes undertaken in the adoption and efficiency of e-Mediated learning are not as radical as the rhetoric would have us believe, but instead are gradual and incremental in practice. This is due to a number of challenges such as a lack of infrastructure, resources and trust, together with resistance to change.

The chapter opens with an introduction to the various definitions of e-Mediated learning and summarizes the rationale behind the study. The next section provides a sociological perspective of the challenges involved in the introduction of technology into traditional organizational settings. Relevant literature on the subject of modernity is reviewed and a case study methodology is used to frame the empirical research. The chapter concludes by highlighting the key themes that have emerged from the study and makes recommendations for further research.

E-MEDIATED LEARNING: SOME DEFINITIONS

e-Mediated learning can be described as the utilization of Web-based information or communications technologies to help support teaching and learning. However, many writers choose to use the term interchangeably with either 'learning technology' (Timms *et al.* 1997; Sosabowski *et al.* 1998; Brusilovsky and Miller 1999), 'educational technology' (Pollock *et al.* 2000; Fetherston 2001; Rosenberg 2001), 'information and communications technology' (ICT) (Stainfield 1997; Goddard *et al.* 1999), 'e learning' (Orsini-Jones 1999), 'online learning' (Goodyear 1999; Laurillard 2000; Salmon 2001) and 'Web-based learning' (Jackson 2002). It is perhaps for this very reason that there is no universal definition. For the purpose of this chapter, the author has decided to use the term 'e-Mediated learning'.

e-Mediated learning technologies can encompass a wide and varied range of technologies to aid the teaching and learning process, such as the use of **email**, **bulletin boards** and **chat rooms**. These can be used on a stand alone basis or incorporated into flexible settings such as a **VLE (virtual learning environment)**. Some of the more widely used VLEs within higher education are **WebCT** and **Blackboard**. These environments provide staff with the option of building a customized learning environment with the following main features.

- resources: supplementary material such as references, links and lecture notes;
- communication tools: chat rooms, mail and bulletin boards;
- assessments: assignments can be submitted and graded online, quizzes and tests can also be created;
- monitoring: academic staff members have the ability to track online student activity.

e-Mediated learning exists within both the public and private sectors. Figure 7.1 identifies the central agencies involved with e-Mediated learning:

1 *The government*
    - The UK government initiative 'Learn Direct' is investing resources and time into ICT centres.
    - UK eU (UK e-Universities) backed by the UK government with £62 million of funding and launched in January 2003, with the aim of bringing UK universities to deliver university education online at a global level (Lambert 2002).
2 *Educational institutions*
    Higher education institutions that are currently exploring how e-Learning can aid their current teaching and learning practices, for example, the introduction of a campus wide VLE at Brunel University.
3 *Academics*
    Individual research interests in e-Mediated learning, for example, Salmon (2000 2001, 2002), Laurillard (2000), Kaur (2002), Lapham (1997) and Grewal (2002, 2003).

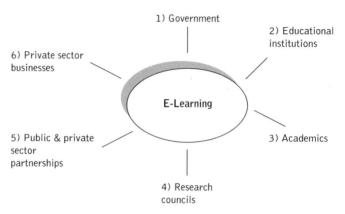

Figure 7.1 *Conceptualization of e-Learning initiatives*
Source: Grewal (2002)

4 *Research councils*

The Higher Education Funding Council (HEFCE) provides funding for special initiatives to support learning and teaching, such as the e-University project. This began in February 2000 as a collaborative project to establish a new way of providing higher education programmes through Web-based learning. The project is designed to give UK higher education the capacity to compete globally with the major virtual and corporate universities being developed in the United States and elsewhere, with the government committing £62 million to the project for 2001–4 (http://www.hefce.ac.uk). (At the time of writing, this project has been suspended.)

5 *Public and private sector partnerships*

- The collaboration between UK universities and Sun Microsystems to build a global university in a project worth £400 million (Kelly 2001). There is substantial recognition of the need to collaborate and establish a partnership, however, there are often problems with partnerships between the universities and the private sector, in terms of differing cultures, expectations and time-scales.

- The Digital Academy was launched in 1999, with substantial private sector and UK government backing. The intention was to provide SMEs with the benefits of cost savings and flexibility to up-skill their employees by introducing e-Mediated learning into the workplace

6 *Private sector businesses*

A substantial amount of activity exists in corporate education. Some of the catalysts for this are technological developments, enhanced interest in lifelong learning in work and huge increases in international demand for higher education. A larger number of corporate universities exist in the USA than in the UK or Europe. The University of Phoenix Online is one such example (www.pheonix.edu).

A distinction needs to be made between private sector and higher education institutions implementing e-Mediated learning. The main aim of the private sector is to make an economic gain, whereas higher education institutions have more of an obligation to their government and citizens, so their motivations are more likely to be determined by these responsibilities. However, they are now faced with increasing competition at a global level in addition to pressure from the state to introduce private sector practices such as providing more of a customer focus amid decreased funding.

E-MEDIATED LEARNING IN HIGHER EDUCATION

As illustrated in Figure 7.2, social, technical, political and economic pressures, competition from both a national and international level, an increasing number of students entering into higher education and decreased funding dictates that the UK higher education sector considers e-Mediated learning. The introduction of tuition fees in the UK means that a more direct 'consumer-based' relationship is being created between the student and the university, and hence the dynamics are changing, a factor which is driving students to expect more efficiency within the system.

Like other sectors of society, higher education is undergoing changes. At the same time, the global market for e-Mediated learning is also expanding, owing to the knowledge-based nature of modern businesses, demographic change and an increasing demand for lifelong learning. However, despite the rhetoric, there is a growing sense that

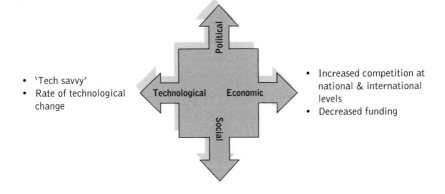

*   Government initiatives, e.g. Learn Direct
*   Research councils, e.g. HEFCE & ESRC

*   'Tech savvy'
*   Rate of technological change

Political

Technological   Economic

Social

*   Increased competition at national & international levels
*   Decreased funding

*   Busy lives not permitting 9–5 attendance
*   Lifelong learning

Figure 7.2 *Factors driving e-Mediated learning within higher education*
Source: Grewal (2003)

109

most higher education institutions are generally taking evolutionary rather than radical steps to implement e-Mediated learning (Goddard *et al.* 1999; Cornford 1999; Cornford and Pollock 2000). The main areas of activity place emphasis upon enhancing staff development opportunities and provide e-Mediated learning tools only as support mechanisms. As the CVCP (2000) highlights: 'There will not be a radical move towards virtual education. Rather the developments in this field are more likely to focus on enhancing access, lifelong learning etc.'

Yet some commentators predict that universities will 'transform themselves' into brokering organizations with no academic staff (Albury 1996). Others argue that e-Mediated learning will transform the landscape of higher education and that change will become inevitable if universities are to remain viable (Liber 2002). At an extreme level, Drucker (1997) claims that universities will cease to exist: 'Thirty years from now the big university campuses will be relics. Universities won't survive. . . . It's as large a change as when we first got the printed book.'

There is an increasing awareness that these elements create both a threat and an opportunity for UK higher education. Around the world, universities and companies are developing new ventures to break into the emerging market for e-Mediated learning. If UK higher education does not respond as efficiently it could lose to others not just the potential to develop new markets but even its share of existing markets. Many students in the UK will continue to want full-time campus-based experience of higher education because of its wider educational and social benefits. Nevertheless, both the overseas and the part-time markets for adult lifelong learning and continuing professional development are exposed to e-delivery and offer the capacity for rapid growth. If the UK higher education sector does not keep adapting to meet the rising demands then others will. If it does respond there are benefits to be gained, however, securing and sustaining such a position demands considerable investment of funds, time and skills.

Despite the growing interest in the technology the rhetoric that e-Mediated learning will 'revolutionize' the existing higher education sector appear ambitious. For example, Laurillard (2001) writing with regard to the Open University, claims that faculty staff can make great time savings: 'Some of our calculations have shown that changing just 20% of the course material to ICT materials increases academic staff time by up to 40%.' However, the preliminary results of the research drawn upon in this chapter challenge the claims made. Specifically, academic staff who used the technology to enhance and support their current teaching practices found the integration of the module into the virtual learning environment (VLE) to be time-consuming in terms of both set-up and maintenance of the site. This indicates that there are significant differences in perception of the efficiency of the technology. The environments in which e-Mediated learning technologies are used may produce varied outcomes depending on the type of technology used, the content, the students, the subject area and the objectives that academic staff have of using the technology. Furthermore, it was found that the wider social and organizational setting, together with the adequacy of supporting infrastructure, play a pivotal role in the underlying success of e-Mediated learning.

110

Many higher education institutions envision e-Mediated learning as a seamless solution to the demanding economic, social and globalization problems that they are facing. Yet some of the challenges being faced by universities are the need for clear quality assurance arrangements to maintain standards, together with funding, development and infrastructure resources. Such infrastructure issues include security, space implications, the internal network, external networks and the access they offer to those within and outside the campus. Data collected in higher education from a 1998 survey of Computer Centre Directors indicated a sector average of one workstation per 11.4 students. Clearly, this indicates a resource issue, as more and more universities are considering e-Mediated learning they need to ensure that they at the very least have the resources to support the new initiatives.

The higher education sector is currently placing greater emphasis on promoting and developing high quality learning and teaching, recognizing the potential contribution of e-Mediated learning in this area. Within higher education, there are many e-related learning and teaching initiatives, at both institutional and national levels. A study commissioned by HEFCE and the University for Industry (Ufi) highlights a low take-up rate of staff adopting this technology, with much of the activity occurring at an experimental level. As such there is a certain amount of scepticism of the extent to which e-Mediated learning can be formally introduced into existing academic structures. In many cases, the desire for change does not actually materialize. It has been argued that the use of e-Mediated learning as an educational technology poses pedagogical challenges, as such the use of e-Mediated learning in university teaching should focus on learning rather than technological issues (Fetherston 2001; Gunstone 1998). It is argued that the first challenge is to reconceptualize the use of e-Mediated learning from a delivery medium to a pedagogical [teaching and learning] tool and academic staff will have to change their current ways of teaching. However, as mentioned earlier, the main use of e-Mediated learning within higher education is as a support mechanism for face-to-face teaching, hence at this stage it not a central part of university teaching and learning. Moreover, adopting e-Mediated learning as a pedagogical tool will require an overhaul of the existing methods of teaching and central support and this may prove to be quite difficult within an inherently political domain.

Rosenberg (2001) suggests that the integration of technology is often prone to failure due to factors such as high costs and persuading staff and students of the benefits of the technology. The fact that evidence on the efficiency of e-Mediated learning is mixed makes it difficult to assess the outcomes of the specific projects. In other words, the more exaggerated claims of some of the advocates (Albury 1996; Drucker 1997; Laurillard 2001) of e-Mediated learning have not been validated. Furthermore, the use of e-mediated learning in teaching does not yet occupy a central role within higher education. This is key to the rhetoric and reality argument underlying the theme of the book.

SOCIAL DYNAMICS

It can be argued from a sociological perspective that the integration of e-Mediated learning into traditional UK universities is a double-edged sword. On one hand there is the argument that the technology is cost-effective and flexible in the sense that it can provide students with access to course materials on a 24/7 basis and is highly scalable. However, on the other hand, introducing e-Mediated learning runs the risk of fragmenting the university and pressurizing the organization into reinstitutionalizing into a more corporate or concrete organization. The rollout of the e-Mediated learning systems generates a demand for more policy. This ends in the tightening up of roles and procedures but also policy applied locally and across the university. Goddard *et al.*'s (1999) study of change at four higher educational institutions in the UK revealed that the case study institutions felt that they could move seamlessly towards virtuality in theory, but practice often showed that the introduction of new e-Mediated learning systems in conjunction with the provision of traditional teaching was extremely problematic. For example, three projects had stalled shortly after they started as the aspects that were crucial for the success of the project, such as guidelines, standards and validating bodies were non-existent and had to be created from scratch. In support of Goddard, Cornford (1999) argues that in an attempt to become virtual, ironically the university becomes so bound up by structures and procedures that it takes on even more characteristics that are indicative of a concrete university:

> It is becoming increasingly clear that the pursuit of the **virtual university** is having a major, perhaps paradoxical impact on the institutional form and sense of identity of the university as it has developed in the twentieth century. Specifically the application of new technologies is generating a myriad of demands for re-institutionalization of the university as a far more 'corporate' one might even say concrete kind of organization.
>
> (Cornford 1999)

It is suggested that building the virtual university appears to require the construction of a far more corporate structure capable of co-ordinated action with formalized roles and standardized practices. Attempting to build the virtual university from the bottom up, course by course without reconstructing the basic structures of the university appears to be laborious and labour intensive.

> Initiatives were confounded by difficulties in co-ordinating a wide range of actors across a large organization made up of diverse and disparate entities [i.e. departments and service units]. It seems that it is the very institution of the university which is at the heart of the problem.
>
> (Cornford 1999)

112

The research carried out by Cornford teases out a number of key issues that have manifested as a result of HE institutions' attempts to become more virtual. The most significant (perhaps ironic) discovery is that there are more procedures and policies involved in creating a virtual university than a traditional university. Cornford and Pollock (2000) unequivocally state that the theory of the virtual university does not work in practice. They suggest that it is the system that conceptualizes the virtual university through complex databases and sets of procedures, but within a traditional university setting it is the individuals with complex identities that are at the heart of the institution, and not the system itself.

The issue of modernity as being a double-edged phenomenon has long been addressed by sociologists such as Marx, Durkheim, Weber and Giddens. The work of both Marx (1818–83) and Durkheim (1858–1917) also stressed that the modern era was a troubled one, but both believed that the advantages outweighed the disadvantages. Max Weber (1976) took a rather more pessimistic outlook towards modernity and saw the modern world paradoxically, in which material progression could only be obtained at the expense of an expansion of bureaucracy that crushed individual creativity and autonomy. More recently and central to this chapter, Giddens' (1996) perspective on modernity argues that although modern institutions have created greater opportunities than any other pre-modern systems, there is also a dark side to these opportunities. Giddens suggests that by incorporating the use of expert systems (which act as disembedding instruments) modern institutions remove the social relations from local contexts of interaction and then restructure these relationships across indefinite periods of time and space. e-Mediated learning technology within a university setting also has a similar effect. For instance, in one of the universities studied, one of the courses that integrated online learning used an assignment tool where students submitted their assignments online. Initial findings showed that many students were concerned with submitting their assignments in this way and felt that their papers might not reach the academic staff for grading. This highlights the critical issue of trust, a subject that will be returned to in more detail in Chapter 11. Trust plays a fundamental role where expert systems are involved, as trust is transferred from the individual to the abstract system and as individuals we are coerced into placing faith into expert systems as we have bounded knowledge of the way in which these systems work. Trust presupposes that an element of risk is involved, but inevitably as e-Mediated learning systems become globalized the decision to opt out of the abstract system is no longer an option. Giddens states that: 'The trust that individuals place in abstract systems is more of a tacit acceptance of circumstances in which other avenues are closed rather than a leap of commitment.'

Scepticism often manifests when an individual encounters technical hitches or cracks in the technology, or when the intended outcomes are not delivered. As such the amount of trust that individuals place in e-Mediated learning systems are likely to be influenced by their experiences at the outset with the abstract system. e-Mediated learning technology cannot provide either the mutuality or intimacy which personal trust relationships offer. This places the academic staff and individuals at access points in a vulnerable position as they attempt to illustrate their faith in the system, because they provide the connection between personal and systems trust. A carefully designed plan together with training can help to minimize the mistakes made by individuals when using the technology. However, there is always an element of risk where both technology and individuals are involved regardless of how well a system is designed or how efficient its operators are. The ramifications of its (e-Mediated learning) implementation and functioning in relation to the operation of other systems and human activities in general cannot be entirely foreseen.

Some of the key themes to emerge from this section can be summarized as follows:

- The integration of e-Mediated learning into traditional UK universities is a double-edged sword.
- Influential sociologists such as Marx, Durkheim, Weber and Giddens have argued that although modernity may have created opportunities for technological advancement, a dark side to these opportunities also exists.
- e-Mediated learning technology acts as a disembedding mechanism, removing social relations from local contexts of interaction and restructuring relations across indefinite periods of time and space.
- The level of trust that individuals place in e-Mediated learning systems is likely to be influenced by their experiences with the abstract systems.
- The take-up rate of staff adopting e-Mediated learning is a critical issue.
- The use of e-Mediated learning as an educational tool poses pedagogical challenges.
- There are evident infrastructure, resourcing and cost issues.

The following section introduces one of our case study universities in order to examine these issues empirically. A case study strategy of investigation based on a combination of quantitative surveys and qualitative semi-structured face-to-face interviews was adopted in order to explore the factors influencing e-Mediated learning at the micro-level. Yin (1984) suggests that 'A case study is an empirical enquiry that investigates a contemporary phenomenon within its real life context when the boundaries between phenomenon and context are not clearly evident and in which multiple sources of evidence are used.'

Quantitative data were collected in the form of questionnaires from undergraduate level 2 and level 3 students in two modules that would be using e-Mediated learning technology for the first time. The questionnaire was administered to determine the current skills level of students and their expectations of using the technology. The qualitative research used semi-structured interviews to explore both students' and staff members' opinions of using the technology.

THE CASE STUDY

The case study organization is a traditional campus-based university in the UK. It is spread out over four campuses and has 17 departments, which belong to four main faculties. There are approximately:

- 9,000 full-time and 6,000 part-time undergraduate students
- 700 full-time and 1,000 part-time postgraduate students
- 200 hundred full-time and 150 part-time research students
- 1,600 international students from 110 countries
- the majority of students are under 24 years of age
- 800 academic staff members
- 150 research staff

The Virtual Learning Environment (VLE) was introduced campus-wide into the case study university in 2002 as part of a 5-year strategic plan. The plan places emphasis on encouraging all departments to provide high quality teaching and learning. As such, a centralized department had been specifically created as part of the university-wide initiative to promote effective teaching and learning practices, out of which the development of e-Mediated learning environments played a large part. At the start of the academic year September 2002, four VLE-based modules were under development. Of those, two were distance learning and entirely Web-based and the other two modules used e-Mediated learning as a support mechanism for face-to-face teaching. One year on, approximately 100 modules are under development in twelve academic departments. The level of activity differs in each department. Some modules are using only the very basic features (for example, the posting of lecture notes) and others are using it more actively by incorporating some of the more advanced tools such as the online assignment submission feature, quizzes and tests. Nevertheless, at this stage the VLE's main function is to support face-to-face teaching. The technology is used on a voluntary basis in all but one department and it is within this department (where usage is compulsory) that e-Mediated learning development is most actively taking place.

The results from the first questionnaire showed:

- the majority (96 per cent) of students were familiar with using email
- only 40 per cent of students had participated in a chat room discussion
- 54 per cent of the students had never contributed to a bulletin board discussion
- 96 per cent had downloaded or printed course materials from a computer network
- 91.3 per cent of the students had never submitted an assignment via a computer network
- 20.5 per cent of students were familiar with using a Web-based calendar
- 39 per cent of students were accustomed to using weblinks.

115

From the questionnaire it was evident that the students were more familiar with using basic functions like email and downloading or printing of course materials, however they were less familiar with some of the advanced tools within the VLE such as online assignment submission and chat room participation. This finding highlights that even if academic staff are willing to use e-Mediated technology, they are limited in the extent to which they can integrate the various tools into their module because the students may not have the skills to use the functions. The solution would be to provide students with more extensive guidelines on how to use the various functions within the VLE.

DISCUSSION

User skills

The results demonstrated that the students were more familiar with using the basic functions of e-Mediated learning. This indicates that for those who did not have the skills to use more of the advanced features of the VLE, training would need to be given before any of the advanced features are included in the Web site design. Some of the students were quite concerned with the general assumption that they are technologically literate. For example, if an element of online assessment was included, such students would be put at a disadvantage, as they are being tested on their technical ability that may have no relation to the module. According to one of the students:

> There is an assumption generally that students are very technical and they know exactly what they're doing with a PC and that's wrong. I know a lot of students that don't know what they're doing with a computer. In a way they can word process and do their essays but that would be it. You ask them about anything else and they don't have a clue. So I think it would be dangerous to assume that oh because they're students they'll know exactly what to do and they'll adapt, perhaps that's true for a number of students but then you've got quite a huge group that really are quite clueless when it comes to computing.

A problem with the email tool within the VLE also caused confusion among those students who were slightly less confident using the technology. In many instances it was presupposed that the mail in the VLE was the same as the university email and thus there was no need to check both. But in fact the mail tool within the VLE was restricted to sending mail to only those students and academic staff who were registered on that particular module. A link did not exist that enabled the mail to be forwarded from the student VLE mail box to the student university mail account.

The technical ability of the staff is another key issue that may prevent them from adopting the technology. For instance, availability of time plays a fundamental part in the willingness of academic staff to use e-Mediated learning as a delivery mechanism. Salomon (2002) has attempted to address the issue of time, suggesting that participants' experience of online time is a crucial factor in determining their rate of participation and competition of Internet courses. She argues that teaching methods need rethinking as both learners and moderators have difficulty in grasping the notion of 'Internet time' as the concepts of 'online' and 'offline' time are different. However, the applicability of her research within a traditional university setting can be questioned as significant differences exist between teaching in a 'distance mode' and in a traditional university setting. For example, the student make-up may differ in the sense that students opting for distance learning courses are usually employed adults and are taking the course to further their professional development, whereas the majority of students within a traditional university setting are full-time undergraduates.

Trust

Initial findings showed that many students were concerned with submitting their assignments via the VLE and felt that their papers might not actually reach the academic staff for grading. This highlights a critical issue of trust. As discussed earlier in the chapter, trust plays a fundamental role where expert systems are involved, as trust is transferred from the individual to the abstract system and as individuals we are coerced into placing faith into expert systems as we have bounded knowledge of the way in which these systems work (Giddens 2001).

Resource issues

Overall the students felt that there should be a balance between face-to-face and e-Mediated learning technology, and the technology should be used as a support tool rather than a substitute for face-to-face teaching. The value of technology lay more in bridging geographical distances, but this is only applicable for those students and academic staff members who have ready Internet access. It may very well be that if online chats/lectures are scheduled then many students will still come on to campus to access a PC, which defeats the purpose of having an online chat/lecture in the first instance. As campus facilities are limited in this respect, a serious lack of resources to facilitate this type of interaction has been exposed.

The preliminary case study findings revealed that there is a need for both additional computing facilities and support staff as developing module Web sites is a complex and time-consuming process. For example one of the interviewees suggested:

> I think staff themselves don't often get the support that they want as quickly as they want you know, they want us in their office and they contact us, we can't get there quick enough to support them in their development.

Therefore a lack of technical support in the developmental stages of using the technology can discourage staff from using e-Mediated learning technologies. In addition, some academic staff members expect technical support staff not only to develop the module Web site but to also maintain it:

> Some people even come with little hand written notes and then they want us to create that into a file and upload their file . . . I'd love to have a team of people that can take on anything any request and run with it and complete and deliver it, quality check, but we don't have those kinds of resources. It makes them very dependent on us if they want to change anything they have to come back and they don't learn and they're always sort of apprehensive about tampering with it but our whole aim is to make them more self sufficient so even if we do the major development work for them our aim is to enable them to do the maintenance at least.

Similar results were obtained across a range of departments in terms of staff willingness to develop e-Mediated learning systems. Some tutors said that until the computers in the labs are improved they cannot make effective use of the VLE, furthermore technical support staff have faced difficulties in finding adequate resources to hold training sessions:

> Because the labs are busy, we try to find time to have a session there with academic staff and we couldn't find a time slot, and even when they did allocate us half a lab students continually came in to use the other computers and we couldn't stop them they were preparing for exams at that time. They were saying look you've got to let us in, we've got to work, so we need enough labs and we need enough computers.

So although staff may be supportive of the technology, they are not as happy about developing the Web bases; once again, this highlights deficiencies in technical support and also in university computing facilities more generally.

Proliferation of systems

The fact that the VLE has been introduced on a voluntary basis is causing tension between the academic staff and students. There are currently various electronic systems where staff can place information relating to their modules. However, the students are concerned with coping with a number of different formats when it comes to accessing information about modules, which in turn affects their decisions about which modules to choose. Generally, the student looks at a study guide for each module and then builds up information on the assessment structure by looking at past exam papers and module content, but the proliferation of systems in use makes it difficult to collate all the necessary information. It was strongly suggested that all academic staff should use the same technology, leading some tutors to feel they are being unduly pressurized into using the VLE by students. One student suggested:

> When you've got something like the VLE which clearly has more features than the others, it really shouldn't be a question of having to drag the lecturers on one by one

kicking and screaming, it should really be them jumping for joy because it makes things that much easier.

The preliminary research findings indicate that much of the current activity in developing VLEs is as a support mechanism for face-to-face teaching. There is a certain amount of scepticism of the extent to which e-Mediated learning can be introduced within existing academic structures. In many cases, the desire for change does not actually materialize. In other words, the more exaggerated claims of some of the advocates of e-Mediated learning in teaching and learning have not been validated. The use of e-Mediated learning does not yet occupy a central role within higher education, suggesting that in this context the rhetoric is not matched by the reality. Dutta (2002) summarizes the issue quite well, suggesting that while the technology to support e-Mediated learning is now at a mature stage, the organizational processes involved in using the technology to deliver effective education lag behind and still need to be fully addressed and developed. As the research presented here demonstrates, it is not the technology itself creating the barriers but rather the absence of institutional commitment coupled with a lack of understanding of the various stakeholders' perspectives of change.

The key themes to emerge can be outlined as follows:

- The real value of e-Mediated learning is as a support tool for face-to-face teaching.
- The level of computing and human resources has a significant impact upon a tutor's decision to adopt e-Mediated learning.
- A certain amount of scepticism exists concerning the extent to which e-Mediated learning can be effectively introduced within existing academic structures, leading some staff to opt out.

CONCLUSION

This chapter has attempted to address some of the sociological issues arising from the integration of e-Mediated learning into higher education. The preliminary findings indicate that it tends to be regarded as a support mechanism for face-to-face teaching and thus does not play a central role at this stage. This suggests that the adoption of e-Mediated learning is gradual and incremental, requiring careful and detailed planning aside from the implementation of a purely technical solution. It is recommended that a student skills analysis is crucial before developing e-Mediated learning technologies and appropriate training or induction programmes then provided to introduce students to the system. For reasons of space this chapter has focused on the sociological dynamics of integrating e-Mediated learning into higher education, further research will develop other key themes such as organizational culture and change management in more detail.

QUESTIONS

Question 1

How might e-Learning initiatives differ between public and private sector organizations and why?

Feedback

The private sector focuses on profit making, whereas the public sector has a responsibility to its government and citizens, therefore public sector motivations may be determined by these responsibilities.

Question 2

What types of structures need to be in place to develop an e-Learning strategy within an organization?

Feedback

- technical infrastructure
- reliable and adequate technology
- senior management support
- staff willingness to adapt
- appropriate skills set
- ongoing support.

Question 3

How can higher educational institutions overcome barriers of adopting e-Learning technology?

Feedback

- through a gradual and incremental introduction of the new system
- ensuring that reliable resources are in place
- involving staff in the decision-making process
- providing adequate training and ongoing technical support.

GLOSSARY

e-Mediated learning technology   The utilization of Web-based, information or communications technology to help support teaching and learning.

Bulletin board   An electronic board where messages and documents can be posted and discussions can take place around specific topics.

Chat rooms   Real-time interaction within a virtual setting.

VLE   Virtual Learning Environment – a Web-based, flexible, integrated environment where technology can be used to foster enquiry, encourage discourse and collaboration.

Blackboard   A Content Management Tool (VLE).

WebCT   A Content Management Tool (VLE).

Lifelong learning   An attitude of mind in which a person engages throughout his or her life.

e-Delivery   Transporting data electronically.

Virtual university   An institution that has no physical presence, i.e. is free from time and spatial barriers.

e-Moderator   An online teacher or facilitator.

BIBLIOGRAPHY

Albury, D. (1996) 'End tenure, start tender', *Times Higher Education Supplement*, 11 October.

Brusilovsky, P. and Miller, P. (1999) 'Web-based testing for distance education', in P. De Bra and J. Leggett (eds) Proceedings of WebNet'99, World Conference of the WWW and Internet, Honolulu, Hawaii, 24–30 October, AACE, pp. 149–54.

Cornford, J. (1999) 'The virtual university is . . . the university made concrete?', *Information, Communication and Society*, 3, 4: 508–25.

Cornford, J. and Pollock, N. (2000) 'Theory and practice of the virtual university', *Ariadne*, issue 24. Available at http://www.ariadne.ac.uk/issue24/virtual-universities/intro.html

CVCP and HEFCE (2000) *The Business of Borderless Education: UK Perspectives*, A study commissioned by the Committee for Vice Chancellors and Principals (CVCP) and the Higher Education Funding Council for England (HEFCE), London.

Drucker, P. (1997) *The Organization of the Future*, San Francisco: Jossey-Bass.

Durkheim, E. (2003) 'Functionalist perspectives', in S. Best, *A Beginner's Guide to Social Theory*, London: Sage.

Dutta, S. (2002) 'Integrating online education with executive management', keynote speech at the 8th International Conference on Technology Supported Learning and Training, Berlin, 27–29 November.

Fetherston, T. (2001) 'Pedagogical challenges for the World Wide Web', *Educational Technology Review*, 9, 1: http://www.aace.org/pus/etr/fetherston.cfm

Giddens, A. (1996) *The Consequences of Modernity*, Cambridge: Polity Press.

Giddens, A. (2001) *Sociology*, 4th edn, Cambridge: Polity Press.

Goodyear, P. (1999) 'New technology in higher education', in A. Eurelings (ed.) *Understanding the Innovation Process in Integrating Information and Communications Technology in Higher Education*, Deventer: Kluwer, pp. 107–36.

Goddard, J., Robins, K., Webster, F. and Charles, D. (1999) *Space, Place and the Virtual University: Full Report of the Research Activities and Results*, London: ESRC.

Grewal, S. K. (2002) 'Experiences of using WebCT', paper presented at Best Practices for Promoting E Learning Seminar in the European Union, Luxembourg, 4 December.

Grewal, S. K. (2003) 'The social dynamics of integrating e-mediated learning into traditional UK universities', paper presented at E-Learn 2003 World Conference on E-Learning in Corporate, Government, Healthcare and Higher Education, Phoenix, Arizona, USA, 7–11 November, Association for the Advancement of Computing in Education.

121

Gunstone, R. F. and Mitchell, I. J. (1998) 'Metacognition and conceptual change', in J. J. Mintzes, J. H. Wandersee and J. D. Novak (eds) *Teaching Science for Understanding*, San Diego: Academic Press, pp. 134–63.

Jackson, R. H. (2002) 'Defining learning-different shades of "Online": a definition protocol', Web Learning Resources Library. Available http://www.outreach.utk.edu/weblearning/

Kaur, A. (2002) 'The evolvement of Open University Malaysia's "E" learning model', paper presented at the Online Educa Conference, Berlin, November–December.

Kelly, J. (2001) 'Sun chosen as web partner for virtual university', *Financial Times*, http://www.ft.com October 19.

Lambert, T. (2002) 'UK e-Universities world-wide delivering the best of UK education online', paper presented at Online Educa Conference, Berlin, November–December.

Laurillard, D. (2001) 'The e University: what have we learned'?, *The International Journal of Management Education*, 1, 2: 3–7.

Laurillard, D. M., and Stratfold, M. (2000) 'Affordances for learning in a non-linear narrative medium', *Journal of Interactive Media in Education*, 2: 1–17.

Liber, O., Holyfield, S., Richardson, P. and Smart, C. (2002) 'The BA in the Internet, learning and organizations: a peer to peer approach to distance learning', paper presented at the Networked Learning Conference, University of Sheffield.

Marx, K. (2003) 'Theorising capitalism', in S. Best, *A Beginner's Guide to Social Theory*, London: Sage.

Miller, P. (1999) 'The CTI and learning technology in the past decade: the director's cut', *Active Learning*, 11, December: 41–42.

Orsini-Jones, M. (1999) 'From reflective learners to reflective lecturers via WebCT', *Active Learning*, 10, July: 32–8.

Pollock, N. (2000) 'The virtual university as timely and accurate information', *Information, Communication and Society*, 3, 3: 1–17.

Rosenberg, M. J. (2001) *e-Learning: Strategies for Delivering Knowledge in the Digital Age*, London: McGraw-Hill.

Salmon, G. (2000) 'The boundary hunters', paper presented at the Online Educa Conference, Berlin, November–December.

Salmon, G. (2001) 'e-moderating: the key to successfully teaching and learning online', paper presented at the e-Learning Summit, Sydney, August.

Salmon, G. (2002) 'Internet land: where the sun never sets', paper presented at the 8th International Conference on Technology Supported Learning and Training, Berlin, 27–29 November.

Sosabowski, M. H., Herson, K. and Lloyd, A. W. (1998) 'Enhancing learning and teaching quality: integration of networked learning technologies into undergraduate module,' *Active Learning*, 8, July: 26–30.

Stainfield, J. (1997) 'Using IT to manage 3rd year module', *Active Learning*, 6, July: 1–5.

Timms, D., Crompton, P., Booth, S. and Allen, P. (1997) 'The implementation of learning technologies: the experience of Project Varsetile', *Active Learning*, 6, July: 1–7.

Weber, M. (1976) in Giddens, A. (1996) *The Consequences of Modernity*, Cambridge: Polity Press.

Yin, R. K. (1984) *Case Study Research, Design and Methods*, London: Sage.

e-Government: from utopian rhetoric to practical realism

NOAH CURTHOYS

KEY LEARNING POINTS

After completing this chapter you will have an understanding of:

- The scale and scope of e-Government activities in the UK and USA
- How significant change projects can be managed
- The extent to which practical e-Government is living up to the early rhetoric

INTRODUCTION

> We are being swept up into a powerful new technology revolution that offers the
> promise of a great social transformation.
>
> (Jeremy Rifkin 2000)

Since the mid-1990s, the adoption of Internet technology in the public sector has driven
a growing wave of institutional reform. This has culminated in an array of portals, targets
and re-engineering that is now known as e-Government. As the rhetoric of change has
shifted from technology to management, so too the scope of performance and policy
intentions has developed; governments increasingly see the Internet as more than a 'bolt-
on' to corporate processes. In some cases it has become the start of a 'step-change' in
public service delivery.

Much of this has evolved in a delicate environment, often linked to one particular
party. In the UK, and as part of the modernization agenda of New Labour, e-Government
often represented a change in status for government technology. The language of
privatization had been superseded by that of service delivery and of a leaner, tougher
machinery of government. For the US, the 'Reinventing Government' programme of
the Clinton–Gore era has morphed into the five-point 'management agenda' of the

Bush–Cheney administration. Although ideological, it is no longer associated with just one party.

With regard to the language of the environment, these countries have been at the forefront of e-Government and each demonstrate a clear move from bald rhetoric to concrete reality. This chapter seeks to outline such a transformation, ranging through rhetorical e-Commerce mimicry, to the more modern reality of better service delivery and stronger government. The quotation from Jeremy Rifkin may have concerned how technology affects society, but his words demonstrate exactly how far these ideas travel: it is equally true of the e-Government agenda.

As it stands, e-Government does indeed represent a new stage for the public sector, at least, and increasingly defines how it fits with the realities of the Information Age. But it is an example of the optimism of the pre-9/11 economy too. This is a messy process of difficult choices that has led to some unexpected results. The aim here is briefly to outline an underlying story of change. Some key conceptual frameworks will be explored to demonstrate how far the new agenda reaches, but this is at heart a tale of technological rhetoric giving way to the demands of practical government.

ORIGINS OF E-GOVERNMENT

Although it is no longer accurate to say that e-Government is a new phenomenon, its recent origins do mean that long-term analysis is still questionable. This affects definitions as much as it does branding and any understanding of the practical reality. It is safe to say, however, that e-Government combines key characteristics of technological development and public administration (see Table 8.1). Basically, it is a bipolar phenomenon: it concentrates on customer service (front-office), and organizational structures (back-office).

Much of the appeal of e-Government is based on the integration of IT capacity, primarily Web sites, intranets and databases, to allow self-service via an IT medium. For government, such relations could range from the traditional online channels (portals and referral links) to **PDAs**, **instant messaging services** (SMS, iMode or IRC) or even **avatars** and intermediaries. What counts in this case is the presence of an electronic framework within which the state interacts with citizens.

The flip-side of this is the back-office element. For this, e-Government technology is largely server based, often assuming common protocols and centralized access. Ultimately, it is 'the use of technology to enhance the access to and delivery of government services to benefit citizens, business partners and employees' (Silcock 2001). In short, some of e-Government is akin to e-Commerce, but set within a multi-institutional and public setting with somewhat different expectations, but often similar financial and technological requirements.

This was a picture of straightforward technological and organizational change. The initial concept is that of revolutionized customer/citizen contact, and re-engineered

Table 8.1 *Bipolar model of e-Government*

	Front-office	Back-office
Customer service	Helplines, payments, advice, forms, personal caseworkers, etc.	Information technologies
Workforce	Customer service	IT, HR, pensions and benefits admin, shared office space, etc.
Intra-government	N/A	IT, shared information, shared office space, databases, etc.

institutional structures and working methods. In many ways, this view of change is inseparable from the wider e-Business phenomena.

Yet e-Government was originally designed as 'digital government' by the US-based National Science Foundation (NSF, see http://www.nsf.gov/pubs/1998/nsf98121/nsf98121.pdf). Following on from an earlier report, *Toward a Digital Government in the 21st Century*, the NSF invited reflection of, *inter alia*, the use of Internet technology to enhance government service provision. Interestingly, digital government was in many ways an approach that had more in common with Al Gore's National Performance Review than it does with today's e-Government reality. The aim was to focus on effectiveness in government, and this was confirmed with the publication of a key workshop's findings on the matter (Dawes 1999). This was in effect the first rhetorical branding of e-Government, albeit in the more academic guise of digital government. The host, Center for Technology in Government at SUNY, provided six recommendations, most of which concerned methodology and funding, but not structural concerns. At this stage, e-Government was still a vocabulary of possibility and conceptual frameworks, albeit one with a spirit of transformative change that was as yet unmatched by reality.

UNITED STATES: REINVENTING E-GOVERNMENT

As the original focus of digital governance thought and action, the US is in many ways the 'mother of e-Government'. At all stages of development it has been central in leading change forward, and as such is justifiably ranked highly in terms of development (Accenture 2003). However, this deserves a caveat. Although development continues apace, the actual provision of e-Government has remained somewhat behind its Anglophone and Nordic colleagues, at least at federal level. There are several reasons for this, but to understand the context it is first necessary to outline some of the recent e-Government landmarks of the US environment.

With the NSF in effect incubating e-Government, it is tempting to focus on their role as the most crucial in sparking US development. However, wider public management concerns gave the real political drive to actually build digital government. The 1990s saw considerable public debate on core government issues – trade relations (mainly with Japan), foreign policy (the post-Cold War identity questions) and the shape of federal government itself (Ross Perot, Newt Gingrich's *Contract With America*, http://www.house.gov/house/Contract/CONTRACT.html). One seminal agenda was the reinventing government ideas first put forward at the start of the decade, and indeed, at the beginning of the new Clinton–Gore administration. Focused on developing entrepreneurial spirit in government at all levels, the idea was to unshackle the restrictive bureaucracy of an industrial world as information technologies revolutionized the use of communications and data (Osborne and Gaebler 1992).

This caught the *Zeitgeist* somewhat and massively influenced the review of public services led by Vice President Gore. The National Performance Review (NPR, see http://acts.poly.edu/cd/npr/np-realtoc.html) was the first plank in 'modernizing government' reforms, and as such provided the political context within which the NSF later launched the digital government programme. It is worth noting that the rhetoric of this agenda was highly linked to the small-business, flexible-working approach of the private sector – indeed of the venture capitalists that ultimately fuelled the dotcom boom.

In terms of e-Government, what this led to in turn was the establishment of a federal links portal, FirstGov (www.firstgov.gov) that acted as a gateway to central government sites. What is important in terms of e-Government development is not what was built (Singapore had long before built a credible version of FirstGov) but the methods and political prioritization given to the project. FirstGov was mandated to be completed within 90 days and even now acts as the linchpin of online federal government, at least for the citizen.

The rhetoric of e-Government was in this case extremely presidential and tied to the heart of government reform. President Clinton personally drove the agenda through the General Services Administration and gave e-Government a legitimacy from the top that had previously been lacking in its language. In his use of political capital to support a project that was quite new to the Washington world, Clinton also massively promoted the underlying environment of FirstGov – namely e-Government in general. It is important to highlight that FirstGov was not the pioneer of government Web sites or e-Government provision in general. As a links page it is in many ways restricted to the bottom level of e-Government (providing information), and each department had Web sites in place long before the portal was built. However, it was the first attempt to consolidate the focus of US citizens in their interaction with the state. Crucially, it was also the first considered branding of e-Government ideals at federal level.

As it now stands, the transition to a more real e-Government is underway, and is largely the result of the Bush administration's *President's Management Agenda*. As a core philosophy of government, and enforced by the Executive Office's Office of Management and Budget (OMB), this contains several items about the procurement and management of federal services and the efficient running of bureaucracy. Some of this has been highly controversial, as with compulsory tendering of services. None the less, e-Government is firmly placed as one of the five key areas of focus for the federal government, and continued excellence is promoted by the OMB's Quicksilver projects which highlight the most successful 25 e-Government initiatives in the US.

UNITED KINGDOM: REBUILDING E-GOVERNMENT

Next to the US, the UK has faced some considerably different issues, albeit with similar underlying themes. The UK's e-Government agenda has been one of the most high profile (and scrutinized) to date. Despite a heritage dating back to the Open Government concept of the Major administration, the UK was not initially at the cutting edge of e-Government development, with efforts in Singapore, the US, Denmark, Sweden, Australia and Canada generally starting first.

However, the election of the Labour administration in 1997 did somewhat change this situation, and relatively soon after, policy developed rapidly. Unlike the US, the initial burst of reform concentrated on technology rather than the business culture of Whitehall. This was not an immediate 'reinvention' of the civil service, and it is notable that the lead agency set up in the late 1990s to pioneer e-Government – the Office of the e-Envoy (OeE) – has achieved much praise around its position as a technical coordinator for standards rather than as a **change agent**.

The major landmarks of this time were first the Modernizing Government paper, and more specifically the e-Government strategy, both issued by the Cabinet Office (2000). Taking forward the principle of joined-up government and electronic services, these set in motion the idea of a step-change in service delivery. In addition, the rhetoric was by this point very much moving into a more commercialized, dotcom language, with targets and goals set at 100 per cent online delivery by first 2008 and then more dramatically by 2005. The initial way forward for this was with a FirstGov-inspired portal.

THINK POINT

Is the Internet the only way 'into' e-Government?

Feedback. While the Internet tends to group key services into single areas (think amazon.com, LastMinute.com or even HotMail) the point about e-Government is that it enables different contact. Instead of needing paper forms to apply for welfare benefits, you can instead go to a service like JobCentrePlus in the UK which provides trained assistance to take you through applications and welfare advice (which may well include electronic systems). Likewise, as discussed in Chapter 3, mobile phones can enable access to specific government services, or even smart cards (like the wireless Oyster travel pass in London) are another contact point.

Lying at the centre of the UK's e-Government agenda, this portal – UKOnline – acts as the main channel to online services. Like FirstGov, the concept is to provide information and links to further, more in-depth sites. For this, the site assumed the role of the old Open Government search engine, albeit with a tighter remit and funding. Indeed, the emphasis here is on strategy, with the OeE originally placing UKOnline as the keystone of e-Government planning. What differentiates this site from its transatlantic counterpart is the additional service element offered by the Government Gateway. To provide secure authentication for government services, the UK has developed an underlying Government Gateway, which is XML-based. This is a national initiative, following a largely consensual approach designed to incorporate all levels of government, and to broaden the overall impact of e-Government. With three initial areas (tax returns, tax credits and land data) the Gateway provides the UK with a transactional portal through which e-Government can be provided.

Funding itself has also been more forthcoming in the UK. Whilst the US has been forced through the congressional budgetary process to take a top-slicing approach (i.e. in 2002 approximately 10 per cent of IT budgets were sought by the OMB for reallocation on e-Government), the UK will have reportedly concentrated £7.5 billion by 2005/6 (Kable 2003). This includes over £1 billion on criminal justice and £2 billion on health.

However, there have been some notable issues for the UK e-Government agenda. For example, whilst procurement and project management have not been too high on the political agenda in the US, for the UK, successive failures of high-profile IT projects have seriously impacted on public perceptions of e-Government. This started with online tax filing with the Inland Revenue, and then moved on through problems with passports to a tax credit breakdown. Even as straightforward an information project as the National Archives' 1901 Census Web site (with a high public interest factor) proved too difficult to engineer for initial demand.

This has entailed an increasing interest in e-Government-related issues by agencies like the Office of Government Commerce (part of HM Treasury) and the Office of the Deputy Prime Minister. The former deals with best practice issues and procurement, whilst the latter has a remit that includes e-Democracy and local e-Government. It is worth noting that the dotcom rhetoric and key players have evolved over time to be replaced by much more potent branches of government that are specialist business units, and speak the language of results.

CONCEPTUALIZING E-GOVERNMENT

Whilst practical experience in the US and UK demonstrates the rhetorical shifts of recent years, theory remains oddly distanced from practice. Unlike e-Business, there is very little literature on e-Government, even now, and no overriding theory of the phenomenon. It is widely seen to signify change for government, but the depth and scope of this remains uncertain. This chapter holds that as a change process within the public sector, e-Government clearly represents a significant and international reform that is perhaps comparable to the Reagan and Thatcher years in the UK and US.

Although the depth of reform may not be as biting as that experienced in the 1980s and 1990s, for example, the significance of e-Government change is hard to ignore. A key question that arises is whether or not the technological changes inherent in the Internet are an extension to these previous administrative reforms. To some extent, this would see e-Government as the final instalment in public sector reform for the foreseeable future – the conclusion, perhaps, to Thatcherite New Public Management.

Although this is one interpretation, a premise of this chapter is that despite much overblown rhetoric, e-Government is indeed more crucial than being a simple endnote to past achievements. With the concentration on effective organization and the step-change in customer service provision already seen within e-Business, e-Government is indeed more akin to a radical leap in government operations. Perhaps it can be equated to the major shifts associated with both the welfare state and privatization – the point is that it is at the least of a similar level of change.

It has been argued that the reforms of the 1980s were nothing more than a reactive process (Pollitt and Bouckaert 2000), or in some cases a 'done deal' of finished reform (Ferlie 1996). For e-Government, this is a heritage of change that has in many ways laid out a foundation that has enabled technological change. It is notable that the states profiled here are some of the leading proponents of e-Government *and* the leading promoters of New Public Management (NPM) styled reform. The recent concentration on results, willingness to invoke and adopt private sector techniques and use of corporate language, rhetoric and concepts, all points to the governance mindset that is mirrored within e-Government programmes.

THINK POINT

Is e-Government limited to the industrialized world? Can you think of good examples from other countries?

Feedback. Some examples might include the ID card system in Singapore, the voting system in Brazil, or the city of Seoul.

Yet the intellectual environment of e-Government goes beyond this rhetorical heritage. For the purposes of this chapter, three particular strands of thinking come together. There are others worthy of consideration, but these are most relevant, perhaps, to the e-Government story as it relates to the rhetorical context. First, the broader information and legal analysis provided by Lawrence Lessig. Second, the evolution of NPM has been joined by a corollary as New Institutional Politics emerges as an alternative framework of analysis. This is supported to some extent by long-standing bureaucratic politics theories. Third, a basic but contextual matrix proposed via the iSociety programme (www.theisociety.net) at The Work Foundation think-tank. As an e-Government theorist, Lessig offers little of direct relevance. His background as a US constitutional lawyer advising on issues like the anti-trust position of Microsoft or cyberspace copyright issues does not immediately register as a focal point for e-Government conceptualization. However, what is of relevance are his initial ideas concerning institutional form within the Internet.

With reference largely to the architecture of the Internet – the skeleton – Lessig paints a picture of tension between control and freedom (Lessig 1999). In this world what counts is how the code of Internet life is regulated to gain the best balance between the two. Too much regulation inhibits the enabling factors; too little and abuses of national laws eclipse the benefits. For Lessig, there are three disabling factors in the proper consideration of how best to build this code – namely, limits to judicial action; legislative scope; and the underlying concepts of the digital age. For e-Government this means a major challenge. How best lawfully to regulate and analyse the major shifts in public sector administration without recourse to these three areas? For the US, constitutional pressures inhibit e-Government. The most visible area is the use of personal data by federal agencies. Privacy considerations inhibit the data storing of transactional services expected by citizens. For the UK, there are similar issues, not resulting from prohibition, but from speed of delivery. Data protection, freedom of information and data handling remain poorly supported areas of statute that require (or have required) considerable upgrades.

The point here is that Lessig provides a critique of Internet planning, and argues for a concentration on the skeletal code of what is built. This is a crucial lesson for e-Government; without getting the public sector code right, both the UK and US may well be creating a constitutional black hole for the future shape of government. Although Lessig is concentrating on the broader realm of the information society, this legal analysis is crucial to both the rhetoric and reality of today's e-Government.

By contrast, Jan-Erik Lane provides both a traditional account of NPM (Lane 2000) and a more extensive analysis of the wider NIP, or New Institutional Politics (Lane and Ersson 2000). Both of these provide a political science framework within which e-Government can be slotted, although it is the latter which is of most use. With the NPM of the 1980s, both the US and UK witnessed considerable change focused on decentralizing executive activity (i.e. benefits payments), privatization (i.e. sale of state-owned assets like telecoms companies) and a wholesale reduction in both public expenditure and investment.

This background is likely to be heavily influential to e-Government initiatives. However, Lane's core conclusions about NIP bear an increasing relevance to the concerns of electronic service delivery. Like Lessig, Lane argues that constitutionalism is crucial to effective government operations. For the NIP, this means one of two outcomes. On the one hand, there could be a thin constitutionalism in which flexible rule-making and variable relations between government, legislature and judiciary dominate. On the other hand, there could be a thick **constitutionalism**, in which relations within the architecture of government are heavily prescribed in formal constitutions.

In addition, NIP holds that institutions are crucial to public life in that they structure behaviour and determine outcomes. This may seem self-evident, but within a fast-moving field like e-Government, institutional strength has a disproportionate influence on behaviour. Combined with the stated form of constitutionalism, the existing government set-up can massively influence the development of e-Government itself.

This has already been seen in the US where rigid forms of budgeting relations between Congress and the incumbent president have delayed investment in e-Government. By contrast, the UK which operates under a more flexible 'thin' system has been able to pump money into the area. This hasn't necessarily guaranteed success, but it does demonstrate where NIP provides a key analysis for those focusing on e-Government. Other issues concerning the role of bureaucracy are important (Halperin 1974; Peters 2001), and help broaden any consideration of e-Government beyond the technical.

The final framework is a basic development matrix, in which e-Government is positioned as both an ideological, historical and institutional development with clear defining boundaries (Curthoys and Crabtree 2003). This doesn't claim that the reforms are identical in each state, rather that a broader context exists in which e-Government change can be analysed. Of note in Table 8.2 is the position e-Government holds as an approach instead of a mechanism, which implies greater rhetorical clout, and with a defined goal, namely to improve public services. Obviously, this is focused on the UK, but similar positioning can be given for the US and the wider developed world.

Table 8.2 e-Government framework

	1945–51	1979–90	1997–
Political leader	Attlee	Thatcher	Blair
Theorist	Keynes	Hayek/ Friedman	Castells
Approach	Bureaucracy	New public management	e-Government
Mechanism	Nationalization	Privatization	Various
Power shift	State centralization	Market freedom, state centralization	Technological innovation, decentralization?
Purpose	Social security	Enterprise creation	Renewed public services

Source: Curthoys and Crabtree (2003)

FROM RHETORIC TO REALITY

Theory and practice may well be two sides of the same coin, and for e-Government there remains some distance between the two. The arguments above all touch on the scope for implementing e-Government change, and it should be stressed that this has been played out in the rhetoric and branding of those services. Indeed, the transition from rhetoric to reality encapsulates some of the broader themes of e-Business reorganization and social upheaval unearthed by the Internet.

Yet, on one level the debate surrounding e-Government has never really changed since that first branding of digital government. The bulk of interested media outlets and several government agencies continue to see e-Government as first and foremost a technological phenomenon. The rhetoric has until very recently been as utopian as such a stance would normally suggest. The descriptions of change are far-ranging, frequently climbing up towards 'transformative' or 'paradigm-shifting'. There is little scope here for either modesty or underselling.

Despite the gap between this rhetoric of change and the reality of e-Government detailed above, each state has undergone a similar process, often copying, learning and leap-frogging from each others' experience. As a public domain, government is often placed within difficult constraints as expenditure, innovation and service provision are tackled. Unlike with traditional business, tough strategic decisions cannot simply be mandated given the consultative and democratic nature of policy-making. The speed of reaction inherent to the private sector still remains some way off – government is after all a provider of monopoly services in which it sets its own targets.

None the less, there are three broad themes which seem to have emerged from the e-Government story in much of the Anglophone world. In terms of rhetoric, e-Government has passed through the initial round of academic discussion, thought and abstract consideration. The image of technologically adept government has long been touted as a theoretical consideration (Bellamy and Taylor 1998; Heeks 1999), and the dry but optimistic ideas of building digital government was a fundamental stage in the creation of a core identity about **social connectedness** and a better quality of governance.

Following that, e-Government appears to have undergone a widespread commercial-ization as the concepts of e-Business permeated into the sales and consultancy culture of the big corporate organizations. Dotcom hype was not limited to the private sector, and even the branding of e-Government has been heavily influenced by the late-1990s world, as the creation of an 'e-Envoy' in the UK illustrates. Indeed, it was at this point that the very term 'e-Government' was first used. To this day there are no particular conventions on spelling or presentation, with variants ranging from 'electronic government' and 'E-Government' to the more widely used 'eGovernment' or 'e-Government'.

However, and of most interest to this issue, it is the third stage which seems to have radicalized that agenda. The academic talk and commercial promises have now given way to a greater realization of the depth of work needed to actually build e-Services. The machinery of government in each state has required much funding to adapt to Internet technology, and the value-added concept of e-Government is in many ways the last benefit to be realized.

This third stage could perhaps be referred to as 'normalization' as government returns to a more traditional sceptical and cut-throat approach to funding. On another level, though, it is an indicator of the growing demand for effective service delivery. The traditional rhetoric of 'levers of power' in government increasingly includes discussion of results-focused e-services. In other words, e-Government has become a reality of power-politics within the bureaucracy itself – not just a management fad or utopian ideal.

What this means is that the rhetoric of electronic change and organizational reform has come some way over the past decade. Perhaps this reflects the internationalization of the agenda, as the original US-focused academic arguments have broadened into a sharper commercial (and multinational) use of consultancy ideologies. Most recently, the dreamy hopes for utopian reform have been seriously displaced by an increasingly voracious demand for effective policy.

THINK POINT

Can you think of any practical examples of e-Government that you use in everyday life?

Feedback. Some examples might include welfare payments (benefits) or transport permits (e.g. the London 'congestion charge').

What were originally targets have become serious hurdles; what was once a vision of efficient government has now become a crucial plank in security efforts. To sum this up somewhat pithily, digital government is dead, and e-Government is working hard to catch up to service delivery goals. Just how hard that is, is evidenced below (Figure 8.1), taken from the most recent Accenture survey of e-Government maturity. It is notable that of the four groupings (service transformation, mature delivery, service availability, basic capability), both the US and UK – despite heavy investment or pioneering work – still remain in the second category.

CONCLUSIONS

Consultancy charts and theories of government notwithstanding, e-Government has come a long way. Despite several core differences in the base rhetoric, there are some underlying themes which this chapter has tried to tease out. First, early e-Government has been characterized within the industry in breathlessly optimistic terms. On the one

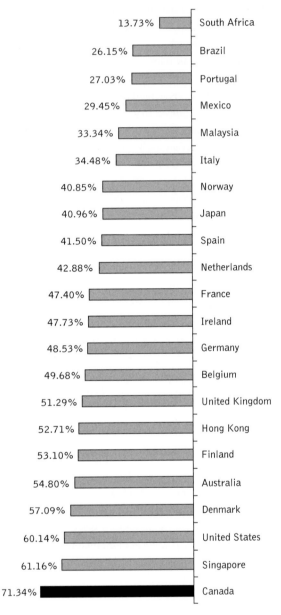

Figure 8.1 *e-Government maturity*
Source: Accenture Report (2003)

hand, there has been the persistent recourse to utopian language as first academic vision and then corporate interest fuelled the agenda. As with much of the dotcom era, the concepts, descriptions and hopes have been wildly inflated in many ways, and core business operability often overlooked.

Second, there has been a discernable power shift since the early days of design and implementation, in which the original lead agencies have steadily transferred control of the agenda to more powerful departments and organizations. In many ways this was somewhat predictable as existing areas of government reclaim the area, or as the e-Government policies are joined to wider reform movements. None the less, e-Government is more visibly led now by parts of government that have more clout, in both the US and UK.

Third, strategic investment for e-Government, particularly in the UK, has now largely led to greater demand for results. Likewise, where dotcom dreams once predicted year-on-year investment in government IT capacity, in the post-9/11 US, efficiencies are increasingly felt. For the US this makes little real difference since original federal funding was never high. For the UK, the provision of what was in effect seed capital for IT, has given way to more long-term investment.

The net result of these three issues means that e-Government rhetoric has largely caught up with the reality. Where change management and organizational design and redesign were always likely to be the key to success in this area, the language of government and vendors has finally moved on from the Brave New World of open possibilities. Service delivery is the reality of technology in the public sector across the Western world, but especially within financially stretched central governments.

This means that for the first time since the seminal NSF thinking on digital government, expectations and likely outcomes are finally drawing together. What was a widely disparaged gulf is now barely visible. Credit for this is debateable, but can perhaps be laid at the door of practical frustration (e-Government was not living up to its utopian marketing), international events (September 11 and the ensuing conflicts in Central Asia and the Middle East), and the more gritty realism of lower growth and some recession-branded economies.

Ultimately, the end result is positive for future e-Government development. Previously, the reforms were set-up to fail as the rhetoric of change was unreachable. Today's atmosphere is far more realistic, and ironically e-Government is likely to be the biggest beneficiary of such lowered expectations.

QUESTIONS

Question 1

Is e-Government and e-Business the same thing? Has all the dotcom rhetoric also affected the public sector?

Feedback

You might want to consider who the 'customers' of government are, and what competition agencies face. Also, are issues like marketing, client management and brand identities relevant for government?

Question 2

How does e-Government affect policies like decentralization or devolution?

Feedback

This depends on the style of e-Government – it is not a simple, one-size-fits-all product. In the US and UK, the technology is based on decentralized information, dispersed via Internet and network infrastructure. However, the effect is to centralize control, with single access points (portals) and identities (authenticated log-on). Devolved areas like Scotland run e-Government, as do national agencies like the Department for Transportation in Washington DC. However, the design is not yet finished.

Question 3

Do you think that electronic services are affected by the way in which a country is run?

Feedback

While the technology might be the same, even small differences can have a major impact on electronic services. For example, in the US it is much harder to collect personal data (normally as 'cookies'), which in turn makes it difficult to personalize e-Government. In the UK it is much easier, and customized log-on pages are therefore easier to provide.

Question 4

To what extent was e-Government a product of the dotcom era, rather than a public management reform?

Feedback

This is difficult to answer as change is still happening. However, it is fair to say that only now in 2004 is e-Government being seen as part of public sector management – both in the US and the UK. It is important to remember that e-Government is as radical as e-Business, and the big changes concern citizens and employees first, rather than 'circuits and wires'. It is a product of government change, rather than the dotcom era.

GLOSSARY

Avatar   An animated Web site figure increasingly used (particularly by online banking services) to handle standard customer queries.

Change agent   An individual (s) responsible for promoting and implementing change.

Constitutionalism   Governmental culture where a written constitution acts as a genuine constraint on state activity.

I-mode   Wireless Internet system used in Japan, Taiwan, Germany, France, Holland, Belgium, Spain and Italy (created by phone company DoCoMo).

IRC   Internet Relay Chat (e.g. MSN or Yahoo Messenger, ICQ or AIM).

P2P   Peer-to-peer (e.g. Kazaa, Napster, MSN Messenger).

PDA   Personal Digital Assistant – an integrated electronic organizer, telephone and Internet connection device such as the BlackBerry or Palm Pilot.

Social connectedness   1 (Social network analysis) this relates to the quantity and structure of ties between people; 2 (social capital) this refers to aggregate ties in a community (e.g. a broader public good). For further discussion of these see http://theworkfoundation.com/research/isociety/social_capital_main.jsp.

BIBLIOGRAPHY

Accenture Report (2003) *eGovernment Leadership: Engaging the Customer*, US: Accenture.

Bellamy, C. and Taylor, J. (1998) *Governing in the Information Age*, Buckingham: Open University Press.

The Cabinet Office (Spring 2000) *E-Government: A Strategic Framework for Public Services in the Information Age*, London: The Stationery Office.

Curthoys, N. and Crabtree, J. (2003) *SmartGov: Renewing Electronic Government for Improved Service Delivery*, London: The Work Foundation.

Dawes, S., Bloniarz, P., Kelly, K. and Fletcher, P. (March 1999) *Some Assembly Required: Building a Digital Government for the 21st Century*, Albany, NY: Center for Technology in Government (NSF Grant 99–181).

Ferlie, E., Ashburner, L., Fitzgerald, L. and Pettigrew, A. (1996) *The New Public Management in Action*, Oxford: Oxford University Press.

Halperin, M. (1974) *Bureaucratic Politics and Foreign Policy*, Washington: The Brookings Institution.

Heeks, R. (1999) *Reinventing Government in the Information Age*, London: Routledge.

Kable Report (2003) *Cost Savings from e-Government in the UK 2003*, London: Kable Ltd.

Lane, J. (2000) *New Public Management*, London: Routledge.

Lane, J. and Ersson, S. (2000) *The New Institutional Politics*, London: Routledge.

Lessig, L. (1999) *Code and Other Laws of Cyberspace*, New York: Basic Books.

Osborne, D. and Gaebler, T. (1992) *Reinventing Government*, New York: Plume.

Peters, B.G. (2001) *The Politics of Bureaucracy*, London: Routledge.

Pollit, C. and Bouckaert, G. (2000) *Public Management Reform*, Oxford: Oxford University Press.

Rifkin, J. (2000) *The End of Work*, London: Penguin.

Silcock, R. (2001) 'What is E-Government?', *Parliamentary Affairs*, 54.

e-Retail: paradoxes for suppliers and consumers

CHARLES DENNIS AND OLIVER RICHARDSON

KEY LEARNING POINTS

After completing this chapter you will have an understanding of:

- How to identify the purpose of a Web site
- How companies can use their Web sites to educate customers
- The reality of online activity for suppliers
- The extent to which the Internet can satisfy shopping motivations
- The positive and negative effects of e-Retailing on social exclusion

INTRODUCTION

The years 1998 to 2002 have seen a 320 per cent increase in the number of Web sites, at the same time as the number of business failures associated with Web-based companies has increased dramatically. These two sets of facts would appear to contradict each other and they provide opposing perspectives on the reality versus rhetoric debate. In this chapter, we will examine the overt reasons why companies have Web sites. This will involve examination of the sites of small businesses, especially those involved in areas of production in rural regions – those types of business that would appear to have most to benefit from expanding their trading horizons by bringing themselves to the attention of a wider public. This examination will differentiate such sites according to their offerings: information; product marketing; sales; service provision; and attempts to attract 'real' visitors to their shop or factory. In the first section we will examine the purposes for which businesses have designed their Web sites and in the second, what actual effect it has had on consumers.

The uses of the Web will be examined by means of an analysis of the Web sites of a number of small rural industries – vineyards, smokeries, herb and other gardens, cheese manufacturers and woodworkers, in order to ascertain to what uses the Web is being put. These industries must have believed at least some of the e-Economy rhetoric; otherwise the sites would not be there. Businesses seek to maintain and expand their markets in order to survive and the Web is one method that has been 'sold' to them as a method by which they can do so. In the latter part of the chapter, we shall examine the reality of how these Web developments are currently affecting high street shopping, and assess the extent to which they really do benefit all sections of the community. In addition to these offerings by suppliers, we will examine the benefits (or otherwise) that such sites bring to potential customers, including groups of people whose homes are outside the areas serviced by physical entities such as shops and banks. The last 10 years has seen a gradual withdrawal of these facilities from many areas – Barclays closed 171 branches in 2000 alone and the potential for the Web-faced services to fill this vacuum and to assist the disadvantaged merits close examination. One might almost ask 'Is the Internet the shopping mall of the future?' The rhetoric suggests that it is. The reality may be considerably different, as we demonstrate below.

INTERNET USE BY BUSINESS TO CONSUMER (B2C) SUPPLIERS

Since its inception, the World Wide Web has presented a challenge to businesses worldwide. According to rhetoric, it is the ideal medium that is destined to replace half of traditional high street shopping by 2010 (Austin 1997) and to revolutionize businesses. Shropshire E-vent (2003) commented:

> Whatever your market sector, the Internet can give you benefits; staff can be totally mobile, important documents can be sent or downloaded, allowing information to be provided quickly. And don't forget purchasing, banking and marketing, and so the list continues; all benefits that allow you to take care of your core business.

The rhetoric goes on; cheap advertising, marketing, information dissemination and sales, including to those people who have no local outlet for the product or service that they require. In theory, the Web would appear to be of benefit to people in all regions, rich or poor, for areas highly or thinly populated, anywhere in the world. Businesses have, in poor economic times, rationalized their operations and closed outlets in areas that they considered marginal. Such rationalization does not remove the demand; it merely makes it more difficult for potential customers to obtain satisfaction. In many areas of former industrial towns for example, the closure of banks, supermarkets and even of job centres means that potential clients are reliant on more expensive corner shops, or on increasingly rare bus services to distant town centres where such services may still exist. Web sites for banks can satisfy such demands, even though they were probably not intended to service such sections of the community. Government sites can supply some information and services, but the unemployed are still expected to travel to a job centre at regular intervals. The reality, to date, is that the Web has not provided a replacement for these services for all groups of people.

Among the early business effects in the e-Economy was the closure of 'real' shops and offices as businesses, believing the rhetoric, sought cheaper methods of sales. In the late 1990s, many viewed the Web as the scene of the next commercial revolution. In an undated paper, Barta *et al.* believed that 'By 2010 it [i.e. the Internet] may account for as many as 25 percent of US retail sales'. In a similar vein, Fulton McDonald (Austin 1997), a retail consultant with IBM, stated: 'The Internet is going to drive half of today's retailers out of business by 2010.'

However, this optimism appears to have been short-lived. By 2000, the newspapers and, indeed the Web itself, were full of articles about the demise of the Internet as a means of commerce. The magazine *Computing* reported that the fastest growing Internet site was one devoted to Web failures (Whittle 2000). The BBC News Web site was packed with articles such as 'Dot.com gold rush ends' (BBC 2000 – Ward) and 'From Boo.com to Boo.gone' (BBC 2000 – Anderson). In a Web mail link system, a discussion contained the comment 'the internet is more potent as a tool for getting ideas about things to buy and getting price comparisons than it is for making purchases' (Robertson-Dunn 2001). From these statements, it would appear that the rhetoric fizzled out, and we could now expect a long, slow decline.

So which set of stories is true? Where does the rhetoric divide from the reality? Is the Web of little business value, or is it just that the initial hype is wearing thin? The jury is still out. Statistics and examination of current Web sites suggest that there is a Web-based future for businesses, but possibly not on the scale imagined. University of Ohio statistics suggest that while the growth of the late 1990s is beginning to tail off in the public sector, the private sector remains buoyant. Levin (2003) also enthused:

Creating a Web site for your business will benefit your bottom line with increased sales, improved customer service and reduced operating costs. It's a service end-users will value, and in this highly competitive marketplace, a web site just might be what keeps your customers from going to another distributor.

If business usage is still growing, despite the much-heralded failures, what then exactly is the Web being used for? Is the Web more rhetoric than reality? Next, we will examine the functions to which it is being put, how specific small industries can benefit and are benefiting from it, and how customers, especially those without local facilities, can gain benefit from the Web-based services provided by such institutions as supermarkets and banks.

E-RETAIL PARADOXES FOR SUPPLIERS

TORONTO, January 25, 2001 — An e-Business survey conducted by Ipsos-Reid on behalf of the Canadian Institute of Chartered Accountants (CICA), Bell Canada, bizSmart and CIBC found that while 77 per cent of small to medium-sized enterprises (SMEs) expect that the Internet will have a positive impact on their businesses over the next 2 years, only 32 per cent have developed a strategy for their Internet presence (Chartered Accountants of Canada 2001). This impact may take several forms. To some, there will be benefit from direct sales, to others, marketing. The majority will benefit in several ways, and in this section, we will examine how different industries gain in different ways. The methods used to gather information in this section are:

1 Questionnaire responses from the owners of over 100 vineyards worldwide by Richardson (2002). The survey included the question 'What do you see as the main purposes of having an Internet site?' This method does not always work as many of the targets regard the emails as 'spam' and ignore them.

2 Direct analysis of over 200 Web sites for five types of rural industry. Industries chosen were cheese production, vineyards, woodworkers, smokeries, herb producers and gardens; all industries which, being largely rural-based and therefore being in areas of comparatively low population, seemed likely to benefit from being brought to the attention of a wider market. The fact that so many have Web sites suggests that the rhetoric of Web salespeople has influenced them in some way.

A comparison of the two research methods can be seen in Table 9.1. The observed tourist use is based on the existence on the site of a map and opening times. It is possible that many owners regard such features as an assistance to direct shoppers and have classed it as sales. However, for the purposes of this survey, 'sales' is taken to involve the provision of some online shopping facilities – either a secure credit-card facility or merely a printable order form. Many sites can be classed as 'marketing' as they are showing specific products as opposed to generic descriptions of product types.

Table 9.1 *Survey results using different methods*

Criteria	Email survey	Observations
Tourist brochure	33%	68.67%
Trade enquiries	4.4%	—
Marketing	63%	91.57%
Sales	49%	51.81%
Future potential	13.3%	—
Education	17%	16.87%

Many sites can also be classed as purely 'informational' – 61 per cent according to the same survey by the Chartered Accountants of Canada (2001). The survey quotes Jim Carroll, author of many books on e-Commerce, as saying that he was not surprised at the absence of anything but information. 'It is a tremendous challenge for any executive to figure out e-Business and how to level the massive and often ridiculous hype that has surrounded anything Internet-related over the past five or six years'. Faced with this, many industries, such as woodworkers and herb gardens have opted to remain as information-only providers, though many of the latter include material aimed at educating the consumer. Other industries have made wider use, although this is by no means a feature of all their members.

Not all products are suitable for Web sales, even though it could be said that all business-related sites are, in some way, seeking to sell, if only indirectly. Geller (1999) cautions against 'forcing a square peg into a round hole' – what sells well in a retail store may not sell online. He asks whether an online shopper will trust your security guarantee, and whether high shipping costs will affect the purchase decision. 'Angela W' (undated), editor of *Online Business Basics* in 'Is your product suitable for the Net' (undated), asks whether there is a more convenient alternative and whether or not the product in question is something that a customer needs to feel or see before making a purchase. Eagle Malls (undated) stress the same point – the Web should not be selling items that can easily be obtained from the corner store, unless there are additional benefits to be had in such transactions. An example of this could be in the purchase of groceries by the disabled, or those without transport. However, even in these cases, the Web will only be a sales success if the twin factors of trust in its financial integrity, and trust in the reliability of the transport system exist. If a perishable product is consistently left, unannounced on the doorstep by a delivery van – or even delivered broken, then repeat business may not be forthcoming. These are factors for the seller to consider. On the customer side of the equation, sales via the Web are only possible if the potential customer has the computer equipment and access to the network. As we shall examine later in the chapter, this is not always the case, especially in the communities that are also being 'hit' by the very shop closures that the Web sites are seeking to replace.

THINK POINT

What 'added value' can the Web give to retail customers?

In his book *E-shock*, De Kare-Silver (2000) has developed a scale by which the suitability of a product for sale via the Web can be measured, involving three criteria:

1 Is it widely known and therefore purchased without sampling or view? (score 0–10).

142

2   Is it 'sense' related, i.e. does it involve taste, smell, sight, sound or touch. Such an unsuitable product could well be wine or cheese from small producers. An Alsace vineyard owner, for example, when asked what were the main obstacles to selling on the Web responded 'Voir le produit, le déguster' (viewing the product and tasting it) (Richardson 2002). However, it need not preclude herbs, which are fairly standard and well-known or products from suppliers that are familiar to the purchaser. It could include small firms that have been used before, for example, whilst on holiday (score 0–10).

3   What is the state of consumer attitudes towards its being purchased electronically, i.e. is it subject to 'conservatism' or the need for social interaction during purchase? For example, a simple bank transaction could be performed online. However, a complex loan might require personal reassurance, and might need a face-to-face situation (score 0–30).

From these items, a score is calculated out of 50 – the higher the score, the more likely it is to be purchased online. De Kare-Silver gave branded drinks a score of 4 for category (1), 8 for (2), and 15 for (3) – a total of 27. This score would not be applicable to all types of wine. For example, it could be argued that a bottle of claret costing £200 would probably be unsuitable for Web sales, since a buyer would most likely want the direct reassurance of a producer or broker when undertaking such an expensive purchase and would score low on category (3). It might fit a standard wine, such as that produced by large companies (for example, Hardys or Montana), since they are generally well known and accepted as being of good value without requiring tasting. However, a wine from smaller wineries, known mainly within their own locality could have greater difficulty. A vineyard in France summed this up with the comment 'Problème de la degustation quant on n'a pas sufisamment de notoriété' (problems of tasting when one is not well known)[1].

Despite the inability of Web users to taste and smell, the Web does give vineyards the opportunity for far more comprehensive tasting notes than are possible in, say, a mail-order catalogue. One would expect wine and cheese and smoked products from small producers to have limited appeal to Web customers. However, this does not stop any of those producers from providing the facilities for 'online' shopping, even though the actual sales through this medium may be limited. In a survey of vineyards across the world, Richardson (2002) found that sales of wine on the Web from vineyard Web sites were largely under 5 per cent of turnover. Inter-state restrictions on the sale of wine from producer to consumer had a major effect on the development of online sales. These restrictions, based on the 21st Amendment, placed alcohol trade in the hands of state legislatures, who have enacted widely differing restrictions. In Florida (2003) for example, direct shipments are classed as a felony, punishable by fines or imprisonment. There are signs of change. In 2003, the California Wine Institute (2003) president, Bobby Koch, declared that 'With the ever-increasing use of the Internet in U.S. households, Wine Institute believes that direct shipments will help to dramatically increase the number of wine brands available to customers'. Legal judgments in the USA also suggest that the Federal authorities are minded to relax the restrictions.

In the wine trade, the larger products mainly do not sell online, for fear of competing directly against their main retail outlets. The smaller ones are willing to experiment, providing that it is relatively inexpensive, whilst the medium-sized producers are attempting to expand marginally by any means available. Some regard the provision of sales as being completely unnecessary, and use the Web merely as an interactive brochure. Bob Lindo of Camel Valley vineyards in Cornwall appears to agree with these sentiments, when summing up how he felt about his site.[2] 'Conclusion – Web site is great – on-line shopping is unnecessary – most people have a phone and a credit card'. Little has changed since then. Many of the wineries interviewed by Richardson (2002) regarded the Web as a cheap method of widening access to information about their products. Some used it for supporting existing agents, especially in the export market. For example, a number used their sites either to describe their wines in great detail. For example, the Hugel Web site (http://www.hugel.com) has a vast array of information about each individual wine, including tasting notes, so that buyers will have a detailed impression of the wine before purchasing, and so that third-party salesman in other countries have a reference point when asked for information by their customers. A similar level of detail is found on the whisky site of Bruichladdich on Islay (www.bruichladdich.com) which provides detailed tasting notes, and, via broadband, live tasting commentaries 'for anyone with the right equipment' and who has obtained the product in advance (Gerrard 2003). For many woodworking sites, marketing appears to the main objective of the site. About half included sales facilities, especially where 'standard' items (for example, walking sticks) were being produced. These sites made extensive use of photographs of products to attract both sales and potential clients seeking bespoke carvings. In virtually no cases were visitor facilities indicated.

THE ROLE OF CUSTOMER EDUCATION

Companies have always educated their customers about their products, but the Internet allows you to reach out and educate more customers in a consistent and timely way. If your products confuse a customer they are unlikely to buy, but if you can help your customer make more educated choices, they are more likely to keep coming back to you. You can consider using e-Learning to offer extra value to your customers direct through your Web site.

(Applications of E-learning 2003)

The 'educational' nature of business sites can manifest in a variety of forms. Some organizations offer courses, others provide information on the way that the product was made. Sites can be deemed educational when there is information about the production of products in general, for example, how they are made, or how they can be used. Wilson

(1996) believes that education is an effective way to sales – the more information about the production methods, place and product is provided, the more people associate the product with quality and will come back to the site. Higgison (2002) refers to **Edumarketing**, which 'educates the consumer to value the process the product supports'. The examples that she provides involve finding a benefit of the product (for example, a tonic wine) and using advertising or sponsorship to bring this benefit to the attention of customers, so making them aware that the product itself will be beneficial to them. *Business World* (2002) puts it more bluntly. In a survey of Asian Internet banking users he found that online education was the ultimate key to success:

> In all surveyed countries, respondents indicated a strong desire for more education and said they would increase online activity as a result. They feel banks have done a poor job on education, convincing them Internet banking is safe, and making sites easy to use.

In other words, using the Web to provide background information about security or product detail will put the customers in the mood to make purchases. Thus educating Web sites may be the key to long-term business success, at least for those consumers with Internet access. Dadoly (2003) comments that 'e-Edumarketing' represents the convergence of e-Learning and marketing to promote a company's online sales and marketing strategy, drive revenue and increase Web site traffic and 'stickiness'. He cites an example that he is developing for the fitness site of Tom Platz, Inc (www. tomplatz.com):

> **Project overview**: Develop Web site and e-Learning program to deliver health & fitness classes and seminars via the Web. Develop and launch marketing program to drive traffic and transactions through Web site.

> **Objectives**: Develop Web presence for Tom Platz targeting fans and fitness enthusiasts. Develop new revenue stream by converting classroom based instructor led bodybuilding and fitness educational content to salable e-Learning lessons.
>
> (Dadoly 2003)

Educational principles would appear to be being used by a number of small industries in order to generate interest in, and knowledge about their products, with a view to generating future sales. This has taken a variety of forms, from providing quizzes, to seeking to answer questions about the use and production of the products. Many herb producers provide details of specific products and their uses, and some cheese-makers present details of their processes. Smokeries too often have detailed descriptions of their processes. For example, Isle of Man Kippers http://www.isleofmankippers.com/kippers-main.htm devote pages to kipper production, the life of the herring and a history of Manx sea fishing. It is almost totally absent from the sites of woodcarvers, possibly

145

because the types of wood and methods of using it are regarded as craft secrets. Other examples of sites with a strong educational content include:

- The De Bortoli pages at www.debortoli.com.au in which there is an examination of the various stages of wine-making, from harvesting to bottling – far more detail than is needed for marketing purposes, but enough to satisfy, for example, a student looking for detailed information on the wine-making process.
- Mount Avoca vineyard in Australia, which goes even further, and provides large amounts of data on climate, geology and the history of wine-making for the benefit of schools and researchers, although in this particular case, the key words are concerned with the wine types, rather than the functions.
- James Arthur in Nebraska (http://www.jamesarthurvineyards.com/about.htm) concentrates on educating wine drinkers in such topics as starting a wine cellar, storing and tasting wine etc. so demystifying a product that, it is felt, may frighten people.

Herb gardens also provide large amounts of information on the potential medicinal and culinary uses of particular herbs. In many cases, this is because the site is marketing plants for people to grow themselves, rather than packaged products. Education as a form of marketing is important as a means of giving potential users the confidence to go out and buy the products. An article in *Businesstown* (2003) comments that 'Ultimate success comes from not only offering the right products and services at the right prices, but also educating your market.' In summary, 'edu-marketing' allows the potential customer to learn about a particular product, become more trusting of the messenger and therefore seek out the product more actively from any one of a number of potential retailers. At least, this is the theory, but is it any more realistic than the hype about effectiveness of the Web, when a large per centage of the population of the world still cannot access it?

WHAT IS THE REALITY OF THE WEB FOR SUPPLIERS?

So far, we have seen that the World Wide Web has been developed for a variety of commercial purposes, sales, tourist 'pointers', services, marketing, education and information. Many small businesses embraced the early rhetoric and developed Web sites with a subset of these purposes and with varying expectations as to its success. Among suppliers, the expectations do not appear to have greatly changed in the last few years. For example, the vineyards questioned in the original survey in 2000 were resurveyed in 2003. None saw much change in either their sales or their expectations. One user, Three Choirs in Gloucestershire, believes that 20 per cent of its business came from people who used the Web and either bought online, or subsequently visited, so for them, the target market (people who actually own computers) has been reached. For such a supplier, maybe the reality has matched the rhetoric. However, Bob Lindo of

Camel Valley Vineyard believes the Web is useful for most purposes except sales, and has taken out his sales facility, commenting that his customers prefer using a telephone.[3] Some businesses have become more cynical and given up expecting the Web to be much more than a shop window. One New Zealand vineyard went as far as to say that 'it is an information, not a sales tool'.[4]

The Web, seen as the great communications and sales medium, may pose as many problems as it solves. It would appear to be a source of cheap advertising, yet its market range is limited by lack of personal computers among the very sector of the community that might benefit from its services because traditional service and retail outlets have closed. Naughton (2002) comments that 45 per cent of British households are Web-connected, but that still leaves 55 per cent that are not. If the 45 per cent includes the majority of the suppliers' target market, then, for them, the rhetoric is justified. However, for the unconnected consumer, it has not improved the situation. The World Summit on the Information Society (2003) pointed out that in the Third World, the connected figure is only 2 per cent. The conclusion of the same report reads:

> Instead of contributing to an increase in everyone's well being, we sometimes notice the opposite effect. The gap between those who have access to information and those who do not is constantly growing and continuing to deepen the already existing division between the rich and poor, instead of bringing them together.

For these people, as we shall see now as we move on to consider the consumer perspective in more detail, there is no reality in the Web – it is still just rhetoric.

E-RETAIL PARADOXES FOR CONSUMERS

One of the major issues associated with moves towards an e-Economy will be the effects of e-Commerce on consumers. Shopping behaviour is changing, but research into the effects has lagged behind. In this part of the chapter, we study the effects of **e-Retailing** on the consumers who would be expected to have most to gain from it (although not the usual targets of e-Retailers): those who tend to be excluded geographically from conventional retail. As noted earlier in this chapter, retail facilities in many local areas have been in decline. From 1986 to 1997 the number of independent retail stores declined by almost 40 per cent (Lang and Rayner 2001). The potential for e-Retailers to fill this vacuum and to assist the disadvantaged merits examination. **Shopping deserts** have been identified (areas with a lack of opportunities for purchasing a range of products and services). These present a significant problem for health and well-being as a causal link has been demonstrated between retail exclusion and poor nutrition. e-Retail has been championed as a possible solution to the shopping deserts problem. As the availability of physical shops declines, it has been suggested that consumers can 'e-Shop' instead. This is presumably an attractive idea for UK consumers, the second biggest e-Shopping nation in the world. In this final part of the chapter we examine two contrasting questions. First, what is the potential for e-Retailers to fill the vacuum of shopping deserts and assist the disadvantaged? Second, will the disadvantaged become further disadvantaged as a result of e-Shopping? We explore the extent to which e-Shopping's promise to the disadvantaged is reality or rhetoric.

Prospects and trends in e-Retail

Online shopping is growing in the UK with sales having reached £3.3 billion (Verdict 2003). This is only 2 per cent of all retail sales but is predicted to rise to between 2.5 per cent and 5 per cent by 2005 (BCSC 2001) and 10 per cent by 2009 (Gibson 1999; Verdict 2003). 'Most people' will buy groceries, books, CDs and even clothes by e-Shopping (RICS 2000). Books, movies and software, high on 'factual search' (Shim *et al.* 2001) are natural for e-Retailing, but groceries and clothing are also increasing (Doidge and Higgins 2000; Verdict 2002). Ninety-four per cent will be at the expense of existing channels (half diverted from catalogues, half from high street – BCSC 2001), only 6 per cent from extra growth (PreFontayne 1999).

Food deserts and shopping deserts

The previous step-change in shopping was the growth in out-of-town shopping in the 1970s and 1980s. Between 1971 and 1992 the number of out-of-town superstores (3000+ square metres sales area) increased from 21 to 719. By 2000 there were 960 (Lang and Rayner 2001). There is a substantial body of research literature tracking the consequent creation of **food deserts** (shopping desert areas, particularly downtown, with a specific lack of opportunities for purchasing a suitable range of nutritional food) in inner cities that has disadvantaged the underprivileged (for example, Opacic and Potter 1986; Hallsworth 1988; Bromley and Thomas 1995; Guy 1996; Reisig and Hobbiss 2000; Rex and Blair 2003). For example, Rex and Blair (2003) mapped every shop selling food in an area of Sandwell (Midlands, UK) with a population of 100,000 people. Most residents did not have access to healthy food such as fresh fruit and vegetables within walking distance (although access to biscuits, chocolate and cigarettes was relatively good). Major ongoing projects are studying the social, nutritional and health consequences of food deserts (reported by, for example, Cannings and Whelan 2001; Dowler *et al.* 2001; Wrigley *et al.* 2003). Studies such as these indicate that there could be physical health disbenefits arising from poor nutrition caused by food deserts.

Tackling social exclusion in British cities has been a major priority for the UK government. Wrigley and colleagues (2003) described the setting up of the Social Exclusion Unit within the Cabinet Office and research highlighting widening inequalities between deprived neighbourhoods and elsewhere. As part of the process of producing *A National Strategy Action Plan* (Social Exclusion Unit 2001a, 2001b), Policy Action Team 13 (PAT 13), led by the Department of Health, released a consultation report which

148

outlined a grim picture of those neighbourhoods in which 'once vibrant local shopping centres or neighbourhood stores that provided a safe place for the local community to meet and access a range of services to meet every day needs have mostly disappeared' (Department of Health 1999). Ministerial statements from the Department of Transport and Regions have described 'tackling social exclusion [as the] new main task for retail planning policy' (Raynsford 2000).

The work of Wrigley and colleagues concerned food deserts. They described the large-scale intervention of a Tesco superstore: successful in improving the diet of the most deprived residents of a former food desert. The study had implications beyond just nutrition, also reporting lifestyle improvements such as increased travel by foot and reduced use of the car. Those authors hope to develop the project beyond just diet, to health and general well-being. The Tesco intervention had an additional benefit not mentioned by Wrigley: the new store is an e-Retail supplier, adding around a couple of dozen extra jobs in a major unemployment black spot. Unfortunately, this type of intervention is unlikely to be a universal solution to the food deserts problem as it is almost axiomatic that not every food desert will be able to host a new grocery superstore.

e-Retail has been suggested as a solution to the shopping deserts problem. As the availability of physical shops declines, it has been suggested that shoppers can e-Shop instead ('let them eat cake'?). Unfortunately, in the current climate, this actually turns out to be a less than ideal solution, because of the 'digital divide'. 'Diffusion of Innovations' theory (Rogers 1995) predicts that the 'laggards', those slowest to take up an innovation such as the Internet, will tend to be older, of lower education level and lower socio-economic status (**SES**) than the average – i.e. the demographic characteristics most prone to social and retail exclusion. Fitch and Fernie (2002) demonstrated that socially excluded tended to have low levels of computer ownership and Internet access (from an analysis of the Scottish Household Survey of 14,500 households). For example, whilst 40 per cent of owner occupied households had computers, only 16 per cent of renters did, and for those in social housing the figure fell to below 13 per cent. Internet access for the lower income households was less than one-tenth of the level of the highest income ones. Retired people and low-income households without children had very low levels of Internet access. Across the UK, 7 per cent of the population is excluded from the use of the Internet (i.e. do not have own access and do not know anyone who could access for them, and are not anti-technology).[5]

Lack of literacy, numeracy and access to credit means that those who most need extra provision are least able to access it by e-Shopping. For example, 11 per cent of households had no bank account and therefore presumably no credit card. The UK as a whole shows a similar divide to that detailed for Scotland, with a greater than 60 per cent difference in Internet adoption between the lowest and highest household income deciles (National Statistics 2001). The existence of the digital divide can be demonstrated on a local level by comparing the penetration of e-Shopping with the level of food-shopping provision in food desert areas. For example, for 85 per cent of the residents of a food desert in Seacroft (Leeds, UK) (Cannings and Whelan 2001; Wrigley *et al. 2003*) penetration of e-Shopping is either 'low' or 'very low' (post-code level analysis by the authors using e-Types e-Shopping stages 4 and 5: e-Types 2003).

The social and hedonic benefits of shopping

THINK POINT

The Web is excellent for purposeful shopping and finding the best deal quickly without wasting time talking or listening to sales people. Is there any reason why e-Shoppers should be interested in the enjoyment or social aspects of e-Shopping?

In our discussion of food deserts above, we have already briefly alluded to the effect of shopping provision on nutrition (and by implication, on health). It can be argued, though, that the implications are wider, involving social and enjoyment benefits of all shopping (including non-food), and that there may be consequent effects on general well-being, health and even mortality. Lunt (2000) found that a main reason for consumers not e-Shopping was that it 'lacks the experiential aspects'. Dennis *et al.* (1999) found that service and experience attributes were more associated with shopping behaviour than were shops and merchandise. Retail forms the heart of UK cities and is a focus for communities (Dennis *et al.* 2002a). A number of studies have drawn attention to the importance of social and affiliation motivations for shopping (e.g. Dennis *et al.* 2001, 2002b, 2002c; Shim and Eastlick 1998; Westbrook and Black 1985). A picture has emerged of the importance of the social aspects of shopping for shoppers' well-being, particularly for females (e.g. Dholakia 1999). Shopping has been demonstrated to be central to the constitution and maintenance of loving relationships within the family (Miller 1998).

Similarly, hedonic aspects such as enjoyment and entertainment have been demonstrated to be important benefits of shopping (for example, Barbin *et al.* 1994; Sit *et al.* 2003), valued by consumers in resource-expenditure terms (for example, Jones 1999; Machleit and Mantel 2001). Customers' positive emotional responses, particularly in terms of pleasure (and consequently impulse purchases of products simply because they are liked), can increase in a store with a pleasant atmosphere compared to an unpleasant one (Ang *et al.* 1997; Spies *et al.* 1997). Work by Professors Gerald Zaltman and Stephen Kosslyn of Harvard University has apparently indicated that pleasant shopping is associated with increased brain activity in the left prefrontal cortex, providing a physical measurement of heightened pleasure (reported in the *Sunday Times*, 8 August 1999). Further details of Zaltman's and Kosslyn's commercially funded work are unfortunately not in the public domain. Nevertheless, Denison (2003) also reported on the beneficial physiological effects of shopping, indicated by levels of the hormone cortisol, associated with excitement. Findings such as these may give literal meaning to

150

the cliché 'retail therapy'! In fact, we will speculate below on possible health benefits that retailing might provide.

Moving from shopping in general to e-Shopping, Kolesar and Galbraith (2000) reviewed the importance of higher level needs such as personal interaction and control, concluding that e-Retailers have difficulty in satisfying customers' needs for these. On the other hand, they pointed out that loyalty and affinity programmes can be successful in satisfying self-esteem and belonging needs. Their study, though, did not gather primary data. Rohm and Swaminathan (2003), in a study comparing a sample of e-Shoppers with non-e-Shoppers found that social interaction, variety seeking and convenience were all significant motivators for e-Shopping. Recreation, although a motivator for bricks shopping, was not significant for e-Shopping. Those authors concluded that e-Shopping appealed more to functional shoppers than to recreational shoppers. This was consistent with the results of Lee's and Tan's (2003) experiment with 179 undergraduate participants. That study found that shoppers were more likely to shop in store (rather than e-Shop) for products/services high in purchase risks. The results, though, were statistically significant only for services rather than tangible products.

On the other hand, we consider that the variety-seeking motivator is consistent with the substantial use of e-Shopping for 'hedonic' goods and services such as books, music and travel. Childers and colleagues (2001) found enjoyment to be a strong predictor of attitude towards e-Shopping. In that study, 'usefulness' and 'enjoyment' were equally predictive of attitude overall. Usefulness was the better predictor for grocery, enjoyment more so for the examples that the authors described as 'hedonic': Amazon (www. amazon.com), Hot Hot Hot (sauces – www.hothothot.com), Wal-Mart (www.walmart. com), K Mart (www.kmart.com) and Bookstore (www.bookstore.com). Social and hedonic motives, important for shopping in general, are, despite some qualification, also significant for e-Shopping.

Parsons (2002) investigated to what extent social motives were valid for e-Shopping. Of five motives (hypothesized based on the well-known social motives from Tauber (1972)), only 'pleasure of bargaining' was not applicable. The other four were significant descriptors of e-Shopping motives. These were: (1) social experiences outside the home; (2) communications with others having a similar interest; (3) peer group attraction; and (4) status and authority. Qualitative investigation indicated that 'status and authority' was a positive motivator in the minds of those shoppers who felt that e-Shopping raised their standing in the eyes of friends and colleagues. Parsons found that there was clear support for the concept of communities on the Internet: 'The ability of online shopping to cater to social experiences outside the home, without actually leaving home, offers a distinct advantage for those unable or unwilling to venture out to physical locations, as well as offering social support.' Parsons concluded that personal and social motives are not only applicable to e-Shopping, but also they are being applied by e-Retailers.

Well-being, health and mortality

The social aspects of shopping are not of trivial importance but are, we contend, literally a matter of life and death. Many studies have demonstrated that socially isolated people have mortality rates between 50 per cent and 300 per cent higher than people who are integrated into social groups (for example, Avlund *et al.* 1998; Berkman 2000; Bowling 1998). Similarly, many researchers have reported that people who are happy are ill less often and recover more quickly (for example, Danner *et al.* 2001; Kiecolt-Glaser *et al.* 2002; Kubzansky and Kawachi 2000). Happiness and increased immune resistance to disease have been demonstrated to be correlated with high activity in the left prefrontal cortex, associated with pleasure and positive thinking (Davidson 2003), the same brain response as apparently associated with pleasant shopping.

Taking SES into account, there is a 'double whammy' for the unfortunate residents of shopping deserts. Low SES is associated with poorer health and higher mortality (through, for example, poorer nutrition, which can be exacerbated by food deserts). Low SES is also correlated with negative emotions, which in turn act to increase illness and mortality (Gallo and Matthews 2003). In addition to the nutrition problems associated with food deserts, lack of access to the emotional benefits of shopping in shopping deserts may therefore also result in health and mortality disbenefits. A reduction in psychological well-being of the already disadvantaged shoppers might be contributing to the physical health problems that researchers have observed in deprived areas. The exclusion debate concerns not only intangible psychological factors but also some of society's real problems. At least one Social Inclusion Partnership in Scotland has set out to address drugs, unemployment and teen pregnancy by focusing on the primary concern of local residents: retailing (Fitch and Fernie 2002). The implication is that a decline in local retail provision might be associated with worsening social problems.

Current e-Shopping research

This section examines the proposition that as shoppers increasingly e-Shop, high streets will lose business, with some shops and shopping centres closing. The reduction in choice is likely to affect non-car-owning and non-computer-owning shoppers disproportionately – further disadvantaging the disadvantaged and exacerbating the shopping deserts problem. Here we present preliminary findings from work-in-progress from two of our e-Shopping studies.

Case study:

The first study is exploring the extent to which disadvantaged shoppers may become further disadvantaged as a result of the growth in e-Shopping (initial results in Dennis *et al.*

2002c) The method used was a questionnaire survey that compared shoppers' opinions of Internet shopping versus 'bricks' shopping centres. The respondents (n = 308) were sixth form (n = 30) and university undergraduate (n = 278) students – the shoppers of tomorrow. One of the main constructs to arise from the qualitative part of the study was: 'Prefer to shop in shopping centres – more enjoyable/sociable'. Comments of shoppers who shop by Internet and in shopping centres included:

- 'Internet shopping is not a personal experience. You cannot try and see what you're buying.'
- 'Internet shopping is convenient but will never replace actual shops. Shopping is not purely to purchase goods/products, but is also a leisure activity and can be very sociable – unlike Internet shopping.'
- 'I would rather use the Internet as a research tool in comparing potential purchases and to search for exclusive products. However, when making purchases, I would rather the physical nature of going into the shop. It is more reliable and the experience is pleasurable.'

The quantitative findings have indicated that respondents rated Internet shopping higher than shopping centres for *favourable prices* and *convenience*. On the other hand, shopping centres were preferred for *positive image* and more emphatically for *customer service*. It is natural for many shoppers to take advantage of the Internet's convenience (buy where you like, someone else delivers) and lower prices arising from the ease of comparing prices. Given the lead that e-Shopping has on these major shopping dimensions, it is perhaps surprising that the shopping centre was ahead on positive image. As discussed above, consumers value the social and experience aspects of shopping which, we contend, contribute to the positive image of conventional shopping.

One striking figure is that 57 per cent of the total sample were e-Shoppers – compared with the UK average for all adults of around 15 per cent (estimated from NetValue 2001). That said, most respondents shopped infrequently by Internet with the modal class reporting purely nominal expenditure. Nevertheless, there were also a substantial number of more committed Internet shoppers, the next highest class reporting a spend of £20 per month on Internet shopping (12 per cent of Internet shoppers, 6.8 per cent of the total sample). The mean expenditure of the Internet shoppers on e-Shopping was £22 per month, compared with £86 per month on conventional shopping. Thus, over half of the student sample shopped on the Internet, spending on average over 20 per cent of their non-food shopping by Internet. The mean expenditure per shopper on Internet shopping was £12 per month for the *total* sample, i.e. including the non-Internet shoppers.

Case study:

Our second study is investigating shoppers' motivations in e-Shopping (preliminary results reported in Dennis and Papamatthaiou 2003). The respondents were again undergraduate students (n = 150). Enjoyment has been found to be one of the main motivations, along with usefulness, ease of use, convenience, navigation, knowledge and ability to make a purchase and the influence of friends and family. The enjoyment dimension consists of three significant elements: 'involvement', 'not boring' and 'fun for its own sake'. In line with previous work drawing attention to 'variety seeking' (Rohm and Swaminathan 2003), the most popular sites were Amazon (www.amazon.co.uk), CD Wow (www.cd-wow.co.uk), eBay (auction, www.ebay.co.uk), Ticketmaster (show tickets, www.ticketmaster.co.uk), Ryanair (www.ryanair.co.uk), Easy Jet (www.easyjet.com) and Opodo (air tickets, www.opodo.co.uk). These products and services are in the category that can be referred to as 'hedonic (Childers *et al.* 2001). Our results indicate that enjoyment can be a motivator for e-Shopping and that our respondents shop more when and where the enjoyment motive is more satisfied.

The UK's top two sites in terms of audience numbers are Amazon and eBay (Nielsen NetRatings 2003). In fact, the worldwide success of eBay has made it the biggest e-Commerce site in the world (NAMNEWS 2003). These sites enthusiastically embrace the 'involvement' aspect of enjoyment with features such as chat rooms, bulletin boards, customer written stories and product reviews, suggestion boxes, and personalization of the Web site offers. eBay is particularly strong on involvement, with visitors spending on average 1 hour and 11 minutes on the site, one of the longest of UK e-Retailers. Visitors return to the site frequently to check on items they are buying or selling. There is also a feedback feature on sellers that helps to build trust. eBay is one of few UK e-Retailers to achieve over 1 billion page views per month. With users finding enough interest to return again and again, it can be postulated that a highly involving site would also be expected to be 'not boring' – and maybe also 'fun for its own sake'.

Our results apply only to the student sample and should not be generalized: students cannot necessarily be considered as disadvantaged. Indeed, these are people who within a few years are likely to be earning and spending significantly more than the general population. Bearing in mind this income effect and the high computer literacy of graduates, as they move into employment our sample should be firmly on the 'advantaged' side of the digital divide. The UK government has stated a target of 50 per cent of young people entering higher education. If our figures could be extrapolated, Internet shopping by people in higher education alone would account for 10 per cent of the value of total non-food shopping by the age cohort (actually, more than this as graduates can be expected to spend more in total than non-graduates). Simply from today's students becoming the shoppers of tomorrow, without considering any other market growth, we estimate that e-Shopping could be set to almost double by 2011 (based on demographic figures from IGD 2001; National Statistics 2000). Allowing for a general market growth rate of only 15 per cent (a very substantial drop from the 50 per cent reported by Verdict 2002), e-Shopping would still reach 10 per cent of total shopping by 2011.

Whilst such extrapolation cannot be justified, it is clear that the results do nothing to allay fears of big increases in the proportion of e-Shopping and the consequent negative effects on the viability and vitality of 'bricks' shopping areas. We have posed the question of whether the disadvantaged will become further disadvantaged as a result of the growth of e-Shopping? Our preliminary surveys have considered a subset of shoppers (students) and found them to be more active e-Shoppers than are the general population. This tentative finding adds evidence to the existence of a digital divide. The qualitative section of our first study supports previous findings that the most important issue affecting Internet shopping is shoppers' preferences for the experience of 'real' shopping. Nevertheless, our second study indicates that e-Shoppers can and do use the Internet to obtain enjoyment benefits.

At the start of this part of the chapter, we set out to examine the potential for e-Retailers to fill the vacuum of shopping deserts and to assist the disadvantaged. There is evidence that tackling food deserts can improve nutrition (and by inference, health and longevity). We contend that addressing the shopping deserts issue can also provide social and pleasure benefits for consumers. These benefits are not trivial, but may also contribute to health benefits. The paradox is that whilst e-Shopping is forecast to lead to worsening shopping deserts problems, in theory the Internet can provide shopping, education (as noted under 'edumarketing' earlier in the chapter) and even social and hedonic benefits for consumers. e-Shopping therefore has the potential to help address the problems of shopping deserts. The problem is that at present the benefits are mainly restricted to the 'haves' rather than the 'have nots'. Over time as Internet access diffuses throughout the population, this might be expected to change. Unfortunately, this is again a problem for shopping deserts. As mentioned above, residents of shopping deserts are likely to have lower SES and education levels, i.e. typical characteristics of the 'laggards' in the take-up of technological innovations (Rogers 1995).

Faster change would be likely to need some form of intervention, such as subsidized Internet access, training and provision of e-Cash. Whilst this would obviously be expensive on a large scale, we recommend further research focusing on a particularly disadvantaged segment of the population. Disabled residents of shopping deserts would be a suitable target group, i.e. people who often already need help with physical shopping. As suggested by Parsons (2002), e-Shopping may provide housebound shoppers not only with functional benefits, but also the important social benefits (and we believe, hedonic benefits also). We contend that this will be a potentially fruitful and worthwhile research area.

CONCLUSIONS

The rhetoric of the Web promoters is that it brings shopping to the home and creates a more equal society. The developers of Web sites have stressed how Web sites can increase sales and can penetrate unseen markets. The message was that, as a supplier, all your competitors could outsell you. As Alter (2002) noted: 'In a few short years, e-business grew from an IBM advertising campaign into a tidal wave of hope and hype, mixed with fear and uncertainty about becoming obsolete and being blindsided by unknown competitors.'

However, could the reality be that by making increasing use of it, businesses are widening the social and economic divisions that, in theory, the Web should be helping to abolish? As has been outlined, the disadvantaged are starved of banks, shops, etc. by the gradual movement of vital services to the Web. Real live shops require people to have transport to reach them, and cash to buy in them. As shops close, or migrate to town peripheries or have to 'reconceptualise cost structures in order to remain competitive' (Kalakota and Whinston 1997) cash is harder to obtain and, because fewer people are using them, transport costs rise for shoppers. The Web by contrast requires the providing company to provide the transport (for the goods) but the means of facilitating the transactions, credit-cards and computers, are lacking from the very groups of society that are suffering most from the shop closures. These groups of society are left with only expensive credit facilities and more expensive 'corner shops' (if they exist at all).

QUESTIONS

Question 1
Do the figures in Table 9.1 give a true picture of the reality of the value of the Web?
Feedback
Figures show what sites appear to be offering. However they do not show what it is delivering to owners. For example, about half have a sales facility, but few seem to be doing much business. Difference in survey and observations suggests many people are providing information that could be used by tourists, but don't think of themselves as tourist-based operations.

Question 2
Are the Web-based hopes of suppliers being realized?
Feedback
Most of the small suppliers seem satisfied, but they are the ones that did not put all their sales and marketing hopes on the Web. There is a need to look at the products – suppliers of 'suitable' products are happy, but the number of failures suggests too much hope and not enough market research. There are still too many 'non-Web' restrictions and bottlenecks so maybe it is a technology too far ahead of the supporting infrastructure.

156

Question 3
Is the Web a success or a failure?

Feedback

Before answering this question, criteria must be set. The Web has an increasing number of sites and a large number of uses. However, by the standards of its own rhetoric, it has failed to achieve the proportion of sales that were predicted.

Question 4
Is Web-based tourist information more or less effective than its printed counterpart?

Feedback

The Web can provide virtual reality visits, large-scale maps and more detailed information. However it cannot reach a large proportion of the population (55 per cent in the UK, 98 per cent worldwide). However, are these people in the target audience for visitors?

Question 5
Why do people shop?

Feedback

To obtain useful benefits, but also for many other reasons – for example, to enjoy the process or to socialize with others.

Question 6
Can 'e-Shopping' satisfy shoppers as much as 'bricks' shopping does?

Feedback

e-Shopping and bricks shopping are different and there is some evidence that e-Shopping does not satisfy recreational motives as well as bricks shopping does. Even so, successful e-Retailers can provide satisfaction for enjoyment and social motives.

Question 7
How can the mechanistic process of e-Shopping satisfy shoppers' social motives?

Feedback

For example, providing social experiences, communication with others having a similar interest, membership of virtual communities.

Question 8
What can e-Retailers do to provide enjoyment and social benefits for e-Shoppers?

Feedback

For example, provide chat rooms and bulleting boards. Provide facilities for product reviews and suggestion boxes. Personalization of offers.

GLOSSARY

Edumarketing   The provision of more information than is needed for strictly marketing purposes. An attempt to educate the customer in the purpose and production of a product, in order to generate an interest and a desire to purchase an example of it.

e-Retailing   The sale of goods and services via Internet or other electronic channels, for personal or household use by consumers.

Food deserts   Shopping desert areas, particularly in inner cities, with a specific lack of opportunities for purchasing a suitable range of nutritional food.

Informational sites   Sites which provide background details of the company and what it does rather than specifics on individual products/prices.

SES   Socio-economic status, i.e. the status of an individual or household in terms of purchasing power and social standing.

Shopping deserts   Areas, particularly in inner cites, with a lack of opportunities for purchasing a range of products and services within a reasonable walking distance – sometimes defined as 500 metres.

NOTES

1   Dopff au Moulin. Email response to online questionnaire on the uses of wine Web sites 11 May 2000.
2   Lindo, B. Response to on-line questionnaire on the uses of wine Web sites (11 May 2000).
3   Lindo, R. Private email from Bob Lindo (bob@camelvalley.com) Sent: Thu 9/4/2003 10:46 AM.
4   Private email from Kawarau Estate Vineyard (wine@kestate.co.nz) sent: 9 March 2003.
5   OxIS (2003) Oxford Internet survey, results of a nationwide survey of Britons aged 14 and older, 23 May–28 June 2003, number of respondents: 2030, Oxford Internet Institute.

BIBLIOGRAPHY

Alter, S. (2002) *Information Systems – the Foundations of e-Business*, Upper Saddle River, NJ: Prentice Hall, p. 227.

Ang, S. H., Leong, S. M. and Lim, J. (1997) 'The mediating influence of pleasure and arousal on layout and signage effects', *Journal of Retailing and Consumer Services*, 4, 1: 13–24.

Applications of E-learning (2000) Online. Available http://www.futuremedia.co.uk/FMsite3/Html/e_learning6.htm (accessed 15 June 2003).

Austin Automated Sales, Inc. (1997) Untitled. Online. Available http://www.austinasi.com/lvl222.html

Avlund, K., Damsgaard, M. T. and Holstein, B. E. (1998) 'Social relations and mortality. an eleven year follow up study of 70-year old men and women in Denmark', *Social Science and Medicine*, 47, 5: 635–43.

Barbin, B. J., Darden, W. R. and Griffin, M. (1994) 'Work and/or fun: measuring hedonic and utilitarian shopping value, *Journal of Consumer Research*, 20: 644–56.

Barta, S., Martin, J., Frye, J. and Wood, M. D. (undated) *Trends in Retail Trade*, Oklahoma State University. Online. Available http://www.agWeb.okstate.edu/pearl/agecon/resource/wf-565.pdf

BBC Website – Anderson, 'Dot.com gold rush ends', Online. Available http:/news.bbc.co.uk/1/hi/business/766098.stm

BBC Website – Ward M., 'From boo.com to boo.gone', Online. Available http://news.bbc.co.uk/1/hi/business/753782.stm (accessed 18 May 2000).

BCSC (2001) *Future Shock or E-Hype: The Impact of Online Shopping on UK Retail Property*, London: British Council of Shopping Centres/The College of Estate Management.

Berkman, L. F. (2000) 'Social support, social networks, social cohesion and health', *Social Work in Health Care*, 31, 2: 3–14.

Bowling, A. (1998) 'The association between social networks and mortality in later life', *Reviews in Clinical Gerontology*, 8, 4: 353–61.

Bromley, D. F. and Thomas, C. J. (1995) 'Small town shopping decline: dependence and inconvenience for the disadvantaged', *The International Review of Retail, Distribution and Consumer Research*, 5, 4: 433.

Businesstown (2003) 'Internet – the World Wide Web: putting the Web to work for you', Online. Available http://www.businesstown.com/internet/basicwork.asp

Business World (2002) 'Asian banks poor at pushing online banking – IDC', Online. Available http://itmatters.com./ph/news/news_03262002f.html

California Wine Institute (2003) 'Wine institute applauds FTC report on direct shipping', Online. Available http://www.wineinstitute.org/communications/statistics/ftc_online.htm (accessed 9 October 2003).

Cannings, E. and Whelan, A. (2001) 'The consequences for households living in food deserts: previous findings and the experience of Seacroft residents', *Food Deserts in British Cities: Identification, Measurement and Perception*, seminar, University of Leeds, 6 April.

Chartered Accountants of Canada (undated) Online. Available http://www.ipsos-reid.com/media/dsp_displaypr_cdn.cfm?id_to_view=1144 (accessed 2 February 2001).

Childers, T. L., Carr, C. L., Peck, J. and Carson, S. (2001) 'Hedonic and utilitarian motivations for online retail shopping behaviour', *Journal of Retailing*, 77: 511–35.

Dadoly, C. (2003) *E-marketing*, Online. Available http://www.dadoly.com/ (accessed 6 October 2003).

Danner, D. D., Snowdon, D. A. and Friesen, W. V. (2001) 'Positive emotions in early life and longevity: findings from the nun study', *Journal of Personality and Social Psychology*, 80, 5: 804–13.

Davidson, R. J., Kabat-Zinn, J., Schumacher, J., Rosenkranz, M., Santorelli, S. F., Urbanowski, F., Harrington, A., Bonus, K. and Sheridan, J. F. (2003) 'Alterations in brain and immune function produced by mindfulness meditation', *Psychosomatic Medicine*, 65: 564–70.

De Kare-Silver, M. (2000) *E-shock. The Electronic Shopping Revolution*, London: Macmillan Business, pp. 71–88.

Denison, T. (2003) 'Men and women arguing when shopping is genetic', *News Shop*, Exeter University. Available www.ex.ac.uk/news/newsshop.htm (accessed 22 September 2003).

Dennis, C. E. and Hilton, J. (2001) 'Shoppers' motivations in choices of shopping centres', *8th International Conference on Recent Advances in Retailing and Services Science*, Vancouver, EIRASS.

Dennis, C. and Pappamatthaiou, E.-K. (2003) 'Shoppers motivations for e-shopping', *Recent Advances in Retailing and Services Science, 6th International Conference*, The European Institute of Retailing and Services Studies, Portland, Oregon, August 7–10.

Dennis, C., Marsland, D. and Cockett, W. (1999) 'Why do people shop where they do?' *Recent Advances in Retailing and Services Science, 6th International Conference*, Puerto Rico, The European Institute of Retailing and Services Studies, Eindhoven, EIRASS.

Dennis, C., Marsland, D. and Cockett, W. (2002a) 'Central place practice: shopping centre attractiveness measures, hinterland boundaries and the UK retail hierarchy', *Journal of Retailing and Consumer Services*, 9, 4: 185–99.

Dennis, C. E., Patel, T. and Hilton, J. (2002b) 'Shoppers' motivations in choices of shopping centres, a qualitative study', *9th International Conference on Recent Advances in Retailing and Services Science*, Heidelberg, EIRASS.

Dennis, C. E., Harris, L. and Sandhu, B. (2002c) 'From bricks to clicks: understanding the e-Consumer', *Qualitative Market Research – An International Journal*, 5 (4).

Department of Health (1999) *Improving Shopping Access for People Living in Deprived Neighbourhoods*, Discussion paper of Policy Action Team 13 of the National Strategy for Neighbourhood Renewal, London: Department of Health.

Dholakia, R. R. (1999) 'Going shopping: key determinants of shopping behaviour and motivations', *International Journal of Retail and Distribution Management*, 27, 4–5: 154.

Doidge, R. and Higgins, C. (2000) *The Big Dot.com Con*, London: Colliers Conrad Ritblat Erdman.

Dowler, E., Blair, A., Rex, D., Donkin, A. and Grundy, C. (2001) 'Mapping access to food in deprived areas for health authority activity: experience from London and Sandwell', *Food Deserts in British Cities: Identification, Measurement and Perception* seminar, University of Leeds, 6 April.

E-vent (2003) Shropshire Internet promotion, Online. Available http://www.e-vent.co.uk

Fitch, D. and Fernie, J. (2002) 'Local stores in Scotland: opinions, prospects', *9th International Conference on Recent Advances in Retailing and Services Science*, Heidelberg, EIRASS.

Gallo, L. C. and Matthews, K. A. (2003) 'Understanding the association between socioeconomic status and physical health: do negative emotions play a role?' *Psychological Bulletin*, 129, 1: 10–51.

Geller, D. (1999) 'The seven deadly sins of e-commerce', *E-commerce Times*, October 1999. Online. Available http://pf.inc.com/articles/1999/10/14379.html

Gerrard, M. (2003) 'Whisky Mac', *Guardian* 5 June.

Gibson, B. (1999) 'Beyond shopping centres – e-commerce', *British Council of Shopping Centres Conference*.

Guy, C. M. (1996) 'Corporate Strategies in food retailing and their local impacts: a case study of Cardiff', *Environment and Planning A*, 28: 1575–1602.

Hallsworth, A. (1988) *The Human Impact of Hypermarkets and Superstores*, Aldershot: Avebury.

Higgison, L. (2002) 'Edumarketing: a win-win concept for associations and corporate sponsors', Online. Available http:///www.tcico.com/pages/edumarketing.htm.

Jones, M. A. (1999) 'Entertaining shopping experiences: an exploratory investigation', *Journal of Retailing and Consumer Services*, 6: 129–39.

Kalakota, R. and Whinston, A. B. (1997) *Electronic Commerce*, Harlow: Addison Wesley Longman.

Kiecolt-Glaser, K., McGuire, L., Robles, T. and Glaser, R. (2002) 'Emotions, morbidity, and mortality: new perspectives from psychoneuroimmunology.' *Annual Review of Psychology*, 53: 83–107.

Kolesar, M. B. and Galbraith, R. W. (2000) 'A services-marketing perspective on e-retailing: implications for e-retailers and directions for further research', *Internet Research: Electronic Networking Applications and Policy*, 10, 5: 424–38.

Kubzansky, L. D. and Kawachi, I. (2000) 'Going to the heart of the matter: do negative emotions cause coronary heart disease?' *Journal of Psychosomatic Research*, 48, 4–5: 323–37.

Lang, T. and Rayner, G. (eds) (2001) *Why Health is the Key to the Future of Food and Farming, Joint Submission to the Policy Commission on the Future of Farming and Food*, December, Online. Available www.ukpha.org.uk.

Lee, K. S. and Tan, S. J. (2003) 'E-retailing versus physical retailing: a theoretical model and empirical test of consumer choice', *Journal of Business Research*, 56, 11: 877–85.

Levin, D. (2003) 'The value of a Web-based storefront for distributors', Online. Available http://www.p21.com/press/edt-storefront.html (accessed 20 june 2003).

Lunt, P. (2000) 'The virtual consumer', *Virtual Society? Delivering the Virtual Promise? From Access to Use in the Virtual Society*, ESRC presentation led by Brunel University, London, 19 June.

Machleit, K. A. and Mantel, S. P. (2001) 'Emotional response and shopping satisfaction: moderating effects of shopper attributions', *Journal of Business Research*, 54: 97–106.

Miller, D. (1998) *A Theory of Shopping*, London: Polity Press.

NAMNEWS (2003) 'US: eBay tells analysts growth can be sustained', *NAMNEWS The Original Newsletter for Key Account Managers*, London: EMR-NAMNEWS, Available www.kamcity.com/namnews (accessed 30 October 2003).

National Statistics (2000) *1998-Based Population Projections*, London: The Stationery Office.

National Statistics (2001) *Internet Access Statistics*, Online. Available www.gov.uk

Naughton, J. (2002) 'Like electricity, the Web is a liberator that's here to stay', Online. Available http://www.paricenter.com/library/papers

NetValue (2001) 'NetValue study on US and European Internet usage', Online. Available www.netvalue.com

Nielsen NetRatings (2003) Online. Available www.nielsen-netratings.com

Opacic, S. and Potter, R. B. (1986) 'Grocery store cognitions of disadvantaged consumer groups: a Reading case study', *Tijdschrift voor Econ. En Soc. Geografie*, 77, 4: 288–98.

Parsons, A. G. (2002) 'Non-functional motives for online shoppers: why we click', *Journal of Consumer Marketing*, 19, 5: 380–92.

PreFontaine, M. (1999) 'Beyond shopping centres – e-commerce', *British Council of Shopping Centres Conference*.

Raynsford, N. (2000) Speech to LGN/NRPF Conference on '*Town Centres': Turning the Lights On'*, Available www.nrpf.org

Reisig, V. M. T. and Hobbiss, A. (2000) 'Food deserts and how to tackle them: a study of one city's approach', *Health Education Journal*, 59, 2: 137–49.

Rex, D. and Blair, A. (2003) 'Unjust des(s)erts: food retailing and neighbourhood health in Sandwell, *International Journal of Retail and Distribution Management*, 3, 9: 459–65.

Richardson, O. (2002) 'Utilization of the World Wide Web by wine producers.' *International Journal of Wine Marketing*, 14, 3: 65–79.

RICS Foundation (2000) *20:20 Visions of the Future*, London: Royal Institute of Chartered Surveyors.

Robertson-Dunn, B. (2001) 'The Net is a commercial failure: study', Online. Available http://www.anu.edu.au/mail-archives/link/link0101/0024.html

Rogers, E. M. (1995) *The Diffusion of Innovations*, 4th edn, New York: Free Press.

Rohm, A. J. and Swaminathan, V. (2004) 'A typology of online shoppers based on shopping motivations,' *Journal of Business Research*, 7: 748–57.

Shim, S. and Eastlick, M. A. (1998) 'The hierarchical influence of personal values on mall shopping attitude and behaviour', *Journal of Retailing*, 74, 1 (Spring): 139–60.

Shim, S., Eastlick, M. A., Lotz, S. L. and Warrington, P. (2001) 'An online prepurchase intentions model: the role of intention to search', *Journal of Retailing*, 77: 397–416.

Sit, J., Merrilees, W. and Birch, D. (2003) 'Entertainment-seeking shopping centre patrons: the missing segments', *International Journal of Retail and Distribution Management*, 31, 2: 80–94.

Social Exclusion Unit (2001a) *A New Commitment to Neighbourhood Renewal – National Strategy Action Plan*, London: The Cabinet Office.

Social Exclusion Unit (2001b) *National Strategy for Neighbourhood Renewal – Policy Action Team Audit*, London: The Cabinet Office.

Spies, K., Hesse, F. and Loesch, K. (1997) 'Store atmosphere, mood and purchasing behaviour', *International Journal of Research in Marketing*, 14: 1–17.

Tauber, E. M. (1972) 'Why do people shop?' *Journal of Marketing*, 36 (October): 46–59.

Verdict (2002) *Verdict on Electronic Shopping 2002*, London: Verdict Research.

Verdict (2003) *Verdict on Electronic Shopping 2003*, London: Verdict Research.

Westbrook, R. A. and Black, W. C. (1985) 'A motivation-based shopper typology', *Journal of Retailing*, 61, 1: 78–103.

Whittle, S. (2000) 'Where did it all go wrong for ClickMango?' *Computing* 10 August.

Wilson, R. F. (1996) 'What is the purpose of your Web site?' Online. Available http://www.wilsonWeb.com/articles/Web-putp.htm.

World Summit on the Information Society (2003) 'The information society . . . a tremendous advantage', Online. Available http://www.wfuna.org/site/wsis/wsis%20presentation.htm.

Wrigley, N., Warm, D. and Margetts, B. (2003) 'Deprivation, diet and food retail access: findings from the Leeds "food deserts" study', *Environment and Planning A*, 35: 151–88.

e-Business processes: information and operations for competitive advantage

SUZANNE MIECZKOWSKA, DAVID BARNES
AND MATTHEW HINTON

KEY LEARNING POINTS

After completing this chapter you should have an understanding of:

- The ways in which organizations are seeking to use the Internet and other ICTs to achieve competitive advantage in the global economy
- Alternative competitive strategies for e-Business and their implementation challenges
- The current trend away from 'pure-play' organizations and towards a more organic, integrated and pragmatic approach to e-Business
- The organizational and contextual variables that can bring success or failure in e-Business

INTRODUCTION

With the advent of the 'new' economy, and its 'super-connectivity' of information breaching the boundaries of time and space, e-Business emerged during the late 1990s as an entirely new business model – sexy, appealing and one from which many organizations sought to capitalize. But the dotcom bubble quickly burst, and with it the aspirations and expectations for e-Business began to return to reality. Part of that new reality is the concern of organizations of all kinds to find ways to use e-Business as an integral component of their business strategy.

Operations management has, in the past, often been regarded as the poor relation of strategy. Nowadays, however, managing an organization's operations is increasingly seen as an effective means to achieve competitive advantage. Managing operations involves the

163

management both of business processes and of information, as well as the people and technological structures that support them. Yet there is evidence from practice that many organizations have implemented e-Business applications in their business operations without fully thinking through their strategic impact.

This chapter uses an operations management perspective to consider some actual applications of e-Business operations within a number of UK organizations. In particular, it focuses on the rhetoric versus the reality of these e-Business applications. It explores what the Internet was supposed to mean for business operations, focusing in particular on:

- dis-intermediation;
- business process management, specifically the internal and external integration of business processes and their supporting information systems;
- relationships between suppliers and customers.

It uses case-based vignettes, largely based on our own research, to illustrate some of the issues and problems that the various case organizations have encountered. The chapter concludes with an overview of the current state of e-Business operations and offers some suggestions for future research.

THE INTERNET AND E-BUSINESS

Today's business environment is very different to that of 20 years ago. Notwithstanding the dotcom crash of 2000, and subsequent economic slowdown, Internet growth continues at an unprecedented rate (Michalak and Jones 2003). All around the world, industries of all kinds, services as well as manufacturers, are subject to the powerful forces unleashed by the technological advances underpinned by the Internet, seemingly buoyed by a relentless tide of liberalization and free trade which is creating a new global economy (Cohen *et al.* 2000; Castells 1996). There is greater availability of information to consumers as well as businesses; and advances in computer processing capability and the availability of public infrastructures for information, especially the Internet, and in recent years, mobile telephony, means that information available for utilization by organizations and individuals is growing exponentially (Sampler and Short 1998). Dutta and Segev (1999) write that the Internet has created 'a unique shared global knowledge and communication space, the likes of which has never existed before' and that it genuinely provides organizations with an opportunity to do things differently. As such, this new economy has given rise to organizations with many new business models (Timmers 1998; Weill and Vitale 2001), and many of these models are direct attempts to harness new technologies for business advantage.

The widespread adoption of the Internet as a communication tool for commercial use is generally referred to as e-Commerce. Some authors (e.g. Chaffey 2002) seek to distinguish between the terms e-Commerce and e-Business, but no such distinction is made within this chapter, where the terms are used more or less interchangeably. Poon and Swatman (1999) define e-Commerce as 'the sharing of business information, maintaining business relationships and conducting business transactions by means of Internet-based technology'. Schniederjans and Cao (2002) are similarly broad, describing e-Commerce as 'the exchange transactions which take place over the Internet primarily using digital technology', including buying, selling and trading of goods, services and information. Both of these definitions effectively capture the essence of the encounter between the customer and the organization, whether in the business-to-business (B2B) or business-to-consumer (B2C) environment.

Shaw *et al.* (1997) summarize electronic activity at two levels: the enterprise level, and the channel/customer interface level. The first of these categories emphasizes what might be termed the 'internal' dimension of e-Business, including the management of the operations of the organization. The second category emphasises the 'external' dimension of e-Commerce, that is to say, the impact that e-Commerce has on the behaviour of the organization in its external environment. Until quite recently, this dimension, with its emphasis on consumer marketing, networks and markets and extra- and intra-organizational systems, seems to have dominated many considerations of e-Commerce.

Phan (2003) offers another, quite similar categorization based on three main types of e-Business application:

1 electronic markets or e-Marketplaces;
2 inter-organizational systems that facilitate the flow of inter- and intra-organizational goods, services, information, communication and collaboration;
3 customer service, including help, handling complaints, tracking orders, etc.

This chapter concentrates mainly on aspects (2) and (3) of externally oriented e-Business. It looks in particular at processes, information flows and communication relationships between organizations and their supply chain (B2B) and retail (B2C) customers.

OPERATIONS MANAGEMENT AND BUSINESS PROCESSES

Operations management can be defined as the design, planning, operation and control of the resources used in the production of goods or services for customers (Johnston *et al.* 1997). An operation can be thought of as an activity in which resource inputs of customers, materials and information are transformed into physical goods and/ or intangible services (Slack *et al.* 2001). As such, any organization can be characterized as a series of business processes that utilize resources in an attempt to achieve the desired outputs (Barnes 2001).

The business process perspective of operations has become popular in recent years. Biazzo (2000) encapsulates the process perspective of operations management by pointing out that a process 'is conceived as a system transforming input into output, one which uses resources, and which is subject to controls'. Childe *et al.* (1994), reviewing a number of definitions of a business process, argue that a business process is characterized mainly by whatever flows through it. Accordingly, Slack *et al.* (1998) claim that business processes can be classified as materials, or customer, or information operations, although in reality they are likely to be a mixture of more than one of these. Business processes are also characterized by the way they cut across organizational boundaries: they are 'the strands of activity that link the operations of an organization to the requirements of its customers' (IMI in Lee and Dale 1998). Thus, business processes cross not only boundaries inside organizations (typically those between functions) but also those between organizations. Figure 10.1 shows the transformation model of a business process.

For many years, corporate strategists have argued that price-based competition (known as **cost leadership**) is not the only means to achieve competitive advantage (Porter 1980, 1985; Porter and Millar 1985; Johnson and Scholes 1999). In the new economy where information communication technologies (ICTs) facilitate low-cost global competition (Castells 1996) and with increasingly saturated marketplaces (Slywotzky 2003), organizations have had to find other ways to compete than those based on cost alone. Porter (1980, 1985) famously categorizes **differentiation** (offering a product or service package that is perceived by customers to add value) and **focus** (i.e. targeting a narrow market segment that the organization is well-placed to serve) as alternative generic strategies to cost leadership. Porter (1985) particularly notes that there is an important role for technology because 'information and information systems are becoming increasingly important tools in differentiation, and bundling information with a product can often enhance differentiation'. Yet information communications technology is increasingly ubiquitous, and so differentiation is not always easy to achieve. As Andreassen and Lindestad (1998) note, 'differentiation through the delivery channel is difficult [when] a growing number of service companies have embarked on a journey of positioning through the communication channel (i.e. advertising and personal selling)'.

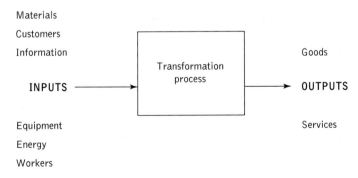

Figure 10.1   *The simple input–output transformation model for operations*

Yet within the existing e-Commerce literature, there is a strong perception that Internet-based technologies can be effectively implemented in the pursuit of strategies based upon differentiation and focus. As Steward *et al.* (1999) say:

> Current forms of commerce are very much a function of yesterday's communication techniques. Companies have built relationships with suppliers, partners and customers using slow, non-interactive and non-automated methods. Companies are now . . . finding ways to integrate new media and on-line communications into their business processes, and even to create entirely new business models that exploit the speed, interactivity and automation of the Internet. Radically new commercial structures are forming.

E-BUSINESS RHETORIC VERSUS E-BUSINESS REALITY

Many organizations believe that the Internet offers significant potential to change the processes that underlie business (Katz and Sofranski 2003). Phan (2003) says that 'most organizations today use Internet technology to redesign their processes in ways that provide new competitive advantage'. And while there is growing recognition that success in e-Business depends on the business processes that facilitate order fulfilment and delivery (Hall 2000; Keating *et al.* 1999), and that customer satisfaction depends on the effective and efficient integration and co-ordination of these processes (McGuffog 1999), there remains a considerable gap between the perceived opportunities that the Internet provides, and what is actually achieved in practice.

It is possible to identify from the literature three key areas where the Internet is thought to change business operations profoundly: (1) **dis-intermediation**: putting sellers and buyers into direct contact and eliminating many of the 'middlemen' from commercial transactions; (2) it will radically influence the design and management of business processes and supporting information systems, both internally within the organization, and externally with supply chain partners; (3) it will significantly improve communication relationships between buyers and sellers, permitting both increased availability and transparency of information.

Mahadevan (2000) defines dis-intermediation as 'the process by which the logistical stream is shortened, leading to better responsiveness and lower costs'. Ryan (2000) notes that dis-intermediation 'signifies major shifts in how we market, sell and deliver products; [that] in many industries, distributors are disappearing and being replaced by electronic media'. Bill Gates (2000) is among many in the IT industry who emphasise that dis-intermediation will be a key feature of the evolving digital economy. Academics too, have noted the financial benefits available from using the power of ICTs to 'cut out the middle man' (Malone *et al.* 1987; Benjamin and Wigand 1995). And Merali *et al.* (2000) write that 'British business is exploiting the Internet . . . in business-to-business e-Commerce the Internet has brought increased productivity and a shorter supply chain'.

167

As well as reduced costs, it is also claimed that Internet-induced dis-intermediation would enable suppliers to get 'an individualized knowledge of the customer' (Jeff Bezos in Tassabehji 2003) and thus create 'valuable information . . . to leverage relationships with customers' (Michael Dell in Margretta 2000). Merali *et al.* (2000) similarly write that the Internet 'has enabled businesses to extend their reach to access customers across traditional boundaries, woo them more selectively and tailor product offerings more closely'. Thus many have come to believe that traditional intermediaries will become an endangered species in electronic markets (Strader and Shaw 1997).

However, it is relatively easy to find examples where the adoption of e-Commerce has not resulted in dis-intermediation. The case of Equipco (below) provides an example of a company that is using the Internet to reinforce the role of the existing intermediaries in its supply chain.

Case study:
EQUIPCO

Equipco manufactures a range of industrial equipment used mostly in fluid processing applications. Its products are technically complex, its customers geographically dispersed, and it sells primarily through local intermediaries who can offer the level of expertise necessary to ensure that customers order the most appropriate equipment for their requirements. Previously, Equipo's intermediaries made enquiries and placed orders via letter, fax or email. Equipco's engineers would advise on product selection using paper-based product information data. These processes of equipment selection, quotation and order entry have now been replaced by a Web-based software tool. This is installed on an individual PC, normally that of the intermediary, although some customers have also installed it. An additional feature of the software tool is its ability to automatically create a Bill of Material for any new product design, thereby saving many hours of work from the pre-manufacturing processes. Thus, the software tool supports Equipco's inter-mediaries, ensures the best technical solutions, and reduces lead times and costs. However, some customers still prefer traditional face-to-face ordering methods. Internally, Equipco's sales and manufacturing information systems are not yet integrated and the manufacturing process does not distinguish between orders received via the Web and those received by conventional means. Equipco hopes its use of e-Commerce will differentiate it from its competitors, as it believes it cannot compete on price alone. As such, it sees e-Commerce as a means of locking-in customers and intermediaries to its Web-based ordering process thereby raising the barriers to exit.

Equipco is dependent on its intermediaries both because of the technically complex ordering process, and because some of its customers (mainly European ones) do not like using the Web-based ordering system, and in fact insist on face-to-face ordering via an Equipco intermediary. Although Equipco's inclination is to rely much less on its intermediaries, it recognizes that this would be prohibitively expensive and impractical. As such, it endeavours to support its existing intermediaries as part of its service-based differentiation strategy.

The case of Legalco (below) offers an illustration of **re-intermediation**, that is to say, the creation of an additional intermediary in the supply chain. Legalco's business model is deliberately predicated and reliant upon various degrees of intermediary relationships between itself and its suppliers.

Case study:
LEGALCO

Legalco is an online business providing a range of legal services. Its main Web site acts as a portal to a number of linked sites that offer online services, provided either free, or at a low and fixed cost by the company. One posts free basic legal information. One enables customers to buy legal services and advice at fixed prices. Another is the company's B2B site, which operates in the settlement of personal injury claims. Another site offers annual subscriptions to a legal advice service and insurance cover for any legal problems that may arise during the subscription period. It also offers fixed-price packages in matrimonial, probate and conveyancing law. Other Web sites link customers to Legalco suppliers who can also provide traditional, face-to-face, legal services, if this is what customers require.

Legalco itself functions as an information intermediary – or 'infomediary' – bringing together information about, and links to, provider services via its own Web site. In addition, Legalco is additionally a kind of technical intermediary – a 'technomediary' – by virtue that its business is also based on its considerable (mainly in-house) technical expertise and proprietary software, of which Legalco owns the intellectual property rights.

Ryan (2000) writes, 'if you are in a business that relies on bricks and mortar, you need to think about how to integrate your existing business model with a virtual presence'. Shim *et al.* (2000) write that 'e-Commerce gives companies improved efficiency and reliability of business processes through transaction automation'. Keating *et al.* (1999) believe that the Internet will enable companies to outsource 'not only the computer running the transaction process, but the process itself [so that] one company's production planning system can be seamlessly merged with another company's inventory management system, and both systems can be managed by a third entity'. Keating (ibid.) also predicts that 'with the Internet as an enabler, the process cycle time can be dramatically collapsed'.

To date, however, most of the consideration of the impact of e-Commerce on operations management has tended to focus primarily on the external links in the supply chain. Limited attention has been given to the management of core internal operations, and there is still little research into how organizations using e-Commerce are adapting their internal business processes. And whilst there was apparent widespread belief that organizations would easily be able to merge conventional business processes into e-Business processes, there is as yet little evidence this is proving to be the reality. Contrary to Hammer's (1990) exhortation, 'don't automate, obliterate', the Internet does not appear to be having a dramatic impact on the redesign of business processes. Rather, as in the case examples that follow, of Shareco and Risk-insure, the Internet is being used to automate and to segregate e-Commerce business processes from conventional ones.

Case study: SHARECO

Shareco is aLondon-based market-maker, trading shares in small and medium-sized companies (SMEs). Previously all share dealing was done over the telephone, but the company has developed a Web site which provides information for investors and enables shares to be traded online. The Web site is mainly aimed at small private investors because Shareco anticipates that its institutional investors will prefer to remain as telephone-based traders. The move to online trading has not yet prompted significant changes to its internal operations and in fact Shareco uses the online channel mainly to trade in what it describes as 'high volume–low value' shares. All share transactions ultimately have to be channelled through Shareco's dealers, whether the orders are received via telephone or via the Web site. Shareco has recently invested in new information systems, which have enabled some reduction of back-office staff. The company's main motivation in using e-Commerce is to tranfer low margin retail (B2C) trade from the telephone dealing system to a discrete online system. If it can achieve high volumes of online business, it believes that this should improve efficiency through lower transaction costs, thereby enabling Shareco to charge lower fees. The overall proportion of business being conducted electronically is still very small, however.

Like Shareco, Risk-insure is also keen to minimize risk to its core business and has, like Shareco, isolated its 'low value–high volume' electronic trade from its main business.

In addition, Risk-insure is also encountering significant preferences in the UK insurance industry for traditional, i.e. face-to-face, business processes.

Case study:
RISK-INSURE

Risk-insure is the UK subsidiary of a multinational insurance broker. It insures against political risks, provides aviation and marine insurance, and conducts some of its business with the major banks. The company has been using an electronic data interchange (EDI) since the early 1990s and has used e-Commerce processes since 1997. Like Shareco the company uses e-Commerce in what it describes as low value business, providing an immediate benefit from automation but with minimal risk to the company. Risk-insure's e-Commerce application is effected mainly through a Web-based quoting structure that the company has established with the insurance underwriters. A structured workflow allows for the establishment of an electronic file and subsequent contract. A consortium of some half dozen underwriters is involved, and the company establishes around 1–2 per cent of its transactions in this way. The quotation process previously took place on a face-to-face basis, supported by paper documentation. Brokers still attach much higher priority to face-to-face clients than they do to completing electronic applications and quotations, thus adding extra time to these processes.

The company's acknowledged motivation for e-Commerce is the threat of competition, coupled with the lower transaction costs available through customer electronic 'self-service'. The company wants to be seen as a leader in an industry that has been slow to embrace technology, yet its e-Business activity is strictly segmented from conventional business activity. The company describes the insurance sector as very conservative, and believes this is a key factor preventing more widespread use of e-Commerce in the industry. Much insurance business has traditionally been based on personal relationships, and so the company feels that this inevitably means a slow and difficult path towards greater e-Business within the industry. The company also believes that a lack of agreed technical standards, coupled with the proliferation of proprietary software, contribute to the slow uptake of new technology within the industry.

Effective e-Business processes are dependent upon effective information systems. An organization's information systems provide the vascular structure and lifeblood for its operations. Yet again, within the literature on e-Commerce information systems, this is an area where there is considerable rhetoric about the impact of the Internet. Mariotti and Sgobbi (2001) note that 'by cutting communication unit costs and enlarging the

171

range of transmissible information, ICTs knock down space and time constraints to interactions among geographically distant actors'. Of the information systems that support internal and external business processes, Chan (2000) observes that 'IT is now taking significant roles in business processes – creating new needs, causing new product development, and commanding new procedures. . . [and that] these internal changes may also lead to broader shifts in products, markets and society as a whole'. While this may be true in some instances, often there are constraining factors which prevent fully effective use of technology-based information systems to manage business processes. These may range from cultural factors, both internally within industries, for example, the slow take-up of technology by the UK insurance industry (*The Economist* 2000; Hulme 2001; Hensmans *et al.* 2001) to financial constraints or lack of time for training.

Pharmco is a company, which despite its small size, is using Internet-based ICTs to link its operations across the globe. However, this use is restricted by internal resource constraints (of both time and money) that are all too typical in the small business sector.

Case study: PHARMCO

Originally founded as a research and development organization Pharmco has recently been licenced to manufacture and sell its products, therapeutic pharmaceuticals. It does not use e-Commerce in sales, but as an internal communication tool between its sites in the UK, USA and Australia. Pharmco operates within a highly regulated environment where documents and inventory need to be strictly and securely managed. In addition to the information systems it has developed to support production processes, the company is developing e-Commerce applications for financial accounting, and setting up links between its various logistics groups and the accounts department, to enable information transfers across key managerial functions. At the moment, the company has not got the necessary management systems in place, and grappling with the technology issues involved in an organization with less than 100 employees worldwide is costly, both in terms of time and money. There are both limited financial resources and insufficient time to fully train staff on the new systems. The result is that Pharmco feels it is not yet making optimum use of internal e-Commerce.

Finman is also a small business. In this case, Finman's intentions of maximizing internal efficiencies by dealing exclusively with its clients on-line has been curtailed by a marked reluctance of many in its industry to forego the traditional ways of doing business.

Case study:
FINMAN

Finman is also a small financial management company established early in 2000 as a dotcom. The company provides finance and accounting functions for other companies and also provides some financial consultancy services. Its main customers are SMEs, often themselves technology, computing or service-based, where many of the business processes would appear to lend themselves to the online model. But while Finman's original intention was to operate a completely online model, it now describes itself as a 'halfway house' because its services are both traditional and e-based. Since start-up, it has had to recognize that some of its clients are not willing, or able, to use a fully online accounting solution and to push an exclusively online model would not be viable. The original motivation in setting up the company was to exploit the benefits of e-Commerce within a highly informationalized environment, but this has to some extent had to be scaled back because of the value many clients put on face-to-face dealing and also because clients' internal information systems support for trans-organizational e-Business accounting processes is either not in place, or is not inter-operable with Finman's own systems.

Finman has also found that there is an issue of getting SME clients to accept the benefits of outsourcing. Technology and integration have been, and remain, key issues. The company's own internal systems are not yet fully integrated because it has been unable to find an appropriate software package. There is also currently limited integration between some of its external business processes and its clients' banks' processes. The issue is not one of client confidentiality, but rather, once again, is about the lack of appropriate software and technology platforms to integrate Finman's business processes with its clients and their bankers.

Both the academic and practitioner literature places considerable emphasis on the anticipated impact of the Internet on relationships between organizations and their B2B and/or B2C customers. As we have already seen, the Internet was not only going to reduce the distance between suppliers and customers by dis-intermediating middlemen, but its opportunities for limitless connectivity led to speculation about greatly enhanced relationships between customers and organizations, through improved informational flows. Customers would, for example, be able to track order progress or obtain product information, on a round-the-clock basis. Organizations would be able to use customer-provided information in order better to tailor their products to particular customers, or to more effectively market their products and services for target, or niche markets.

The case of ARB offers an example of a company which is trying to do exactly this.

Case study:
ARB

Serving a specialist market of relatively few customers ARB is a major European producer of metal products. It uses the Internet via an industry portal, developed in conjuction with a number of its European competitors. The portal offers a one-stop facility for users, specifiers and buyers by facilitating access to all the participating companies's Web sites. The intention is to offer multiple products via a group of suppliers, in this way offering choice to customers, and minimizing some of the costs of establishing an e-Channel for each of the suppliers. This European collaboration is intended to enable all participating companies to compete more effectively with producers in other parts of the world, and encourage greater use of products made from its own, rather than from alternative materials.

ARB's Web site enables customers to make enquiries, request and receive quotations, place orders, receive acknowledgements, test certificates, despatch notes and invoices. Additionally, customers can register order queries and complaints, whether these concern the quantity or quality of goods despatched. The Web site is primarily aimed at automating existing processes, thereby taking out costs, increasing the quality of information, reducing errors, and speeding the order and payment cycle. The intention is to be fully customer-centric: providing customers with as much access as possible to information both pre- and post-order, and during the delivery period. ARB's manufacturing processes are unaffected by the Web site, but customers can track and trace their orders in the manufacturing process. ARB hopes its Web site will offer an improved service to its customers and reduce its transaction costs, helping it to survive in a fiercely competitive market.

ARB believes e-Commerce will enable it to reconfigure its supply chain to be more efficient, reducing costs, adding value for its customers, and thereby encouraging customer loyalty. Internally this has meant changing processes and information systems so that they work for the benefit of the customers. However, as with Finman, some of ARB's target clients do not have the necessary information systems in place to allow maximum inter-operability. In some instances, ARB had already provided EDI-based information support systems for some of its longstanding, important customers. The result of having installed this costly infrastructure now means that ARB is having, in some instances, to use an **extensible mark-up language (XML)** platform with those of its B2B customers that it is anxious to retain. This is because ARB's investment in the EDI systems is too costly to abandon, at least while its Internet-based operations are in a relatively early stage, and while ARB itself still faces an uncertain and unpredictable market in its industry sector.

Similarly to ARB, the case of E-insure also illustrates that the Internet does not necessarily provide either instantaneous, or easy, integration with external customers and supply chain partners. E-insure has, like ARB, had to build a special infrastructure to maintain links with its clients. It describes this infrastructure as an 'invisible portal'.

Case study:
E-INSURE

E-insure is a dotcom start up, spun out from a parent company whose main business is export credit insurance. E-insure is an attempt to harness the connectivity of the Internet to develop business that is considered to be outside of the parent company's clicks-and-mortar operation. E-insure services companies that trade online. Its product offering is based on proprietary software that enables it to screen and verify potential purchasers for credit worthiness, and insure the credit risks. It operates as an invisible portal, through which its clients can interface with their customers using the clients' own Web sites. This enables its clients to utilize their own names as they are recognized brand traders, rather than using E-insure's own brand, which is not sufficiently recognizable. E-insure does not describe itself as a dotcom, but rather an online provider of services to dotcoms. In fact, it is tending to move away from a pure-play online model and back towards a clicks-and-mortar business model, as it expands its service provision to clients. As such, finding a fit between this separate online venture and the parent company's business remains as unresolved issue for both E-insure and Creditinsure. The parent company feels that there is still a degree of competition between itself and the spin-off, and this has created a degree of ill-will.

Clothingco is another company that, despite good intentions, has found it difficult to achieve the dramatic improvements in communications with both suppliers and customers promised by Internet advocates.

Case study:
CLOTHINGCO

Selling specialist clothing, Clothingco is mainly aimed at the older customer and at those who may have difficulty finding what they require elsewhere. The company began its life as a mail-order business and still retains its printed catalogue alongside the online operations. The company feels that this approach allows customers to 'look through the shop window', find what they require and order in the way they are most comfortable with. The company says it is aiming, as far as possible, for a person-to-person (P2P) focus. Technology has been, and remains, a key concern for the company. Online customers email their order, and those ordering from the printed catalogue order by telephone or post. Whatever the method received, all orders have to be rekeyed into the company's main system. The company would like a much more integrated system, but as yet it has not attained this. It feels that this is partly due to bad computer advice at start-up.

The company has no Internet links with its suppliers and has to fax all of its orders to suppliers. Again, this is due to integration issues that are not entirely within Clothingco's ability to resolve. On the one hand, the company's own internal systems are not set up for email ordering from suppliers, but on the other, it describes some of the suppliers as being 'in the Stone Age' and not prepared to do business online, or with a small company. The company outsources its delivery, Web site design and computer maintenance operations.

The company feels that it has a reasonable knowledge of its customers, although it would like more, maintaining that 'until you've sold to a lot of customers, the figures don't mean anything'. It feels that there is insufficient volume of sales either to build up a meaningful picture, or to justify spending money on extra marketing. The lack of customer information is in part attributabe to the inefficient information systems that are currently in place.

AN EMERGING PICTURE

While the case examples in this chapter cannot be treated as a representative sample, and the generalizability of the findings has not been fully tested, the case organizations do provide some indications of an emerging picture, and areas for further empirical research.

It appears that Hammer's (1990) exhortation to 'obliterate' existing business process is misjudged, at least when applied to e-Business. Both the literature and empirical research show that many companies have not been able – and do not wish – to impose e-Business processes overnight. They are, in Hammer's (1990) words, still 'paving the cow paths'. This is perhaps especially the case post-2000 where much of the initial hype and excitement have now been tempered by a more reserved and pragmatic view of e-Commerce. It seems likely that companies are anxious to avoid the risks associated with a 'big bang' approach to adoption of e-Commerce. There is evidence that companies are taking a more holistic and incremental approach to implementing e-Business processes, either by developing them organically, out of existing business processes, or by running e-Business processes as discrete applications. This is because organizations are conscious of constraints of finance, technology and organizational and/or industry culture, while at the same time they seek to tailor products and services to customer needs and expectations, via strategies not only of cost limitation, but increasingly through approaches based on differentiation and/or focus.

While there is no doubt that the Internet has provided a new channel for the conduct of B2B and B2C information transaction exchanges, and in this respect has had a discernible impact on the speed, location and volume of information communication, it remains debatable whether there is as yet real evidence of Steward *et al.*'s 'radical new commercial structures'.

Focusing on the three topics that have been given special prominence in this chapter points to the future direction of e-Business operations. The picture that is emerging is one in which:

- there is re-intermediation as well as dis-intermediation.

Whilst the rhetoric was initially one of dis-intermediation, there appears to be an increasing trend within both the academic and practitioner literature to acknowledge that it is not so much a case of dis- but rather, of re-intermediation (e.g. Chirchu and Kauffman 1999; Subirana and Carvajal 2000; Jallat and Capek 2001). While writers such as Janssen and Sol (2000) write that 'traditional physical intermediaries are threatened by direct communication between sellers and buyers', a conflicting view highlights the ascent of 'white van man', i.e. of traditional road-based delivery operations, as a direct consequence of online retail shopping (Clark 2003). UK government transport statistics appear to support this, showing that good vehicles traffic in urban areas increased on major roads by 6.2 per cent between quarter 2 of 2002 and the same quarter of 2003; and light van traffic, 'representing 11 per cent of all motor vehicles, increased by 5.9 per cent in the second quarter of 2003 compared to the same time' in 2002 (Department for Transport 2003).

In terms of any identifiable trend, the terms **infomediary** and **cybermediary** are in increasingly common usage (see, for example, Sarkar *et al.* 1996; Hagel and Rayport 1997). The roles of a cybermediary in the context of re-intermediation due to the Internet can be illustrated by reference to two online booksellers, Amazon.com and abebooks.com.

Case study:
AMAZON

The well-known online bookseller Amazon.com is often regarded as the template for online business. Amazon's success is based on its dis-intermediation of the supply chain by combining the role of wholesalers and retailers, acting as a single link online intermediary between publishers and individual consumers (Tassabehji 2003). The Web-based business model offers easy purchasing, a huge selection and fast delivery. The cost-savings Amazon's model achieves also allows it to sustain a price advantage over many traditional

177

booksellers. Amazon is in fact not so much a force of dis-intermediation, as a cybermediary merchant fulfilling informational, transactional and logistical operations. Part of the reason for Amazon's success is because it has been able to establish a trust role in the marketplace by creating a strong brand name. Although customization of its products is at best highly limited, its software enables it to achieve a higher degree of personalization of its service. For example, on re-entering the Web site, returning customers are met with a personal greeting and suggested purchase offerings. Amazon also facilitates some customer-to-customer (C2C) interaction. This is not direct C2C interaction, but takes the form of customer reviews of books. Customers are invited to review a book or CD, and these reviews are published alongside the price and ordering information for each product. In this way, Amazon uses its customers to spread word of mouth about its products.

Although Amazon has used its first-mover advantage to achieve market leadership, the case of Abebooks (www.abebooks.com) illustrates that, in contrast to the Amazon model, there is still scope for other kinds of cybermediaries, whose success is based on re-intermediation.

 Case study:
ABEBOOKS

Abebooks is the world's largest online marketplace for used, rare and out-of-print books. Abebooks links approximately 10,000 independent booksellers from around the world via the Internet through a massive searchable database of over 40 million books. The Web site acts as a virtual meeting place for buyers and sellers, helping small independent players to compete with bookselling superstores. Buyers who visit Abebooks do not see a single corporate book retailer – instead they see a network of independent booksellers. Booksellers upload their inventory data to the Abebooks database, specifying information about each book including condition and price. Bookbuyers can search the Web site to find the book they want. Once they have located the book they want, the buyer contacts the bookseller and makes their purchase through direct communication, usually by email. The bookseller ships the book directly to the buyer from their own shelves, and receives their full listed price. Booksellers can process credit-card payments themselves, or, for small fee, opt to have Abebooks process these payments on their behalf. Abebook's role is essentially that of almost a pure infomediary. Its transactional role is solely facilitative.

Amazon and Abebooks join Legalco as examples of companies whose intermediary activities and business models have capitalized on the opportunities to reconfigure the supply chain offered by the Internet. However, other companies, such as Equipco, who are keen to use a dis-intermediated model of e-Business cannot do so, because of customer preference and also (curiously enough since the Internet is thought to break this barrier down as well) because of the geographic distance between customers and a need for locally based sales intermediaries. With regard to dis-intermediation, it is becoming increasingly clear that the picture painted of an intermediary-free environment is not in fact a reality of current e-Business practice.

- Significant barriers to integration remain.

Regarding the management of business processes and information systems, the rhetoric has been one in which the information flows facilitated by the ICTs of the Internet would enable all the business processes within and between organizations to be linked effortlessly together in one interconnected 'wired' world. However, the reality of current e-Business practice does not seem to indicate a world of seamless interaction and integration. Often, companies run their e-Operations as a discrete set of processes, quite separate from their traditional operations. There seems to be a real failure to capitalize on the benefits available from maximizing information systems integration. Such integration is inhibited by both technological and business barriers.

Information systems integration can be limited internally due to the inadequacy of long established and expensive legacy systems, as is the case in Equipco; or it may be due to the limitations of more recently acquired technology, as is the case in Pharmco, Finman and Clothingco. Externally, integration can be limited due to inadequacies in the information systems of customers and/or suppliers (for example, Finman, ARB, Clothingco). For companies like Risk-insure, it can be the lack of agreed industry standards that is holding back greater integration with supply network partners.

However, some companies choose to maintain separate e-processes for primarily business reasons. For example, Risk-insure does this as it wants to limit the risk to its existing business relationships with supply network partners who have a strong preference for traditional trading processes. On the other hand, some companies have set up quite separate e-Processes in order to penetrate new market segments (for example, Shareco). In contrast, Finman is an example of a dotcom that has been driven away from its original pure-play model by the preferences of some of its customers.

Thus, the reality is that companies are having to evolve a variety of approaches to overcome the very real barriers that still exist to achieving business process and information systems integration.

- More and faster communication (but is it better?).

Concerning communication relationships between suppliers and customers, this is arguably the area where, to date, the Internet has achieved the greatest impact, and

179

where at least some of the rhetoric about e-Commerce appears to match the reality. Certainly speed and ease of Internet-based communication have helped information flows. Use of Internet-based ICTs such as e-Commerce can facilitate the flow of much more information, more speedily than ever before. This can be particularly helpful in improving communications with customers. In customer service operations this can improve companies' ability to respond accurately, reliability and speedily – and usually at much lower cost than was previously possible. The case of ARB is a useful illustration of this. However, at the same time, many organizations speak of 'information overload'. It is certainly the case that for some organizations, the inability to integrate conventional and e-Business processes, often leads to repetition in the handling of information – for example, both Shareco and Clothingco still rely on paper-based operations to process customer orders, whether these orders arrive electronically, or by conventional channels. Unless such multi-channel communication is handled carefully, it risks confusion, both externally with customers and internally with staff. Replication of business processes will almost certainly also lead to higher operating costs.

A NEW E-BUSINESS REALITY?

Ultimately, any organization must judge the success of e-Commerce in its business operations against the extent to which its use better enables it to achieve its strategic objectives. In terms of Porter's (1985) generic strategies, these objectives might be based on cost leadership, differentiation or focus. Adoption of e-Commerce usually has the potential to reduce operating costs significantly. (As we have already noted, a significant caveat to this is where e-Commerce replicates existing channels, as this is likely to increase rather than reduce costs.) As such, use of e-Commerce in operations seems essential to support low cost business strategy. However, as e-Commerce technology is available to all, its use can only provide an initial advantage over competitors. As its use becomes ubiquitous any such advantage seems doomed to fade. It seems that many companies are recognizing that the adoption of e-Commerce is necessary to avoid being at an operational cost disadvantage.

A sustainable competitive advantage seems more likely to accrue where e-Commerce can be used to support a business strategy based on differentiation or focus through superior customer service. The cases used in this chapter offer some examples of this. Clothingco, Shareco, Legalco, Finman, Pharmco and E-insure are all aiming to use e-Commerce to penetrate targeted market segments. ARB, Equipco and Risk-insure are trying to use e-Commerce to defend existing market segments. All these companies would claim to offer a product/service package that is in some way differentiated through its online customer service operations. All these companies see e-Commerce as a means of adding value for their customers in order to access new online markets, or to increase the loyalty of existing customers and raise exit barriers. They all see the use of e-Commerce as offering the means of gaining a competitive advantage by enhancing their customer service operations. Internet-based ICTs enable them to communicate and interact with their customers, both directly and via their supply chain intermediaries, more often, more fully and more intimately than ever before.

The theme throughout this chapter is that the initial rhetoric about the impact of e-Commerce on the management of business operations is, for the most part, not borne out in the present reality. It has turned out to be far more complex than the Internet prophets' initial predictions. Existing supply network relationships have been challenged and in some cases changed, but not always in the ways envisaged. Business process integration within and between organizations has not proved to be as easy to achieve as initially was believed and significant barriers still remain. The Internet has facilitated more and faster information flows, but whether this achieves better communication is more questionable. Although cost savings are on offer from the use of e-Commerce, particularly where the replication of business processes can be avoided, this seems unlikely to lead to any sustainable competitive advantage over the longer duration. Where e-Commerce is becoming more and more ubiquitous, the route to a sustainable competitive advantage seems more likely to be achieved through the use of e-Commerce to improve service to customers by adding value in support of business strategies based on differentiation and focus.

So what of the future? There seems little doubt that most, if not all business will become e-Businesses, in the sense that the use of Internet-based ICTs will become near universal. Those organizations not using the Internet in some capacity in their operations will be considered exceptional, if not a little eccentric. On the other hand, it also seems likely that the completely online (i.e. pureplay dotcom) business will be rare indeed. The vast majority of businesses will require some kind of real world presence, in their back-office if not their front-office operations. As such, all business will have to learn how to manage e-Operations. On the evidence of current trends as exemplified by the cases mentioned in this chapter, companies are still struggling to implement e-Business practices that best enable their operations to support their business strategies. Despite the early rhetoric, the reality is that there appears to be no one best way to implement and manage e-Business processes. As with many other facets of business activity, e-Business seems to operate on a contingency model; its management depending on factors specific to each case. The struggle to understand how best to manage e-Operations seems likely to continue for some time yet, as the use of e-Commerce in business operations is still in its infancy. Despite the publicity enjoyed by pioneering dotcoms and early converts to clicks-and-mortar e-Business models, fully fledged e-Businesses as yet remain the exception rather than the rule. Even where established businesses have embraced e-Commerce, online trading revenues typically represent no more than 5 per cent of their activities (e.g. when measured by sales turnover). For the UK as a whole, even when a very broad definition of e-Commerce is applied, i.e. where e-Commerce is not just Internet-based transactions, but transactions via *any* computer-mediated channel, the figures show national revenues of around 7.2 per cent in the business sector and 2.4 per cent in the retail sector (OECD 2003).

Our studies indicate that there is much more to learn about managing e-operations. In particular, there is a need to gain a better understanding of the organizational and contextual variables that affect the management of e-Business operations. In establishing operations for e-Business, most, if not all, of the case companies cited in this chapter have had to work within the confines and preferences of both industry and organizational culture, and in so doing have had to accommodate existing or inherited processes and information systems. There are also issues of industry standards – or rather, a lack of such standards – and often this is coupled with working practices that both organizations and their customers may be loathe to change. Clearly, there is much scope for further research into how such organizational and contextual issues affect e-Commerce adoption and operations.

Other areas ripe for study are how best to implement e-Commerce within business operations, how to realize the best mixture of bricks and clicks operations and how to measure the performance of e-Business operations. Whilst there is general acceptance that e-Business is here to stay, many organizations are still grappling with the question of how best e-Commerce applications can be made to fit within the processes and strategy designed for the core business. And once the degree of fit with the core business and conventional processes has been achieved, the all important question of how to measure the performance of e-Business operations remains. This is an area where there is very scant literature, and where 'the lack of concrete data on gains from channel integration highlights a fundamental issue in the evolution of electronic commerce' (Steinfield *et al.* 2002).

By addressing these and similar issues, academic researchers can play their part in helping practitioners to learn how to make best use of e-Commerce in their operations and to avoid the many pitfalls that lie in wait for the unwary or the naïve. There is a balance that can yet be achieved between the rhetoric and the reality of e-Business operations.

CONCLUSION

The chapter has examined the rhetoric about the impact of e-Commerce, versus the reality of how organizations appear to be managing e-Business processes. This shows that:

- In the global economy, many organizations are seeking to use the Internet and other ICTs to achieve competitive advantage.
- e-Business competitive strategy appears to be based more on a strategy of differentiation, rather than cost reduction, where it was anticipated that the Internet would enable:
  1 greater dis-intermediation and reduction of middlemen
  2 improved business processes
  3 greater transparency of information between organizations and their customers.

182

- While some of the above has come to pass, it is by no means a universal outcome of e-Business and many organizations are not only reliant on new forms of intermediaries, but have been unable to wholly integrate e-Business operations with conventional ones, for a number of reasons including cost, lack of standards, and employee and/or customer resistance; and a super-abundance of information, not all of which is either needed, or can be used.
- There has been a marked reduction in the number of pure-play dotcom organizations and the trend now appear to be for an organic, integrated and pragmatic approach to e-Business.
- More understanding is needed of the organizational and contextual variables that can bring success or failure in e-Business; and greater examination needs to be made of how organizations are using e-Business internally, how best to implement e-Business processes, and how to measure the performance of e-Business processes

N.B. To protect the confidentiality of some of the case companies, pseudonyms have been adopted and some of the case details have been disguised.

GLOSSARY

Cost leadership   The strategy of aiming to be the lowest cost producer.

Cybermediary   An electronically based intermediary, such as the holiday company Lastminute.com.

Differentiation   The strategy of offering a product or service package that is perceived by customers to add value.

Dis-intermediation   Cutting out the middleman and selling direct from supplier to customer, for example, Amazon.

Extensible Mark Up Language (XML)   Language which codes computer text such that it can be read on Web pages.

Focus   The strategy of targeting a narrow market segment that the organization is well-placed to serve.

Infomediary   A company which provides essential details to enable a buyer to make an informed purchase decision.

Operations management   The design, planning, operation and control of the resources used in the production of goods or services for customers.

Re-intermediation   The introduction of a new middleman into the value chain, an example would be Lastminute.com.

BIBLIOGRAPHY

Andreassen, T. W. and Lindestad, B. (1998) 'Customer loyalty and complex services: the impact of corporate image on quality, customer satisfaction and loyalty for customers with varying degrees of service expertise', *International Journal of Service Industry Management*, 9, 1: 7–23.

Barnes, D. (ed.) (2001) 'Business processes', in *Understanding Business: Processes*, London and New York: Routledge.

Benjamin, R. and Wigand, R. (1995) 'Electronic markets and virtual value chains on the information superhighway', *Sloan Management Review*, 36, 2: 62–72.

Biazzo, S. (2000) 'Approaches to business process analysis: a review', *Business Process Management*, 6, 12: 99–112.

Castells, M. (1996) *The Information Age: Economy, Society and Culture. Volume 1, The Rise of Network Society*, Oxford: Blackwell.

Chaffey, D. (2002) *E-Business and e-Commerce Management: Strategy, Implementation and Practice*, Harlow: Financial Times/Prentice Hall.

Chan, S. L. (2000) 'Information technology in business processes', *Business Process Management Journal*, 6, 3: 224–37.

Childe, S., Maull, R. and Bennett, J. (1994) 'Frameworks for understanding business process re-engineering', *International Journal of Operations and Production Management*, 14, 12: 22–34.

Chirchu, A. M. and Kauffmann, R. J. (1999) 'Strategies for net middlemen in the intermediation/disintermediation/reintermediation cycle', *International Journal of Electronic Markets*, 9, 1/2: 109–17.

Clark, A. (2003) 'Internet shopping fuels "white van man"', *Guardian*, 'Media Guardian', 8 August. Accessed 15 August at: http://media.guardian.co.uk/Print/0,3858,4728950,00.html

Cohen, S., DeLong, J. B. and Zysman, J. (2000) 'Tools for thought: what is new and important about the e-conomy', *Berkeley Roundtable on the International Economy*, Working Paper no. 138, Berkeley: University of California.

Department for Transport (2003) *Traffic in Great Britain: Quarter 2 2003*, London: Department for Transport.

Dutta, S., and Segev, A. (1999) 'Business transformation on the Internet', *European Management Journal*, 17, 5: 466–76.

The Economist (2000) *Run for e-cover*, 355 (8174).

Gates, B. (2000) *Business @ the Speed of Thought: Succeeding in the Digital Age*, London: Penguin Business.

Hagel, J. and Rayport, J. F. (1997) 'The new infomediaries', *McKinsey Quarterly*, 4: 54–70.

Hall, J. (2000) 'Are your processes fit for e-commerce', *Management Services*, April: 12–16.

Hammer, M. (1990) 'Reengineering work: don't automate, obliterate', *Harvard Business Review*, July–August: 104–12.

Hensmans, M., van den Bosch, F. A. J. and Wolberda, H. W. (2001) 'Clicks vs. bricks in the emerging online financial services industry', *Long Range Planning*, 34: 231–47.

Hulme, G. V. (2001) 'Insurers write new tech policy', *InformationWeek*, 855: 159ff.

Jallat, F. and Capek, M. J. (2001) 'Disintermediation in question: new economy, new networks, new middlemen', *Business Horizons*, March–April: 55–60.

Janssen, M. and Sol, H. M. (2000) 'Evaluating the role of intermediaries in the electronic value chain', *Internet Research*, 10, 15: 406–17.

Johnson, G. and Scholes, K. (1999) *Exploring Corporate Strategy*, 5th edn, Hemel Hempstead: Prentice Hall.

Johnston, R., Chambers, S., Harland, C., Harrison, A. and Slack, N. (1997) *Cases in Operations Management*, London: Pitman.

Katz, J. A. and Safranski, S. (2003) 'Standardization in the midst of innovation: structural implications of the Internet for SMEs', *Futures*, 35: 323–40.

Keating, M., Metz, P. D., Holcomb, C., Nicholson, M. and Jones, D. L. (1999) 'How electronic commerce is transforming business processes', *Prism*, 1: 41–51.

Lee, R. G. and Dale, B. G. (1998) 'Business process management: a review & evaluation', *British Process Management Journal*, 4, 3: 214–25.

McGuffog, T. (1999) 'E-commerce and the value chain', *Manufacturing Engineer*, 78, 4: 157–60.

Mahadevan, B. (2000) 'Business models for Internet-based e-commerce', *California Management Review*, 42, 4: 55–69.

Malone, T., Yates, J. and Benjamin, R. (1987) 'Electronic markets and electronic hierarchies', *Communications of the ACM*, 30: 484–97.

Margretta, J. (2000) 'The power of virtual integration', *Harvard Business Review*, March–April: 73–84.

Mariotti, S. and Sgobbi, F. (2001) 'Alternative paths for the growth of e-commerce', *Futures*, 33: 109–25.

Merali, Y., Arnott, D., Croom, S., Galliers, B. and Levy, M. (2000) *Hot Topics*, Vol. 2, Warwick: Warwick Business School.

Michalak, W. and Jones, K. (2003) 'Canadian e-commerce', *International Journal of Retail & Distribution Management*, 31, 1: 5–15.

OECD (2002) *Measuring the Information Economy*, Paris: OECD Publications.

Phan, D. D. (2003) 'E-business development for competitive advantages: a case study', *Information & Management*, 40: 581–90.

Poon, S. and Swatman, P. (1999) 'An exploratory study of small business Internet commerce issues', *Information & Management*, 35: 9–18.

Porter, M. (1980) *Competitive Strategy: Techniques for Analyzing Industries and Competitors*, New York: The Free Press.

Porter, M. (1985) *Competitive Advantage*, London: Simon and Schuster.

Porter, M. E. and Millar, V. E. (1985) 'How information gives you competitive advantage', *Harvard Business Review*, July–August: 149–60.

Ryan, C. (2000) 'How disintermediation is changing the rules of marketing, sales and distribution', *Interactive Marketing*, 1, 4: 368–74.

Sampler, J. L. and Short, J.E. (1998) 'Strategy in dynamic information-intensive environments', *Journal of Management Studies*, 35, 4: 429–36.

Sarkar, M. B., Butler, B. and Steinfield, C. (1996) 'Intermediaries and cybermediaries: a contingency role for mediating players in the electronic marketplace', *Journal of Computer Mediated Communications*, 1. Accessed online (June 2003): http://jcmc.huji.il/vol1/issue3/sarkar.html.

Schniederjans, M. J. and Cao, Q. (2002) *e-Commerce Operations Management*, River Edge, NJ: World Scientific.

Shaw, M. J., Gardner, D. M. and Thomas, H. (1997) 'Research opportunities in electronic commerce', *Decision Support Systems*, 21: 149–56.

Shim, S. S. Y., Pendyala, V. S., Sundaram, M. and Gao, J. Z. (2000) 'Business-to-business e-commerce frameworks', *Computer*, 33, 10: 40–7.

185

Slack, N., Chambers, S., Harland, C., Harrison, A. and Johnston, R. (1998) *Operations Management*, Harlow: Financial Times/Prentice Hall.

Slack, N., Chambers, S. and Johnston, R. (2001) *Operations Management*, Harlow: Pearson Education.

Slywotzky, A. (2003) *How To Grow When Markets Don't: Discovering the New Drivers of Growth*, New York: Warner Books.

Steinfield, C., Bouwman, H. and Adelaar, T. (2002) 'The dynamics of click-and-mortar electronic commerce: opportunities and management strategies', *International Journal of Electronic Commerce*, 7, 1: 93–119.

Steward, S., Callaghan, J. and Rea, T. (1999) 'The ecommerce revolution', *BT Technology Journal*, 17, 3: 124–32.

Strader, T. J., and Shaw, M. J. (1997) 'Characteristics of electronic markets', *Decision Support Systems*, 21: 185–98.

Subirana, B. and Carvajal, P. (2000) 'Transaction streams: theory and examples related to confidence in Internet-based electronic commerce', *Journal of Information Technology*, 15: 3–16.

Tassabehji, R. (2003) *Applying e-commerce in business*, London: Sage.

Timmers, P. (1998) 'Business models for electronic markets', *Electronic Markets*, 8, 2: 3–8.

Weill, P. and Vitale, M. (2001) *Place to Space: Migrating to Ebusiness Models*, Cambridge, MA: Harvard Business School.

Chapter 11

Building trust in stakeholder relationships: are call centres sweat shops or massage parlours?

ANGELA AYIOS AND LISA HARRIS

KEY LEARNING POINTS

After completing this chapter you will have an understanding of:

- The importance of trust in business relationships
- Why trust is particularly crucial in e-Business contexts
- The influence of technology upon employee motivation and performance
- The role of internal marketing in building and sustaining trust
- The provision of quality service in a multi-channel environment

INTRODUCTION

While press attention has focused on the achievements (and, more recently, the struggles) of Internet entrepreneurs, little mention has been made of the service workers who make up the bulk of the demand for labour in the e-Economy.

This chapter will examine the 'rhetoric or reality?' issue in the context of recent call centre expansion that has taken place to service e-Business operations. We argue that a high quality, integrated service provision is required across a multi-channel environment in order for e-Business reality to stand any chance of living up to the rhetoric.

Specifically, we begin by defining the various forms of trust along a continuum from 'low trust' to 'high trust' and then locate the discussion in the evolving e-Business context. We go on to examine recent developments in call centres, focusing upon both internal relationships between management and staff and also relationships between staff and customers. We then discuss how emerging e-Business technologies and new ways of working provide opportunities for building a high degree of trust expressed in more emotional terms. We pose the key question of whether the caring attitudes and behaviours identified as so essential to building durable bases for customer trust can be routinely achieved in a call centre environment. We argue that competitive advantage can be gained if the customer perception is of a caring organization concerned with meeting individual needs – particularly in an industry sector often associated with 'sweat shop' working conditions and control-based management practices. However, we conclude that if e-Business reality is really to live up to the rhetoric, it requires a 'high-trust' environment developed by effective utilization of multi-channel technological capabilities, together with human resource management policies which encourage rather than stifle **emotional intelligence**. This is currently a tall order for all but the most progressive call centre operations.

FORMS OF TRUST

Trust can be said to exist on a continuum ranging from weaker, fragile trust, which is commonly based on, for example, rules, contracts and institutions, through to more durable, emotionally based trust, aligned with social and cultural groupings and norms, kinship and family, and/or high positive evaluations of good character and goodwill. In between these two poles is a centre point of trusting expectations and behaviours, which revolve around knowledge gathered through repeated interactions over time. Such a knowledge base permits more cognitive, rational bases for trust to emerge centred on calculations and expectations arising out of competent performance of duties. This is illustrated in Figure 11.1, the trust continuum.

Low (calculative) trust:	Intermediate (knowledge-based) trust:	Strong (affect-based) trust:
Contracts	Formal contractual elements fulfilled	Emotional bonds
Insurance		Family/personal kinship ties
The courts/legal system	History of interaction	Shared norms, eg religion,
Job descriptions/ qualifications	Knowledge gained of partners' behaviour	
High monitoring		Showing (reciprocal)
Hierarchy and detailed	Consistency	interpersonal care & concern
specification of job roles	Reliability	Honest intentions
Assumptions of opportunism	Competence	Personally chosen behaviour

Figure 11.1 *The trust continuum*

In practice, these types of trust operate in business life in various ways. For example, some business-to-business relationships may start at the low trust end of the continuum, and move through to intermediate trust and even end up at strong trust, as would be the case, for example, in certain joint venture arrangements, in which partners wish to trust each other without constant high levels of surveillance by each party over the other. Commonly, after a period of a number of years, 'expatriate' staff would be withdrawn from key positions, which are then handed over to local managers, save, perhaps, for the CEO position or something similar. Within a business, individuals are probably initially employed on a low-trust basis, with their CV and qualifications being the determining factor (although this may not necessarily be the case in certain industries or cultures). Once they have 'proved' themselves, and knowledge has been gained regarding, for example their competence and reliability, then trust in them may become stronger, and they may be promoted and/or given more latitude and/or be monitored less. If they continue to prove reliable and trustworthy, and show other more 'moral' characteristics such as honesty and kindness, and/or develop close ties with their 'bosses', becoming part of the 'clan', then that trust will be more dense and durable, their position will be more assured. In external relationships between a business's employees and its customers, then the enduring mark of the relationship will be low-trust, contractual and formal devices, but if staff show competence, if the forms of the agreement are adhered to over time, and if interactions between representatives of the company and its customers become characterized by more emotional and well-intentioned ties, then stronger customer trust and loyalty will result. We will suggest later in the chapter that e-Business developments provide opportunities for modern call centres to develop trust in this way.

Calculative trust

Trust at its most basic relies on contracts and the courts, documents and procedures, and high levels of monitoring and control. In fact, some would question whether this represents trust at all (Husted 1998). It has been named, for example, calculative or calculus-based trust (Lewicki and Bunker 1996; Child 1998), fragile trust (Ring and Van de Ven 1994; Ring 1996), institutional trust (Zucker 1986), and deterrence-based trust (Shapiro *et al.* 1992; Sheppard and Tuchinsky 1996). Such trust revolves around the question of whether the other parties to the relationship will carry out their contractual agreement (Sako 1998), and is grounded in measures that prevent undesired action, for example, through contracts and the courts, to ensure consistency of behaviour (Lewicki and Bunker 1996). Perceptions of risk and the possibility of opportunistic behaviour are mitigated by resort to these formal devices, so that economic actors are able to conduct business with each other in 'guarded ways' (Ring 1996). As he puts it: 'these parties trust, but make rationally calculated side-bets about the real degree of trustworthiness expected from each other' (p. 153).

An example of this in practice would be customer concern regarding fulfilment of contractual obligations, security of payment systems and the privacy of personal data, which is of particular importance to online trading. The *Guardian Online* (5 September 2003) reported that recent Forrester research found that consumers' confidence in the integrity of e-Business had actually fallen since 2001. It concluded that companies needed to work much harder to re-establish trust. Without trust being achieved at this most basic and calculative of levels, it has no opportunity to develop at a deeper level.

Knowledge-based trust

Trust at the intermediate range of the continuum assumes that trust at its most basic and formal level has been achieved, and parties to a relationship wish to continue interacting, with the 'trustor' having built a degree of confidence in the 'trustee's' ability to deliver what has been formally promised. Calculative bases are a platform for gaining knowledge as to whether partners fulfil the terms of their contract and adhere to or disappoint the formal relationship expectations. Out of this, if contracts and expectations are not compromised, a belief develops that there are 'good rational reasons' for vesting trust in another (Lewis and Weigert 1985) and partners are able to deepen their level of trust. In such a formulation of trust, partners have already positively evaluated the extent to which institutional and formal elements are being properly adhered to, and go on to seek out further evidence that a partner is trustworthy. With calculative requirements for trust development fulfilled, the trustor has the opportunity to gain more knowledge of how the trustee fulfils their duties in their interests, or otherwise. Such trust has been named process-based trust (Zucker 1986), knowledge-based trust (Shapiro *et al*. 1992; Sheppard and Tuchinsky 1996; Lewicki and Bunker 1996), competence-based trust and cognitive or cognition-based trust (Lewis and Weigert 1985; McAllister 1995).

The development of such trust requires time, based largely on repeated interactions between the parties (Lewicki and Bunker 1996). These repeated interactions permit the trustor to develop a view as to the trustee's consistency of behaviour and reliability: 'Inconsistencies between words and action decrease trust' (McGregor 1967 cited in Mishra 1996: 268). And to be reliable, to keep one's word in business life, one at least needs to be competent – partners need to gain knowledge that the other party is capable of doing what it says it will do (Sako 1988), and will do it. As a result, 'judgments about trust in working relationships become specific based on accumulation of interactions, specific incidents, problems, and events' (Gabarro 1987 cited in Mishra 1996: 268).

The importance of this accumulation of a positive experience of process and performance, carried out in the customer's best interests, is readily visible in the e-Business context. For example, the customer reviews and recommendations provided by Amazon, and more recently, the published buyer feedback and rating of a seller's performance, together with water-tight payment systems, has encouraged even 'net-novices' to try out e-Bay's online auction service.

Affect-based trust

The trustor, having observed that the trustee has fulfilled all of the relevant contractual and procedural requirements of their partnership, and having had time to accumulate knowledge of the trustee's consistent and reliable performance of their duties, may be prepared to extend a deepened form of trust to the trustee if they consider it desirable or appropriate. The most intense and durable form of trust has been named, for example, characteristic-based trust (Zucker 1986), emotional trust (Lewis and Weigert 1985), affect-based trust (McAllister 1995), identification-based trust ((Shapiro *et al.* 1992, Sheppard and Tuchinsky 1996; Lewicki and Bunker 1996), resilient trust (Ring and Van de Ven 1994; Ring 1996) and extended trust (Brenkert 1998; Humphrey and Schmitz 1998).

Trusting behaviour at this end of the trust spectrum comprises a more emotional basis of interaction between trustee and trustor. At its most durable, this type of trust is linked closely with the person: ethnicity, family background or religious grouping are often significant factors (see, for example, Zucker 1986). On a daily basis, this trust will be characterized by, for example, efforts to demonstrate interpersonal care and concern (McAllister 1995). How does such trust operate in the business environment? Sako foresees this as a context in which parties to the relationship 'make an open-ended commitment to take initiatives for mutual benefit while refraining from unfair advantage taking' (1998: 89). As a result, partners perceive and feel subject to genuine intentions not to harm, but rather look out for and help the other party.

McAllister formulates the background to such perceptions thus:

> insights into the motives of relationship partners provide foundations for affect-based trust . . . behaviour recognized as personally chosen rather than role-prescribed, serving to meet legitimate needs, and demonstrating interpersonal care and concern rather than enlightened self-interest may be critical for the development of affect-based trust.
>
> (1995: 26)

He explains that this is limited to contexts of frequent interaction, where there are enough social data to permit confident attributions to be made. Out of such interaction, partners to a business relationship come to believe in the other's goodwill (Ring 1996). As a result, such trust occupies the opposite end of the spectrum to the more rational, calculative bases for trust, so that trust comes to be 'a non-calculative reliance in the moral integrity, or goodwill, of others on whom economic actors depend for the realization of collective and individual goals when they deal with future, unpredictable issues' (1996: 156). For example, call centre staff working for telecoms giant Orange actually welcome the monitoring of their work because it provides concrete evidence of the high quality service that they know is provided – in other words it is an opportunity to showcase their skills by winning industry awards! Online communities provide further

191

evidence of affective trust, for example, actively participating Cisco customers actually use the facility to resolve queries posed by other customers.

Trust as presented here, then, operates along a continuum, starting from highly calculative, low-trust bases at one end, moving through accumulated knowledge of the skills and reliability of partners and greater trust, and at the far end, based on the development of emotional trust either as a result of close relationships arising out of repeated interaction and the resultant perception of goodwill, or as a consequence of social, cultural and kinship ties. The definition of trust to be employed here will be Boon and Holmes' (1991: 194) definition of trust as 'a state involving confident positive expectations about another's motives with respect to oneself in situations entailing risk' (cited in Lewicki and Bunker 1996: 117). For convenience, this chapter will name the three distinct modes of the operation of trust identified in this section as calculative trust, knowledge-based trust (Lewicki and Bunker 1996) and affect-based or affective trust (McAllister 1995).

BUSINESSES, BRANDS AND TRUST

During the 1990s, Koehn commented that trust was very likely to become that decade's 'buzzword'. Her prediction seems to have been timely. From the government, to hospitals, through the media, the exam system, and ultimately to business, trust seems to have become the next big thing. 'Building big trust brings big bucks', appears to be the mantra. This fact is easily borne out in practice. Two of our major supermarket chains have run radio advertising campaigns that build on this very notion – by suggesting that the shop assistant talking over the tannoy knows all of the shop's customers personally, the implication is that this is a cosy, local community, where everyone knows each other, where relationships are firm – and where affective trust is high. 'Trust us', they are saying, 'you are part of our community'. As the foregoing analysis has shown, where trust is high customers are more likely to stay loyal to the company, overlook the odd mistake here and there, report positively to friends and relatives about their service, and become quite the advocate for the company. Who would not want this as a source of competitive advantage?

But is this a realistic proposition? Kipnis (1996) does not think so. From banks to telephone companies, from holiday firms to electricity suppliers, from customer care and online shopping to checking our mortgage – these days 'we frequently have to trust strangers to get things done . . . people who are neither close friends, family, nor members of the same tribe or caste . . . Trust under these circumstances may be unnatural' (Kipnis 1996: 40–1). This bothers us: 'having to trust other people is bothersome . . . We believe it is better to control our world than for our world to control us. The requirement that we trust others introduces unwanted uncertainty into our lives. It means that other people control outcomes that we value. It gives people power over us' (1996: 40). People may be bothered by trusting strangers because it feels unnatural, and they will be highly calculative in their approach to such strangers when embarking on any kind of business relationship with them, however, they may be desirous of finding a company with whom they can develop a relationship of trust, and they may indeed be motivated to trust. How does that higher form of trust come about?

The initial assessment and behaviour of a customer towards a business will be calculative – a good reputation, a recommendation from a friend, or an attractive deal will get the customer in, but at this stage the customer will be directing attention towards whether the formal elements of the deal are adhered to – whether the product is 'fit for the purpose', whether what was expected to be delivered is being delivered, whether the service provision fulfils its promises, whether the claim is worth the paper or computer screen it is written on. At this point, the customer is protecting his or herself from 'opportunism', in the sense of failure to deliver what is promised. Fortunately for the customer, this is generally protected in law and regulation:

> control tends to be exercised by making untrustworthy behaviour costly for trustees. Regulatory agencies, professional boards of ethics, and civil laws . . . threats of fines, prison terms, or loss of license for untrustworthy behaviour. I would describe these regulatory agencies as the outward manifestation of people's inner disquiet at the need to trust others.
>
> (Kipnis 1996: 43)

For the business, it is not just the formal institutional guarantors that curb opportunistic behaviour – reputation too has become key to maintaining business competitiveness, and if customers are failed in sufficient quantity to not return to the business, or even worse require recourse to the courts and regulators, then reputation will be lost, trust will be broken and regaining that ground will be nigh on impossible.

For businesses, it is easy to overlook the 'basics' of trust building that occur at the calculative levels – these are, in Herzberg's terms, the 'hygiene factors' of good business. If you do not get the basics right – if the product is not fit for the purpose, if the person answering the telephone cannot satisfy a customer's query or complaint, if the consumer's needs are poorly met, then trust is undermined at the outset. Trust at this stage is at its weakest, and customers may easily withdraw their custom, or if they do stay, they remain at this low-trust level, subjecting all of their interactions with the business to close surveillance, expecting the worse, mindful of recourse to contract documents, guarantees, and possibly 'bad mouthing' the business and its representatives. Businesses wishing to trade on trust do not want this state of affairs, and at the outset they need to bring customers to the point where they trust a business to carry out what it said it would do. As the trust continuum above has shown, once calculative bases for trust have been honoured, customers feel ready to move on to the next level of trust if they so wish, and we would argue that they are motivated to trust beyond the merest calculative levels. Having gathered knowledge, through repeated interactions, we come to 'trust, with cautious faith, people who have interacted reliably with us in the past' (Bromiley and

Cummings 1992: 41) At this stage, customers are heartened, and more inclined to invest trust, if some further elements of trustworthy behaviour become evident.

What are these further elements? Returning to the conceptualization of trust above, words such as reliability, competence and consistency emerge as key factors. When interacting with representatives of the organization providing a service, customers seek evidence of their capabilities to do the job well. In personal encounters over the telephone, for example, this would be shown perhaps through not having to explain again the entire conversation held 10 days ago with another representative, not waiting to be rerouted to 'another department', actually being able to get a resolution to any problem being raised, and knowing that they will not be subject to rudeness, indifference or hard selling. If customers are using an electronic medium, they need to feel able to navigate the site, access their own information, feel it is secure, be confident it is accurate and consistent and so on. All of the foregoing creates an impression of competence, reliability and consistency – an integrated approach and satisfying content across all channels.

If trust is occurring at this level, a more emotional bond of trust has the potential to be created and affective bases for trust start to look achievable. Once the customer has in his or her head the image of a company that delivered on what it said it would do, in which interactions with staff or online communications are competent, consistent, reliable and with a pleasing or satisfying outcome, what moves them on to that extra step of actually feeling a resilient bond of trust with the company? A key element of this type of trust when it exists outside of familial and kinship ties is that of interpersonal care and concern – especially if this is beyond role-prescribed boundaries (McAllister 1995). When a company, through its staff and other customer intermediaries, proves its commitment to its customers through mechanisms that have customer benefit at heart, and which do not take advantage of customers, then more durable, affective bases of trust will be developed. Customers will come to perceive 'goodwill' towards them being exercised by a company if, for example, telephone agents are viewed as working in the customer's best interests, doing everything in their power to 'solve' a problem rather than pass the buck, departing from scripted transactions into personal exchanges appropriate to the interaction (of a positive nature!), empowered to compensate customers or make non-standard decisions. In such a situation, where the company's representatives are seen to be working for, rather than against the customer, expectations of opportunism come to be minimized, and a belief in caring competence and professionalism come to be maximized. This is one of the great advantages of resilient-type trust – even if a mistake is made, in circumstances where the customer has been able over time to develop relationships with the company's representatives, rather than work only on the basis of arm's-length contacts, then they would tend to take the more generous approach of 'I know you didn't *mean* to make a mistake', rather than taking the view that this is 'typical', as is more the norm at the calculative levels of trust. This type of customer trust can translate into customer loyalty, as they feel more closely aligned with the company, and come to identify more with their choice of provider – a very powerful source of competitive advantage.

194

This section has looked at the development of trust from the customer perspective. It has shown that if a company gets the basics right, through delivering on its promises and sticking to the agreement, then this provides a basis for the development of more durable, knowledge-based trust, which in turn has the potential to create a more emotional bond with the customer. But to move beyond these weaker calculus-based levels of trust, customers need to have faith in the competence and goodwill of the representatives of the company with whom they interact. In terms of technology-dependent interactions and transactions, these issues are magnified still further, and customers will seek out reliability and consistency. In terms of interactions and transactions with human representatives of the company, they will additionally seek out competence, and, if optimal trust levels are to be achieved, a degree of interpersonal care and concern. In order to address the 'rhetoric or reality' debate then, we will now examine this issue of ascending levels of trust in the context of the growth of call centres to support e-Business operations.

THINK POINT

from your own experience, what factors actually determine whether you trust a business with your custom or not?

CALL CENTRES – SWEAT SHOPS OR MASSAGE PARLOURS?

As noted earlier, while press attention has focused on the achievements and struggles of Internet entrepreneurs, relatively little mention has been made of the service workers who make up the bulk of the demand for labour in the 'new' economy. Many people work in call centres that have been dubbed 'the new sweat shops' or **electronic panopticons** (Bain and Taylor 2000). Call centre services fall into two main categories – outbound (cold-calling to potential customers) and inbound (taking calls from customers with queries and problems). According to the *Guardian Online* (17 August 2003) the call centre industry continues to grow by 22 per cent a year on average, making it one of the fastest growing sectors in the UK. Call centres currently employ half a million people in the UK, or 3 per cent of the workforce in northern England and Scotland. Of these workers, 70 per cent are under the age of 35 and women, salaries range from £7,800 to £21,000 (the average is £13,000–14,000), and 30 per cent are part-timers.

The reason behind banks such as HSBC pushing telephone and Internet banking operations (through highly successful subsidiary First Direct) is one of cost. These channels are much cheaper for banks than traditional branch banking. Customer relationship management company Talisma estimates that interaction with a customer

195

face-to-face costs $300 a time, a phone conversation costs $53, an Internet chat $30, text chat $10, email $3, and self-help on the Internet 10 cents. On this basis, in the early days of e-Commerce, the long-term future of the telephone call centre was questioned. However, online banking is still principally used for simple transactions, and when it comes to pensions or life insurance, customers prefer to talk to someone or meet face-to-face. For example, both Lloyds TSB and Barclays suffered from significant customer dissatisfaction and adverse publicity when branches were replaced by ATM machines in rural areas.

With the growth of call centres, however, a number of problems have arisen on both a human and a technical level. In these service-intensive organizations the power is in the hands of lower-level, front-line employees upon whose handling of service encounters managers must depend for the achievement of organizational objectives. Customer expectations are rising; many now expect an immediate response to queries at any time of the day or night, and are unimpressed, for example, if a company's Web site does not display the most up-to-date product information and availability. This puts pressure on firms to ensure customer service call centres are adequately and efficiently staffed, and also that their Web sites are easy to navigate and contain the information that the customer seeks. As Piercy (2000) notes: 'Too many employees who deal directly with customers are damaging the product, service or corporate brand every time they open their mouths'.

There can also be conflict between technical and business areas. For example, operators can blame the system for not working properly, while IT managers blame the high turnover of staff – bored by the repetitive nature of the work – for their inability to use a system to its full capability. According to McEwan (2001):

advisers read from a pre-prepared script shown on their personal computer screen . . . advisers were required to answer two telephone enquiries every minute for over 55 minutes in every hour throughout their working day, or else risk dismissal.

the nature of the work and the layout of the workplace only allowed minimum contact between advisers, who were physically isolated from each other and could only communicate with each other at the start and end of a working shift.

advisers at the Scottish call centre could not leave their work station without a supervisor's permission, had to raise their hand for a drink of water which was brought to them by their supervisor; and . . . any time spent in the toilet or on a meal-break was deducted from their paid hours of employment.

The above quotes typify what has come to be regarded as 'normal' operation for call centres, and there continue to be vociferous claims that whatever the rhetoric about the 'new' economy, such practices are still much in evidence today. As noted by Cornelius in Chapter 5, recent research has even suggested that employees may be selected on the basis of docility and malleability. Traditionally, many service industries have relied heavily

196

on 'scripts', and staff are monitored in order to assess how tightly they comply with them. However, these scripts are usually perceived to be inauthentic, just going through the motions, by customers. So for example, in the call centre, the script reigns supreme. This offers the advantage of consistency of service, but at a low, inauthentic or even 'phoney' level. Within the call centre, more opportunity for authentic, individualized responses to customer demands is likely to afford competitive advantage, but can only be delivered if the employee is trained, feels committed and has an appropriate degree of autonomy about how the work is undertaken.

Part of the rhetoric surrounding the e-Economy suggests that rapid technological developments provide call centres with the potential to grow into 'Customer Contact Centres'. According to Simon Rancoroni, an industry consultant, 'We're going to need to interact across a number of different media. The call centre agent will start to co-browse; to send email and text messages. . . . Up until now a call centre operator didn't need to spell'. In September 2000, Halifax spent £90 million launching Intelligent Finance (www.if.co.uk) which was the first organization in Europe to offer five integrated customer communication channels; telephone agents, interactive voice response, Internet, mobile phones and email. At Capital One, a financial services company which handles more than one million calls per week, callers are automatically routed to specialist agent teams depending on the predicted nature of their call based upon past experience. A recent Datamonitor study predicted that 40 per cent of all 75,000 call centres in the UK would be Web-enabled by the end of 2003 in order to provide multi-media customer access points. In theory, this means that a customer should be able to choose whether to 'click to talk' (speak to an employee by telephone) 'click to email' (send a query and receive a response by email) or 'click to chat' (interact with an employee by **instant messaging**). Of critical importance in terms of perceived service quality and the building of trust is for these channels to be seamless, so that a customer can switch from one to another without repeating the story. It is also important for a log to be kept of earlier conversations so that an agent is always aware of the history of the query and what stage has been reached in resolving it. It is also possible for specific customers to be flagged according to their perceived value, so that differing service levels can be applied accordingly. However, such integrated service offerings are currently at an early stage of development and remain elusive in the mainstream of business life.

THINK POINT

What are the dangers of multi-channel services being just a **Potemkin Village**? (see Glossary for more detail!) A Potemkin Village is a glossy façade hiding a lack of substance. If a company's multi-channel marketing strategy does not actually deliver on its promises in terms of integration of service offering, then it probably does more harm than good to the brand.

197

As the scope and role of call centres expands so (potentially) does that of the staff. For example, BT is introducing multi-function centres so that rather than being put through to different departments for each query, the same person can answer a whole range of queries. The training of staff thus needs to be given a role of greater and greater importance. Companies are now realizing that call centre employees are the face (or voice) of the company as far as customers are concerned. This not only has benefits for the customer, it also makes the call centre job more interesting. In many call centres there is no longer a script with standard responses, and staff are encouraged to speak freely. For example, at the RAC call centre they start with 'How can I help you?' and then take it from there. On one occasion when a customer had broken down, the call centre employee (or 'customer services specialist' as they are called at the RAC) sensing that she was upset, asked what was wrong. It turned out that it was her birthday, so the employee called the patrol man and mentioned that it would be a nice idea if he said 'happy birthday' when he reached her. He stopped off on the way and bought her a birthday bouquet of flowers. This is now touted as a 'true embodiment' of RAC brand values.

Recently, many firms (e.g. BT, Aviva and Prudential) have moved their call centre operations to India where costs are 30 per cent lower than in the UK. Labour costs are lower still (70 to 80 per cent cheaper than the UK), which make up two-thirds of the call centre costs. Telecoms and infrastructure share the remaining third equally. Indeed, India is ideal for low-cost outsourcing, as it has a huge population of highly technical and English-speaking workers (they have 7.1 million bilingual graduates enrolled in higher education). Indian call centres also attract applicants of graduate calibre, partly because the jobs are marketed as IT positions. Many of the Indian call centre staff have received special training. For example, staff dealing with UK customers are given accent training, as well as crash courses in pubs, football and soap story lines, so that they can hold 'up to the minute' conversations with the customers. Such policies have raised issues of trust internally as UK staff fear for the future of their jobs, with BT staff, for example, taking industrial action. Other challenges currently facing the industry include the increasing popularity of 'V-Reps' (automated agents) which save staffing costs but rather obviously lack the human touch, and also the difficulty of managing the issue of customer expectations. For example, after UK building society Nationwide upgraded its Web site to provide more detailed information to customers, its call centre was flooded with enquiries from people who wanted further information based on the new data that had been made available. Staff became discouraged as both the quantity and level of difficulty of their work rapidly increased.

DISCUSSION

Writing in 1974, Fox claimed that the vast majority of work environments were characterized by low-discretion work roles and low trust. Much has changed since then, and today, the predominance of rational, low-trust, high-monitoring models in the workplace has been usurped even in the manufacturing industry. And then along came call centres in an apparent throwback to 'old fashioned' modes of working. They fit Fox's model perfectly:

> Fox (1974) characterizes work roles in the 'low-trust-low-discretion syndrome' as consisting of five related elements, of which the first is key:
> (a) role occupants perceive management as behaving as if they believe workers cannot be trusted, of their own volition, to deliver desired work performance, and hence:
> (c) there is specific definition of job activities and close supervision;
> (d) co-ordination of the occupant's with other activities is constrained by standardized rules and routines;
> (e) failures draw punishment because they are presumed to stem from careless indifference to job rules and organizational goals; and
> (f) conflict with superiors handled by bargaining of an adversarial nature.
>
> (Marsden 1998: 177)

Traditional call centres are clearly structured around the fear of what will happen when the employees 'open their mouths': 'the underlying logic of the call centre system is that at some level, employee autonomy is counter-productive to corporate goals' (Houlihan 2001). There is clearly no belief that they will either do the work, or do it well, and so close control is employed as a way of overcoming this. Marsden comments that although managerial control is increased through this reduction in worker's discretion, worker flexibility is also reduced. And if there is one thing the foregoing model of customer–business trust development has suggested very strongly, it is that for trust to be durable, workers need to be interpersonal in their approach – they need to be flexible. There is a clear conflict here. Marsden describes the approach taken by traditional call centres as the 'work post rule', in which each task is unambiguously assigned to different 'posts' to control opportunism. While this close specification of tasks is viewed as reining in attempts by employees to reduce their realm of responsibility, it also tends to rein in their tendency to take on further tasks and responsibilities. Clearly, there is little basis for the establishment of trust, other than at the lowest, most formally calculative levels in such a system – and there is evidence that such systems will be subverted (however controlling they may be), for example, through cutting off customers (see Houlihan 2000 for an in-depth discussion of these issues). As a result even calculative trust with customers will be lost. This is the worst type of customer relations a company could possibly wish for.

Getting closer to the customer is often proclaimed as one of the key objectives of e-Business, be it through telephonic or electronic contacts. Human resource management approaches need to help to facilitate knowledge sharing and good internal employee relations, as well-informed, well-trained, competent and satisfied employees are more

199

likely to deliver 'authentic' service. The work of **emotional labourers**, those for whom changing the mood of others is central to the primary task (Hochschild 1983), has been well documented for flight attendants in the airline industry, and for nurses also (Smith 1992). Within Hochschild's work, there are implicit bi-polar labour processes, one of which includes 'authentic' and 'inauthentic' behaviour. As Cornelius notes in Chapter 5, customers universally warm to and value more authentic behaviour from service providers. Parallels can be drawn here with the earlier discussion of 'low' and 'high' levels trust which has particular significance in an e-Business context.

In recent years, a rhetoric has emerged around the call centre which is characterized by words such as empowerment, Total Quality Management, teambuilding, etc. – we seem to be moving on to a new model:

> Frenkel et al. (1998, 1999) . . . explored the coexistence of two opposing images of call centre organizing (the bureaucratic form and the empowered worker model) which they ultimately interpret as a combined new form, the 'mass customized bureaucracy', a 'best of breeds', providing a combination of standardization and flexibility in how work is carried out.
>
> (Houlihan 2000)

Such models equate with Marsden's 'competence rank rule', which sees tasks flexibly allocated within a work group that takes overall responsibility for the fulfilment of a particular function (1998: 182). Workers in a Japanese plant were shown by Koike and Inoki (1990) to work very effectively on this basis:

> workers are responsible for the production of an entire part using many machines, and also rotate between different production areas. Skill and worker rank are measured by the range of activities a worker can undertake, and her or his ability to deal with unusual operations and to teach other workers, and is not tied to individual work posts. And the tacit nature of these skills means management has to give workers a good deal of autonomy.
>
> (cited in Marsden 1998: 185)

The key point is that it is the tacit nature of the skills sets that needs to be captured and developed. The recognition of tacit knowledge and skills, in some respects, marks a revolution in our thinking about what we want to curb and control in business. No longer should 'control' in business truly be equated with controlling opportunism, what it needs to be about these days is controlling – or rather leveraging – tacit knowledge and skills. Or, in the trust terminology described above, it is about leveraging competence. And competence means a whole lot more than just completing a narrow range of mechanical skills to do one's job. Competence in the modern e-Business service context comprises the mechanical skills to do the job and to use the technology, and to offer that technology to the customer – but we have reached a stage where this level of

200

competence has little more status than reading and writing. These days, organizations implementing effective e-Business strategies must have complex technology capable of delivering sophisticated customer relationship management (CRM) systems. Cigna in the US, for example, lost 10 per cent of its membership in 2002 when it failed to implement its new customer self-service system properly. As noted earlier, technology needs to be in place that first of all accurately forecasts call volumes and staffing needs, and then, once the phone has been picked up, the agent should have information on the customer they are dealing with, when they last contacted them and why, whether they are talkative or to the point, what actions the customer or organization has already taken, who progressed their case and so on. Customers do not want to start their query from scratch every time they make a phone call. This is a very sophisticated level of competence, but building trust of a durable kind in e-Business is highly reliant on such competence, and the perception of knowledge of and care for the customers, along with the consistency of approach and reliability of service that this engenders.

This state of affairs clearly gives rise to a need for staff who can deliver on the promises that such systems make. Such technology releases the potential for trust to be created out of the person who picks up the telephone – their attitude, their motivation, their buy-in to the corporate mission of serving the customer, their knowledge of the needs of the customer and how best to serve them – staff are enabled in this context to release their own competence and knowledge, and to build more human bases for reliable and consistent service delivery. Competence and knowledge-based trust, in the e-Business context, has gained a whole new dimension. In addition to the technical 'hygiene factors' of a reliable and appropriate technological system supporting the business, and customer service 'ambassadors' who know how to use it, matters then come down to interpersonal skills, and these are the skills that the modern business seeks to enable and capitalize on as a source of competitive advantage. In the e-Business context, these are becoming the core skills sets – after all, anyone can answer a phone – it is what happens after that which defines business success.

How is such business success achieved? It is by now well-known in the e-Business context that the organic nature of human contact cannot be predicted through a highly scripted, low-trust, high-monitoring approach. The rise of emotional intelligence as a recognizable business skill in the more empowered models of call centre management is evidence of this fact. For example, reviewing evidence provided by Higgs of the positive relationship between job role performance and emotional intelligence indicators such as conscientiousness, resilience, motivation and sensitivity, Chris Stephenson, head of HR operations at Egg, admitted that with a large part of the work being about relationship building, emotional intelligence has a valid contribution to make (Higgs 2003). Further, Capital One's quality assurance procedures consider agents' abilities to empathize, use their cognitive skills, and seek out ways to satisfy customers (Throne 2001). These types of words, which are now turning up in the strategic vocabulary of e-Business, are words that belong in the higher levels of the knowledge-based and affect-based trust categorizations.

201

THINK POINT

It is of note that Higgs uncovered a negative relationship between intuitiveness and performance, which could be attributed to the heavy use of scripts and standard procedures restricting high levels of intuitiveness. His subsequent conclusion that call centres reliant on highly scripted interactions should change their recruitment policies to employ people with lower levels of emotional intelligence so as to circumvent this 'problem' seems somewhat back to front. Such people may feel frustrated, and even go 'off script' to serve the customer, thus failing to meet their formal targets, it is suggested, and so should be avoided. Surely the policy recommendation should be that such formal operating policies are to be avoided, rather than emotionally intelligent employees? What do you think?

This compelling logic is echoed – with different terminology – in the marketing literature. The basic premise behind **internal marketing** is that a company's communications with its customers and other external stakeholders are unlikely to be effective unless employees within the firm are aware of (and prepared to buy into) the message that the firm is trying to put across. It is currently fashionable to refer to employees as **internal customers**. If all employees are clear about the company's mission, objectives and strategy then there is a much better chance that customers will get the same message. Research by Piercy (2002) showed that firms whose employees understood organizational goals had considerably higher returns on capital than those where employees felt excluded or uninformed. He also noted that while more than 20 per cent of a firm's communications are actually with itself rather than with external stakeholders, internal communications were rarely accorded the same degree of attention and resources as external communications.

It is often suggested that internal communications can be enhanced through induction programmes, training courses, benefits, the use of Intranets or through working in cross-functional teams. However, things are rarely that simple. Payne regards a supportive organizational culture as a key ingredient in the success of internal marketing:

Internal marketing involves creating, developing and maintaining an organizational service culture that will lead to the right service personnel performing the service in the right way. It tells employees how to respond to new, unforeseen and even awkward situations. Service culture has a vital impact on how service-oriented employees act and thus how well they perform their tasks as 'part-time marketers'.

(1995: 48–9)

Inappropriate cultural norms can militate against successful relationship building. Too often, customer care programmes are instigated as a 'quick fix', without making any changes in management behaviour, or attempts to evaluate the success of programme. For example, answering the telephone within a set number of rings does not necessarily mean that a quality service is provided to the customer. In what may be regarded as the ultimate integration of internal marketing and customer relationship marketing Ulrich (1989) advises giving customers a major role in staff recruitment, promotion and development, appraisal and reward systems. While this policy may be too radical for many organizations, it can be seen from this discussion that a suitable internal climate is a necessary first step in the development of a customer orientation, rarely a simple task for an established organization. So, in a traditional call centre environment where staff work under constant surveillance and are denied the chance to express individual thoughts, what chance do CRM systems have that are reliant on the build up of trust?

Traditional 'sweat shop' models of highly scripted and routinized e-Commerce working environments operate at the low-trust end of the trust continuum. For many call centre workers, such working conditions continue to be the e-Business reality – interactions are strictly monitored and controlled, staff are expected to comply with the formal demands and standardized responses designed to limit their perceived opportunism and incompetence, and aggressive performance targets are aimed at channelling these closely specified job boundaries in the 'right' direction to achieve organizational ends. The working models are typical of the low-trust, low-discretion modes described by Fox and Marsden, and suffer from the same dire outcomes of workers working 'to the words of the manual' – bored staff blame the system when things go wrong, avoid serving difficult customers, control and minimize customer needs, evade performance targets through devious means, and do not deviate from the script even if this is evidently required. Employee goals, customer goals and organizational goals clearly do not converge in such a context. Looked at in this way, employee control seems as counter-productive to corporate goals as the dreaded employee autonomy. Customers who are cut off, their queries unanswered, the system failing to meet their needs, and with a standardized response ringing in their ears will not be having the formal, calculative, contractual elements of even a low-trust model being fulfilled. They will not trust such an organization, its products, or its services and neither will other potential customers when the news spreads.

E-businesses are now recognizing this, and, while the sweat shop model undoubtedly still continues, a new rhetoric has emerged which recognizes the central importance of the skills of the individual employee to deliver true customer service. The professed new models find call centre workers with their jobs enhanced and enriched through a multi-skilling approach, in a multi-channel environment, based on work communities which take on a variety of tasks and offer employees the training and autonomy to see issues through from beginning to end. Capital One, for example, seeks to provide a 'close-knit community' of workers, who are called 'associates' and who are encouraged to 'have fun' at work. The aim is to create camaraderie among staff and generate an atmosphere in which ideas can be freely exchanged, staff retained and productivity boosted. In return, managers are required to understand what staff want from their careers, and set objectives to develop and achieve this (Throne 2001). Similarly, attributes such as conscientiousness, resilience, motivation and sensitivity have come to be recognized as key skills in **emotional intelligence** – an area increasingly being seen as ripe for development in an industry mediated by ever more complex technology, but where relationship building is the key.

> A consultant for a major corporation recently gave a lecture on 'the importance of trusting your employees' to several hundred executives of one of America's largest corporations. There was an appreciative but stunned silence, and then one of them – asking for all of them – queried, 'But how do we control them?'. It is a telling question that indicates that they did not understand the main point of the lecture, that trust is the very opposite of control. Or, perhaps, they understood well enough, but suffered a lack of nerve when it came time to think through its implications.
>
> (Flores and Solomon 1998: 206)

CONCLUSION

Thus, in terms of the 'reality/rhetoric' debate, the key question is can the caring, concerned, interpersonal attitudes and behaviours, so essential to building durable bases for customer trust, be routinely achieved in the modern call centre environment? If call centres are indeed high-pressure work environments characterized by routinization, scripting, computer-based monitoring and intensive performance targets, in which difficult customers are cut off and complicated callers have services withheld (Houlihan 2000), can such a rational, low-trust organizational culture translate into a high-trust external face and deliver on e-Business promises? On the basis of the evidence presented above, the answer would appear to be unequivocally in the negative, indicating that in the call centre context at least, the reality of e-Business does not match the rhetoric.

What many of the espoused attributes of the new rhetoric described above have in common is that they reside in the stronger trust end of the trust continuum described at the beginning of this chapter. Intermediate-type trust is built through competence – in the e-Commerce context, the competence demands on the available technology are very high, requiring the capability to deliver seamless service channels, round-the-clock, up-to-date information and customer solutions in a way that not only matches the often vigorous marketing rhetoric, but also creates an experience of reliability and consistency among customers. Further, by attempting to put into practice notions of community and camaraderie, through recognizing that technology can release employees' personal attributes, skills and aspirations, e-Businesses are permitting the inauthentic, scripted interactions of the 'old style' call centres to be replaced with more genuine forms of human interaction. Properly implemented, releasing this human element has the potential to generate the more durable forms of affective trust described in the trust

204

model presented here. Customer trust and loyalty then has the potential to become an achievable business reality in the new economy rather than mere rhetoric.

QUESTIONS

Question 1
Can you think of any examples of when call centre operations might provide a poor quality of service to customers?

Feedback
- poor demand management, whereby calls may not even be answered in busy periods!;
- answer phones with complicated automated menu systems;
- making customers listen to advertisements (or bad music!) while held in a queue;
- employees unhelpful or badly trained;
- lack of integration between online and offline operations, for example, resulting in differential pricing across a range of channels.

Question 2
How might a modern call centre try to attract and retain a high calibre of staff?

Feedback
- structure work so that specific teams handle different types of call, allowing scope for job variety and acquisition of new skills;
- multi-channel working environments can provide a more challenging job specification, requiring IT skills as well as interpersonal skills;
- provide suitable reward schemes for both quantity and quality of work;
- ensure transparency of any employee surveillance operations;
- flexible working hours and bonus packages.

Question 3
From a customer perspective, what particular features of a Web site can help to build trust?

Feedback
- clearly displayed and transparent privacy policies, for example, to detail company policy with regard to customer data management;
- encrypted area of the Web site to handle payments;
- display of 'physical evidence' such as service quality awards, photos of staff or premises;
- options to call a 'real person' if required.

GLOSSARY

Electronic panopticon   The original panopticon was a glass-sided prison which allowed inmates to be covertly viewed at all times. An electronic equivalent could be software which monitors how long call centre employees take for breaks.

Emotional intelligence   Higgs and Dulewicz developed the Emotional Intelligence questionnaire in 1998, which measures seven elements of human behaviour:

- self awareness – awareness of your own feelings and of how others respond to you;
- emotional resilience – ability to keep going in difficult situations;
- motivation – ability to pursue longer-term goals;
- interpersonal sensitivity – understanding others' feelings and having empathy;
- influence – ability to influence others through interaction;
- intuitiveness – ability to make decisions with limited or ambiguous information;
- conscientiousness – integrity and correlation between words and actions.

Emotional labour   The type of work whereby an employee's ability to control his own feelings – and at the same time influence the mood of others – is an essential feature.

Internal customers   A term given to employees which recognizes their importance in terms of presenting the 'face' of the organization to customers, and hence the need for effective training, progression and reward policies if good staff are to be retained.

Internal marketing   Closely related to the above. The basic principle behind internal marketing is that satisfied customers are only created by satisfied employees, and effective communications with customers have to start with effective internal communications. A basic example could be a specific promotion that is advertised in the press, thereby generating enquiries from customers which staff ought to have been pre-warned about if the business is to retain its credibility.

Instant messaging   A peer-to-peer (P2P) electronic tool allowing real time text-based conversations online between individuals. Business applications are currently in their infancy, but pose significant marketing potential.

Potemkin Village   'An impressive showy facade designed to mask undesirable facts' (www.wordsmith.org, 3/11/03). (After Prince Potemkin, who erected cardboard villages to give an illusion of prosperity for impressing his lover Queen Catherine II on her visit to Ukraine and Crimea in 1787.)

BIBLIOGRAPHY

Bain, B. and Taylor, P. (2000) 'Entrapped by the "electronic panopticon"? Worker resistance in the call centre', *New Technology, Work and Employment*, 17, 3: 170–85.

Boon, S. D. and Holmes, J. G. (1991) 'The dynamics of interpersonal trust: resolving uncertainty in the face of risk', in R. A. Hinde and J. Groebel (eds) *Cooperation and Prosocial Behavior*, Cambridge: Cambridge University Press, pp. 190–211.

Brenkert, G. G. (1998), 'International business', *Business Ethics Quarterly*, 8, 2: 293–317.

Bromiley, P. and Cummings, L. L. (1992) *Transactions Cost in Organizations with Trust*, Discussion Paper No. 128, Minneapolis: University of Minnesota, Strategic Management Research Center.

Child, J. (1998) 'Trust and international strategic alliances: the case of sino-foreign joint ventures', in C. Lane and R. Bachmann (eds) *Trust Within and Between Organizations: Conceptual Issues and Empirical Applications*, Oxford: Oxford University Press, pp. 241–73.

Flores, F. and Solomon, R. C. (1998) 'Creating trust', *Business Ethics Quarterly*, 8, 2: 205–32.

Fox, A. (1974) *Beyond Contract: Work, Power and Trust Relations*, London: Faber and Faber.

Higgs, M. (2003) 'Good call', *People Management*, 23 January: 48.

Hochschild, A. R. (1983) *The Managed Heart: The Commercialisation of Human Feeling*, Berkeley: University of California Press.

Houlihan, M. (2001) 'Managing to manage? Stories from the call centre floor', *Journal of European Industrial Training*, Bradford.

Humphrey, J. and Schmitz, H. (1998) 'Trust and inter-firm relations in developing and transition economies', *The Journal of Development Studies*, 34, 4: 32–61.

Husted, B. W. (1998) 'The ethical limits of trust in business relations', *Business Ethics Quarterly*, 8, 2: 233–48.

Kipnis, D. (1996) 'Trust and technology', in R. M. Kramer and T. R. Tyler (eds) *Trust in Organizations: Frontiers of Theory and Research*, Thousand Oaks, CA: Sage Publications, pp. 67–84.

Lewicki, R. J. and Bunker, B. B. (1996) 'Developing and maintaining trust in work relationships', in R. M. Kramer and T. R. Tyler (eds) *Trust in Organizations: Frontiers of Theory and Research*, Thousand Oaks, CA: Sage Publications, pp. 114–39.

Lewis, D. and Weigert, A. (1985) 'Trust as a social reality', *Social Forces*, 63, 4: 967–85.

McAllister, D. J. (1995) 'Affect- and cognition-based trust as foundations for inter-personal cooperation in organizations', *Academy of Management Journal*, 38: 24–59.

McEwan, T. (2001) *Managing Values and Beliefs in Organisations*, Harlow: Pearson Education.

Marsden, D. (1998) 'Understanding the role of interfirm institutions in sustaining trust within the employment relationship', in C. Lane and R. Bachmann (eds) *Trust Within and Between Organizations: Conceptual Issues and Empirical Applications*, Oxford: Oxford University Press.

Mishra, A. K. (1996) 'Organizational responses to crisis: The centrality of trust', in R. M. Kramer and T. R. Tyler (eds) *Trust in Organizations: Frontiers of Theory and Research*, Thousand Oaks, CA: Sage Publications, pp. 261–87.

Payne, R. (1995) *Advances in Relationship Marketing*, London: Kogan Page.

Piercy, N. (2000) *Market-Led Strategic Change*, 2nd edn, London: Butterworth Heinemann.

Ring, P. S. (1996) 'Fragile and resilient trust and their roles in economic exchange', *Business and Society*, 35, 2: 148–75.

Ring, P. S. and Van de Ven, A. H. (1994) 'Developmental processes of cooperative interorganizational relationships', *Academy of Management Review*, 19, 1: 90–118.

Sako, M. (1998) 'Does trust improve business performance?', in C. Lane and R. Bachmann (eds) *Trust Within and Between Organizations: Conceptual Issues and Empirical Applications*, Oxford: Oxford University Press, pp. 88–117.

Shapiro, D., Sheppard, B. H. and Cheraskin, L. (1992) 'Business on a handshake', *Negotiation Journal*, 8, 4: 365–77.

Sheppard, B. H. and Tuchinsky, M. (1996) 'Micro-OB and the network organization', cited in J. Sydow 'Understanding the constitution of interorganizational trust', in C. Lane and R. Bachmann (eds) *Trust Within and Between Organizations: Conceptual Issues and Empirical Applications*, Oxford: Oxford University Press, pp. 31–63.

Smith, P. (1992) *The Emotional Labour of Nursing*, Basingstoke: Macmillan.

Throne, A. (2001) 'Capital One's call centre soars to new heights', *Call Center Magazine*, San Francisco, March.

Ulrich, D. (1989) 'Tie the corporate knot: gaining complete customer commitment', *Sloan Management Review*, 19–27.

Zucker, L. G. (1986) 'Production of trust: institutional sources of economic structure, 1840 to 1920', *Research in Organizational Behavior*, 8: 53–111.

Where do we go from here? Embedding the rhetoric of the e-Economy in the reality of business activity

LESLIE BUDD AND LISA HARRIS

In George Orwell's famous book, *1984*, the central character Winston Smith notices three slogans of the ruling Party:

WAR IS PEACE
FREEDOM IS SLAVERY
IGNORANCE IS STRENGTH

In his book the reversal of normal language is the basis of 'Newspeak', the official language of Oceania, Orwell's fictitious totalitarian state. The plethora of literature, debates and pronouncements of the new economy and the e-Economy has generated its own Newspeak in which there is confusion of language and meaning. The cheerleaders for the weightless economy, the digital economy, the knowledge economy, the information age and the network society appear to believe rhetoric is enough. Rhetoric is a very useful linguistic device, but attempting to unscramble the meaning of the language of the e-Economy is trying at times, particularly when it is, in contemporary parlance, 'sexed up'. Partly it is a matter of reading what the complex technologies and associated processes actually are and mean. Mainly, it is because the potential of new technologies is reported in a 'gee whiz' gushing style: 'it's all new and it's all out there: wow!' Most philosophy of science textbooks suggest knowledge proceeds through critical discourse. That is, each phase of knowledge is subject to a critical interrogation to examine its continuing relevance. The rhetoricians of the e-Economy tend not to do this.

This book has taken a wide-ranging and critical approach to understanding the business reality of the e-Economy. At the outset we defined the e-Economy as a subset of the new economy and one that is much more tightly tied to ICT infrastructure, delivery systems and business processes. The new economy was defined as a much broader entity in which the e-Economy impacts on output and investment decisions of firms,

209

consumption patterns, organizational structures, culture and behaviour, labour markets and the public domain. Both the e-Economy and the new economy have to negotiate the interaction of 'the economy of virtuality and the economy of reality', as we titled our opening chapter. The greatest challenge for business is how to embed the rhetoric in the everyday reality of its operations. It is insufficient for business merely to rebrand itself as, for example, a 'new service company', 'virtual organization' or 'digital enterprise'. The rise of the e-Economy and the new economy does not invalidate the universal problems of trust and governance and how stakeholder relationships are engaged within their trajectory, as Angela Ayios and Lisa Harris point out in Chapter 11. The greatest danger to business reality is what we term 'technological entropy'. That is, the over-whelming promise of ICT and its unlimited delivery potential overwhelms judgement because of a tendency to believe that technological innovation of itself will create greater dynamic performance. The result is that the rapid application of technology and a constant desire to update the technology leads to a stationary or even declining state because the adaptation costs become too high.

The tendency towards 'technological over-determination' through excess enthusiasm about new gadgetry is a function of all ages, old and new, as Leslie Budd argued in Chapter 1. Yet, technology is socially and culturally shaped. Mobile telephony may be the ubiquitous communications accessory of our times but the take-up of newer versions is determined by social practice, particularly for the prospects of mobile phones enabling e-Citizenship developments, as argued by Jane Vincent in Chapter 3. Equally, the social practices around shopping will determine the take up of e-Retail, as Charles Dennis and Oliver Richardson remind us in Chapter 9. The Schumpetarian process of creative destruction underpins much of human ingenuity in the trajectory of innovation. This process is culturally located in enterprise, articulated by Patricia Lewis in Chapter 2, and in the shift to e-Government as shown by Noah Curthoys in Chapter 8.

The prospect for the development of virtual learning environments (VLEs) is heavily determined by the institutional setting in which these environments evolve. The universal nature of the network society supposedly threatens large public bureaucratic organizations, for example, by global corporations creating opportunities for borderless education. Yet as Simran Grewal demonstrates in her analysis of the impact of VLEs on a traditional university in Chapter 7, and Martin Harris argues in his examination of the digitization of the services of a world famous public library, in Chapter 6, it is the degree of institutional appropriateness and embeddedness that will determine the roll out of virtual and digital media.

In the new 'sexed up' techno-world, businesses have to face the prosaic everyday reality of leading organizations, managing people and undertaking operations. The prospect of the e-Economy does not change that fact. Call centre staff, who feel they operate in 'sweat shops' and whose work-life balance is severely constrained will not respond positively to the 'whiz-bang' rhetoric of being foot soldiers in the war of the new. Rather, contextual human resources policies and appropriate working conditions will enable their capabilities to be recognized (and rewarded) to their and the employers mutual benefit, as Nelarine Cornelius suggests in Chapter 5. Similarly, despite the rhetoric of management as leadership, sustaining the competitive advantage of e-Economy businesses will depend on market and organizational context, not the technology itself, as developed by Lefki Papcharalambous in Chapter 4. Finally at the end of the day, businesses are involved in real operations, not some imagined movements across networks. Mieczkowska, Barnes and Hinton show in Chapter 10 that sectoral context is crucial for e-Business operations, as also is the need to take an incremental approach to the seductive promise of ICT for operations management.

It is apparent, however, that the rhetoric of the e-Economy can be a useful device for informing business of the development of reality occasioned by the application and use of ICT and associated media, processes and practice, but to have any true resonance or purchase this rhetoric has to be embedded in the reality of business. This is the key lesson to be learned from the narrative that this book has articulated. We have taken a heterodox approach to narrate an analysis of the rhetoric and business reality of the e-Economy. Our journey has ranged from economics, culture, social shaping, leadership, human resource management, e-Learning and digitized knowledge processes, e-Government, retail and marketing, operations management, trust and stakeholder relationships. In dancing around this circle, theories, concepts, ideas, practice and policies swap partners. The dance of time allows us to navigate around the rhetoric. This equally applies to any new claim through history. The claims of the e-Economy have to be taken seriously, but business reality provides us with a rather better roadmap.

Index